food@home

food@home

Christine Dann

CANTERBURY UNIVERSITY PRESS

First published in 2012
CANTERBURY UNIVERSITY PRESS
University of Canterbury
Private Bag 4800, Christchurch
NEW ZEALAND
www.cup.canterbury.ac.nz

ISBN 978-1-927145-03-6

A catalogue record for this book is available from the
National Library of New Zealand.

Cover photos: Christine Dann

Book design and layout: Quentin Wilson, Christchurch
Printed in China through Bookbuilders

CONTENTS

Acknowledgements   *8*

Preface   *9*

Chapter One: Culinary Confusion   *11*

An everyday christmas dinner   *11*

Zombie food rising   *12*

Killer diets   *14*

No more bad-news food   *16*

Bringing our food back home   *17*

A food@home journey in time . . .   *18*

. . . and in space   *20*

Recipe: Raspberry muffins   *21*

Chapter Two: Growing@Home   *25*

Yes, we have some bananas   *25*

Mission possible: backyard self-sufficiency   *26*

Grown with aroha   *30*

Grown at work   *31*

Grown in boxes   *32*

Grown close to town: sustainable small-holders   *34*

Growing good gardeners   *38*

Recipe: Dill mayonnaise   *43*

Chapter Three: Community@Garden *47*

Maara Maori *47*

From little things, big things grow *51*

Growing together: community gardens *53*

The spirit of growing sustainably *56*

Growing greener cities *58*

Recipe: Ranui Community Garden's Mexican spiced kumara soup *61*

Chapter Four: Dining@Home *65*

Our home dining heritage *65*

A short shift in home dining *69*

Crisis in home dining – crisis in health *71*

Three principles for good food *74*

A cheese (dis)course *76*

Cultivating taste *78*

Recipe: Anna Thomas's Caesar salad *82*

Chapter Five: Cooking@Home *85*

Recovering kitchen skills *85*

Getting it from the garden 1: Planning *86*

Getting it from the garden 2: Harvesting and keeping *87*

Kitchen literacy 1: Cooking skills *88*

Kitchen literacy 2: Recipes *89*

Kitchen literacy 3: Ingredients *94*

Box: Super seed sources *99*

Recipe: Digby Law's carrot cake with cream cheese icing *100*

Chapter Six: Almost@Home *105*

Reclaiming real markets *105*

Super-special shopping *113*

Fresh food to your door *117*

Box: 10 Reasons to shop at your local farmers' market *115*

Recipe: Nigel Slater's spicy eggplant and tomatoes *121*

Chapter Seven: Food@Large   *125*

   Food explorations   *125*
   Foraging freely   *126*
   Sustainable swapping   *129*
   Friendly freeganism   *130*
   Convivial kitchens   *132*
   SOLE food on the menu   *134*
   SOLE drink in the glass   *137*

   Box: My wild and free pantry   *131*
   Recipe: Elderflower cordial   *139*

Chapter Eight: Alimentary Action   *143*

   Creating more eating options   *143*
   Alimentary activism   *144*
   Healthy policy prescriptions   *147*
   The home front   *155*
   Time for (a Victorian afternoon) tea   *158*

   Recipe: Bread and butter pickles   *160*

Appendix I: A New Zealand Kitchen Garden Planning Guide   *165*
Appendix II: A Guide to Harvesting and Keeping Home-grown
                  Fruit and Vegetables   *171*
Endnotes   *189*
Recommended reading   *199*
Index   *203*

ACKNOWLEDGEMENTS

This book is dedicated to the loving memory of two men who were keen vegetable gardeners, good fathers and outstanding citizens. They are my father, Brownie (E. E.) Dann, and my late friend and colleague Rod Donald, member of parliament and Green Party co-leader. They both enjoyed putting effort into growing fresh food organically, even when they had so many other calls on their time, for they both (in their different ways) lived lives of service to their local communities and their country. They both also inspired and supported me in my efforts to garden well and to be of service to others. May their legacy live on.

During the course of researching this book I met many people skilled at producing and preparing good food, and equally dedicated to serving their communities, from organising farmers' markets and community gardens to teaching others to garden and cook. I thank them again for their time in talking to me and showing me what they do, so that I could share it with a wider audience. (Thanks are also due to those people for feeding me so well while I was on the job!)

Thanks and love also to my partner in life, Martin Oelderink, who for 20 years has been giving me a hand in the garden and cooking dinner from it – and taste-testing all my new recipes. While I was writing this book he rebuilt an old garden shed and created a brand-new glasshouse, plus a much better tool- and food-storage shed. Already we have eaten tomatoes, basil, eggplants and peppers from the glasshouse and some fabulous rockmelons and watermelons.

May your garden grow as well, may all your weeds make wonderful compost, and may all your dinners contain something delicious from the garden.

Christine Dann
February 2012

PREFACE

A food evolution is taking place in New Zealand.

Right now, right here, new ways of producing, preparing and sharing food are slowly but surely being established. Some of the new ways are not too different from some of the good old ways, which have been displaced over the past century by the industrial food system. That system has a short historical shelf life because it depends on oil – and oil is an energy source we will not always be able to depend on. Furthermore, the oil-dependent diet is not a healthy diet for humans, or for the Earth. It's time to move on to something better. Food grown and prepared at home, or close to home, is better in so many ways than food from a distant factory. This book covers many of those ways, which are happening now in your home – Aotearoa New Zealand.

CHAPTER ONE

Culinary Confusion

An everyday Christmas dinner

Every Christmas morning when I was growing up my father would go into the garden and dig new potatoes and carrots and pick peas for our dinner. As soon as I was old enough to do so, my job was to sit on the back steps in the sun and shell the peas into a pot. Quite a few never made it there, for freshly picked raw peas are so delicious. The peas went into the kitchen and the pods went straight to the compost heap.

An hour or two later our family sat down to a big midday dinner of roast lamb or beef and fresh vegetables – the classic Sunday dinner, with a few trimmings. Dessert often featured seasonal fruits – raspberry trifle or strawberry-topped pavlova – and there were always bowls of fresh cherries. In winter, apple-based desserts were common for Sunday dinners – crumbles, pies, tarts, baked apples.

All around New Zealand half a century ago, on Christmas Day and on weekends, most families of British heritage ate a meal like this, based on the best locally grown meat and produce. A good deal of the produce came from backyard fruit and vegetable gardens. The 1956 census recorded that over 60 per cent of New Zealand households had such gardens. The rest was generally bought from a local greengrocer's shop, within walking distance of home. The greengrocer's stock could be almost as fresh as home-grown vegetables, since the greengrocers selected their stock at early-morning auctions, buying produce that had been picked just the day before. In summertime they would sell big wooden cases of seasonal fruit, mainly peaches, apricots, pears, sent direct from the orchards. Some of this was eaten fresh, but most was preserved at home for winter eating. Bottling fruit, and turning fruit and vegetables into jams, pickles and other preserves, was all part of the skill-set of the average home cook, who had usually been taught these and all her other cooking and baking skills by her female relatives at home and by trained cookery teachers at school.

The British culinary tradition in which most home cooks were working had already begun to degenerate by the time New Zealand was colonised in the 19th century, and was certainly significantly debased by the time the country itself became a contributor to an industrialising and globalising food system in the late 19th century. Industrially produced and processed foods – biscuits, jams, confectionery, sausages, proprietary breakfast cereals, canned fruit and vegetables, sauces, canned fish and meat, canned soups – began to occupy increasing amounts of grocery shelf space from the early 1900s, but 50 years later they were still considered inferior, in flavour or nutritional value or both, to their fresh and home-produced equivalents. Unless the home cook was a very bad one, this was certainly true.

Zombie food rising

It is just as true now, and yet the majority of New Zealanders today do not grow fruit and vegetables, and get most of their 'fresh' food from supermarkets. We eat more and more food made in factories (which is the bulk of what supermarkets sell), or cooked in factory-like fast-food chains. This food has the same names as food we used to cook ourselves, but it is very different in both taste and nutritional value.

The differences in taste may be considered subjective and therefore unimportant – although I will argue in this book that good taste and good nutrition are intimately linked. Hence rediscovering the connection between the two is vital to our health and well-being.

The differences in nutritional value are not subjective. They can be measured in terms of the levels of fat, salt, sugar, carbohydrate, protein and micro-nutrients (vitamins, minerals, anti-oxidants) present, and also, in the industrially produced foods, their non-nutritional components, which include pesticide and herbicide residues, veterinary chemical residues, synthetic flavourings, preservatives, emulsifiers, anti-caking agents, enzymes, acidity regulators, firming agents, colourings and other substances not used in the home kitchen or garden.

If you were given the following ingredients, would you know what you could make with them? Wheat flour, sugar, canola oil, food acid 330, yeast, sesame seeds, iodised salt, anti-caking agent 535, dough conditioner (emulsifiers 471, 472e, 481), mineral salts 170 and 516, enzymes 1100, 1101 and 1104, ascorbic acid, preservative 262, beef, iceberg lettuce, soybean oil, pickles, vinegar, modified corn starch, high fructose corn syrup, egg yolks, corn syrup, spice, spice extracts, vegetable gum 415, preservative 202, onion extract, paprika extract, dehydrated garlic, hydrolised proteins, cheese, milk solids, non-fat milk solids, emulsifiers (331, soy lecithin), flavour, acidity regulator 260, colours 160b and 160c, preservative 200, gherkins, firming agent 509, preservative 211, dehydrated white onion – and water.

These are the ingredients of a Big Mac, including the bun and sauce, on sale in every McDonald's in New Zealand.[1] There is nothing fresh about this food, or the food at the supermarket in packages with similarly long lists of ingredients. It contains almost nothing of real nutritional value. Whatever taste it has comes largely from chemicals, not from the natural flavours of the few authentic and traditional ingredients. Scientific and popular debates about the safety or otherwise of these non-nutritional additives to industrially produced food have been raging for decades. Some additives have been banned as a result, and others continue to be used only because the food industry is a powerful political lobbyist.[2] Even when one particular additive can be shown not to kill lab rats that eat small doses for a few weeks, no one has any idea how this additive may combine and react with other additives and affect human health over the long term.

It is impossible to conduct sufficiently rigorous experiments on humans to prove it one way or the other, although the poor health of folk who live largely on fast-food diets certainly is suggestive, but even if we could, what would be the point? The additives are only used to make food that is long dead last a bit longer and look as though it is alive. This zombie food contains none of the essential micro-nutrients present in fresh food, and its energy-to-nutrition ratio is shocking. One Big Mac, for example, contains a quarter of the calories/kiloJoules (energy) a man requires for a day, and a lot of those come from fat (over a third of the recommended total daily intake of fat, and 42 per cent of the recommended daily intake of saturated fat). The rest come from carbohydrates (the flour in the bun, the sugars in the sauces and pickles), and these carry no other nutrients. The only essential mineral micro-nutrient one can be sure of finding in a Big Mac is sodium – 47 per cent of the recommended daily intake.

Experiments to prove that this food is no more alive than cardboard can easily be conducted at home. Leave a McDonald's hamburger bun (or any other bread made the industrial way with bleached white flour, food acids, anti-caking agents, emulsifiers, preservatives etc on an open shelf at home. It will become as hard as cardboard and, like cardboard, it will not attract other life forms, such as the fungi or moulds that are attracted to 'real' food.

I have yet to prove whether a whole hamburger made in New Zealand will last as well as they do in the US, where one living room in Vermont sports a collection of hamburgers from McDonald's and Burger King that have stayed intact for 10 years or more, without attracting moulds or decaying in any way.[3]

Killer diets

Humans are not meant to eat food that is mouldy, but we are meant to eat food that could go mouldy – because that means it contains nutrients. We are also not designed to eat food that is so high in energy and so low in essential nutrients. The results of eating this way can be seen at both the individual and the national level. A study of all causes of death in New Zealand in 1997 attributed around 30 per cent of deaths to the joint effect of dietary factors, of which 6 per cent related to inadequate fruit and vegetable consumption.[4] Low fruit and vegetable consumption is implicated in the three leading causes of death in New Zealand today: cancer, ischaemic heart disease and cerebrovascular disease (strokes). The World Health Organisation estimates that low intake of fruit and vegetables causes about 19 per cent of gastrointestinal cancer, 31 per cent of ischaemic heart disease and 11 per cent of strokes.[5] The top three diet-related killer diseases now have a fourth companion in New Zealand – Type II diabetes. In 2007, 17,625 New Zealanders died from these four diseases – and 480 from the next-largest category of predictable and preventable deaths: transport accidents.[6] Yet where does the most prevention effort go?

At the individual level there seems to be little knowledge of the role of diet in causing the killer diseases, and huge ignorance about how different industrial foods are from traditional foods with the same name. Bread is a classic example. So are eggs and chickens from battery farms compared with the free-range equivalent. Hence there is confusion about what to eat and how much of it to eat. Furthermore, choices about what to eat may be hugely constrained by income and even physical access to fresh, healthy foods at affordable prices. In countries like New Zealand, where bad foods often have a lower ticket price than quality foods, it is the poor who are the biggest casualties of diet-related diseases.

When people worry about their diet and what it is doing to them, the usual concern these days is over carrying surplus weight. There is no doubt that the industrial diet, with its poor energy-to-nutrient ratio, is great for gaining weight, although anyone who is genuinely underweight and needs to bulk up would be well advised to avoid fast food and choose genuinely nutritious high-energy foods. Just how much impact the switch towards the industrial diet has had on individual New Zealand waistlines has been documented by Auckland weight-loss instructor Carolyn Gibson, who noticed in the late 2000s that the dietary instructions she was giving to her students no longer seemed to be working the way they had for the preceding 20 years. She also noticed that her late-2000s intake of students had much more weight to lose than her mid-1980s intake. Back then the average initial weight of her clients was 68.4kg and they wanted to lose 8–10kg, going down to 58–60kg. Twenty-five years later the average initial weight was 92.7kg and clients were choosing an average goal weight of 70kg – 2kg heavier than the starting weight of the 1980s clients. Gibson concluded correctly that her recipes and weight-loss instructions were not at fault; rather there had been big changes to everyday foods, which made them more energy dense and less nutritious.

Gibson's observations are scientifically supported by the 2008/09 New Zealand Adult Nutrition Survey (released in September 2011), which surveyed the dietary habits of 4721 New Zealanders over the age of 15, and compared them with previous similar surveys. With regard to fruit and vegetable intake the survey found that 41 per cent of males and 28 per cent of females were not eating the recommended three or more servings of vegetables per day, while 45 per cent of males and 33 per cent of females were not eating the recommended two or more servings of fruit per day. Although respondents appeared to be eating less high-energy food than those surveyed in previous years, successive surveys have shown a steady rise in both mean weights and obesity rates. In 1997 the mean weight for males was 80.4kg and for females 68.7kg. In 2008–09 this has increased to 85.1kg for men and 72.6kg for women. The percentage of the population classified as obese has risen from 17 to 27.7 per cent for males and from 20.6 to 27.8 for females.[7]

There is still considerable scientific debate about just how much weight above the dangerously low cosmetic norms set by models and film stars is too much. There is also plenty of evidence that weight loss or low weight by themselves are no guarantor of good health. I believe that the focus needs to shift from the visual effects of poor diet to an examination of why that diet is so poor, and where and how the overweight can find good alternatives to it, that deliver more nutrients with less energy.

This is urgent for adults, but it is even more vital for children. Fat children were rare when I was at school in the 1950s and 1960s, and most of those who were overweight had an untreated metabolic condition, such as severe hypothyroidism. Now some 8 per cent of New Zealand children are classified as obese, which means that any primary school class will have on average two obese children. There will also be two or three other very fat children who are not technically obese. Fat children, like fat adults, are at greater risk of developing Type II diabetes. But the consequences for children are more severe, since the complications associated with this disease can be fatal and will hit them at an earlier age. No parent would want such a death for their child, and yet many parents today are feeding themselves and their children on the industrial diet that leads to this outcome.

They are not doing this wilfully, because they want their children to die before them, but because the industrial food system has made high-energy/low-nutrient foods very cheap, and very easy to access. There are more fresh-food outlets and fewer fast-food outlets in wealthy suburbs than in poor areas in New Zealand, and unsurprisingly poor people are more likely to have difficulty in affording quality food. The 2008/09 New Zealand Adult Nutrition Survey found that 'food insecurity' (not being able to afford to eat properly all the time) increased significantly in New Zealand between 1997 and 2008–09. In 1997 only 1.6 per cent of adult males were living in 'food insecure' households, but by 2009 this has increased to 5.6 per cent. For females there was an even bigger increase, from 3.8 per cent to 8.8. per cent.[8] Disturbingly for the health future of New Zealanders, food insecurity was more common among young adults than older ones. It is a tragic irony of the industrial food system that being overweight, not underweight, is now a prime marker of being unable to afford to eat properly.

No more bad-news food

Poor nutrition and slow-killer diseases are not the only problem related to the industrial diet. From the perspective of other species, and the environment as a whole, the picture is not pretty either. To take just one example, the total number and geographical range of wild birds have been severely reduced wherever industrial farming dominates the landscape. Their habitats are destroyed and agricultural chemicals in their environment and food chain kill them at all stages of life, from the egg to the mature bird. The devastating effect that industrial farming has on birds and other wildlife was first brought to the world's attention by Rachel Carson in 1962 in her book *Silent Spring*. Unfortunately the killing has not stopped and even greater threats have arisen as new chemicals, and genetically engineered plants, have been released into the environment.[9]

Domesticated birds are also the victims of industrial farming, with chickens brutally abused by battery farming methods. The eggs and meat they produce are inferior in taste and nutritional value to that from birds raised humanely and able to express their natural behaviours, and they are also contaminated by the veterinary chemicals used to keep them alive, if not exactly well. In fact they frequently succumb to disease. Battery chicken farms are also breeding grounds for new and dangerous diseases that threaten humans, such as the H1N1 avian flu strain.[10]

There is a lot more bad news to share about the industrial food system, but that would take another book, or rather a whole library of them. There are many excellent recent books on the subject, and these are included in the Recommended Reading list at the end of this book. This book is about the good news. Another, better food system is possible, and it is evolving in New Zealand right now. If New Zealanders are dying slow and unpleasant deaths because our national diet is too low in fruit and vegetables and too high in animal foods, refined sugars and starches and highly processed foods, what is the solution? More to the point – who is putting the solution into practice right now, what are they doing and how can the rest of us get a piece of the action?

Bringing our food back home

I have spent the best part of three years investigating these questions on a national scale. I have also been putting the answers into practice myself for much longer than that, since I have been aware for many years that the industrial food system is not nutritious, delicious or environmentally sustainable. The industrial food system is broken in many places. It cannot be rebuilt again from its environmentally unsustainable foundations of heavy fossil fuel usage and huge burdens of waste, pollution and water extraction. But replacing it means putting something better in each of those many broken places. That means we have to start not only in the paddock or garden, but also on the plate and at every point in the system in between, including food distribution, marketing, preparation and education.

That's a lot of different places to have to create alternatives, and hence there is a danger that changes will be worked on in isolation, without making the vital connections needed to create a viable alternative system. Is there a way of simplifying our understanding of what needs to be done, so that we can join up the dots?

I believe there is, and that is why the word home is in the title of this book. The industrial food system has taken food production, preparation and distribution too far from home – too far from each household and too far from each town or city. Every one of the evolving alternatives to that system springing up in New Zealand today can be understood as a way of bringing our food back home, where it belongs. Farmers' markets, Community Supported Agriculture, foraging, farm-gate sales and food trails, box schemes, community gardens and community cafés are all ways to produce, prepare or find food close to home. The food obtained this way is mainly vegetables and fruit, which we need to eat more of. This produce is also truly fresh – almost as fresh as home-grown and -prepared produce, which is the other big dimension of a homely food system.

Having tasted the quality of close-to-home food I don't need further convincing that producing and preparing fresh food at home, or obtaining it locally, is the most effective way of safeguarding and enhancing human health and our rapidly degrading natural environment. It is also, ultimately, more efficient and more economical than the industrial food system, when the huge costs of environmental damage, resource wastage and treating diet-related diseases are set against the convenience of having supermarkets and fast-food chains dispensing food-like items 24/7.

It is also much, much more pleasurable, as the thousands and thousands of Kiwis who are rediscovering the joys of home growing and cooking can attest.

A food@home journey in time . . .

I have known these pleasures from an early age, ever since my dad gave me some radish seeds and showed me how to plant them when I was five or six years old. I have been growing some of my food at home ever since. Even when home was a student flat four blocks from Cathedral Square in the centre of Christchurch, and my vege garden was a 5 x 5-metre backyard patch of dirt that was initially better at producing 19th-century rubbish – old bottles, nails, rusty horseshoes, broken crockery and the like – than vegetables.

I have been cooking food at home since the age of seven or eight, when my mum showed me how to bake scones, and had me mixing salad dressings and turning the handle on the mincer that minced the vegetables for our Sunday night vegetable soup. It is not surprising, then, that eventually I put these long-term gardening and cooking interests together and in 1991 I wrote a cooking-from-the-garden cookbook. What is surprising is that this book, *A Cottage Garden Cook Book*,[11] was only the third book, among the hundreds of cooking and gardening books produced in New Zealand to that date, to make this explicit garden-to-kitchen link. There was a 12-year gap between the production of the first of those books, *The Cook's Garden*, in 1980[12] and my book, and then an even bigger gap of 16 years until the next garden-to-kitchen book, *The Grower's Cookbook*, was produced in 2008.[13] (Read more about these books in Chapter 6, Cooking@Home.)

During this time New Zealanders produced less and less food at home, ate fewer home-cooked meals and consumed more restaurant and takeaway meals and snacks that were high in fat, salt and sugar and low on fresh produce. Then, somewhere around the turn of the 21st century, dissatisfaction with what the industrial food system was dishing up began to grow. Business at organic grocery stores started to boom. At Piko Wholefoods in Christchurch they had to take on more staff and expand the shop. The wish to avoid genetically engineered food, along with allergic reactions to industrially produced foods, were just two reasons the increasing number of customers gave for choosing to shop at Piko rather than the supermarket.

On the home growing and cooking front, *New Zealand Gardener* magazine, under its new editor Lynda Hallinan, shifted focus from grand ornamental gardens to home food production and preparation and boosted its circulation during a recession when other magazines were losing readers.

Between the first and second national conferences of the Farmers' Market Association of New Zealand, in 2006 and 2008, the number of markets doubled. Food gardens started to appear in schools that had never had one, or not for 50 years or more. They also started to appear in unlikely places such as church grounds, neighbourhood parks and workplaces.

These changes towards a close-to-home food system do not yet constitute a revolution, for most Kiwis still rely on the industrial food system for the bulk of their daily diet. But I believe there is an *evolution* towards more healthy and sustainable foodways, and that when the majority are eating SOLE (Seasonal, Organic, Local, Ethical) food the revolution will be complete. It took around 150 years to create the industrial food system as we know it today, with its global production and distribution of unhealthy foods at great environmental and social cost. It may take this long to replace it, but there are good reasons why the change could and should happen sooner.

At the end of the great food evolution process it is unlikely that we will all be producing most of our food at home, as our farming ancestors did two centuries ago. But it is likely that almost all of our food will be produced and bought locally, where 'local' means produced no more than 200km from the point of purchase, and purchased within 1km of home. Things worked very well this way only 50 years ago, and they will probably work that way again within the next 50 years. We will grow – and cook and eat – more of our own food at home and within community settings. Eating 'locally' already costs less in dollar terms than eating food from the industrial food system. As energy costs rise, industrially produced and distributed food will cost more, so now is a good time to start making the switch to the healthier local alternative. Precious petrol, and money, can then be conserved for a monthly trip to the country to buy food at the source, or to forage for wild foods.

. . . and in space

While researching this book I took virtual journeys backwards and forwards in time and also some real and virtual road trips to see food alternatives in action and to learn from and about the people creating them. My aim was to study at least one example of every form of close-to-home food alternative in some detail and to find other examples to round out the picture whenever I could. I was not aiming to create a guide to every commercial source of SOLE food (farmers' markets, farm-gate sales, specialty stores etc), as there are already guidebooks that do that. And certainly not to all the many, many private and community examples of close-to-home food production and preparation. That would be an impossible task, and completely unnecessary.

Instead I have tried to create a guide to the emerging new food system. With this map in hand, readers will be able to take their own journeys to the initiatives that interest them most or, even better, create their own map and destinations. I am continuing to record my own explorations into growing and cooking better food at home on my blog, http://ecogardenernz.blogspot.com (The Eco Gardener), and welcome you to travel with me there, as well as through this book.

Raspberry muffins

Ingredients

1 large egg

½ cup mild oil (e.g. light olive oil)

¼ cup melted butter OR sour cream

grated rind and juice of 1 large orange (½ cup juice)

½ cup yoghurt

1 ½ cups fresh berries

2 cups flour

2 tsp baking powder

½ cup sugar

¼ tsp salt

Method

Heat oven to 210°C; put the rack just below the middle.

Grease muffin tins well (12 large or 24 small).

In a large bowl, mix together all the wet ingredients. Gently fold in the berries.

Sift together the dry ingredients and mix them quickly into the wet ingredients.

Spoon into muffin tins.

Bake 12–15 minutes.

Cool in the tins 4–5 minutes before removing to a rack.

To serve

Dust with icing sugar and top with a raspberry; OR (fancy version) dust with icing sugar, make a split across the centre of the top and fill with whipped cream topped with a raspberry.

Rich fruit breads are popular
at Christmas time in northern
Europe. My Yule Bread (from my
Cottage Garden Cookbook) is
based on a Danish recipe.

Pumpkin and squash variety
from Running Brook Seeds.

Auckland Botanic Gardens - traditional potato varieties and
crookneck squashes are a feature of this part of the gardens'
autumn harvest display.

Waiheke Island – 'organoponico' raised beds with slots for hoops to carry netting are a great way to protect and enhance soil in a high-rainfall area, and also to keep insects and birds off the plants.

Pumpkins, carrots and silverbeet snuggle up in my garden.

Brandywine tomatoes ripening.

Garlic plait – taller than a man!

CHAPTER TWO

Growing@Home

Yes, we have some bananas

On a cool spring evening in a small Auckland back yard Bronwen proudly showed me her banana tree, complete with a huge stem of baby bananas. Beside it a grapefruit tree dripped with fruit. Behind that a small enclosure held half a dozen hens, which keep the family in omelettes. There is not much room for lawn in this back yard, as half of the limited flat area is devoted to the vege garden. This doesn't mean there is no space for the family to relax, because on the slope at the back of the section, sheltering under big trees, is an impressive curved stone bench-seat where they can all gather. It's perfect for resting on as the sun goes down, while admiring the productive little farmlet below.

Hundreds of kilometres to the south, in Golden Bay, on a sunny but definitely not tropical June day, I stopped to admire more banana palms, this time growing on a north-facing slope sheltered by manuka trees. Aline showed me how she had made little clearings among the manuka for other frost-tender fruit trees, including tamarillo, cherimoya, babaco, papaya, fig, date, pomegranate, carob, rose apple, red guava, casana, vanilla and citrus trees. There are also some tea bushes. As well as having shelter from the manuka, and a sunny orientation, the trees are given further protection from frost by being above a rill of clear running water that cuts across the slope. This is part of the mini-hydro system that provides the power for all Aline's electrical appliances. It also helps keep any moisture in the air from freezing – and it makes a perfect spot for growing wasabi.

It was a frosty winter morning at Purau on Banks Peninsula when I visited organic grower, teacher and adviser Holger Kahl. He was smiling because he had just eaten his first home-grown banana. His was grown against the north wall of his house, which is a straw-bale construction with thick plastered walls and wide eaves that make a warm micro-climate for the banana palm.

By the time I paid my next visit to Bronwen her bananas had all been devoured. I was assured they were very good and I was left to wonder if they were as good as the other bananas I've eaten in places like Thailand and Brazil that were grown close to where they were consumed – not picked hard and green, transported thousands of kilometres across the ocean and then gassed before they were unloaded in New Zealand. (This is to make them ripen and to kill any insects that have survived the horrendous spray regime that goes with growing bananas on huge plantations.) The beautiful golden bananas New Zealanders love so much have a disturbing industrial back-story, which is one of the reasons I am thrilled to find that it's possible to grow them successfully in places as different as an Auckland back yard, a Golden Bay farm and a Purau garden.

Mission possible: backyard self-sufficiency

It's good news for those who want to source most of their food *really* close to home – as in just outside the back door. Or the front door, come to that. That's how it is for self-sufficiency enthusiast and gardening editor, writer and presenter Lynda Hallinan, who conducted a one-year experiment in living off her land – all 733 inner-Auckland square metres of it. I'd call Lynda the poster-girl for the current New Zealand renaissance in home food growing if that didn't sound a bit trivialising given the inspiring example she set for her readers when in 2007 she took up a challenge to spend only $10 a week on bought food, and get the rest from her garden.

You can read about the ongoing experiment in back issues of *New Zealand Gardener*, and on Lynda's blog.[1] In some ways she was in an ideal position to do this: young, fit, no kids, owning her own home and garden. In other ways she was in the worst position: editing one of New Zealand's top magazines and taking up all the speaking and other engagements that go with that full-time, high-stress occupation. A lesser woman would have laughed at the very suggestion of adding self-provisioning to her existing workload, but Lynda pulled on her garden boots and got to, working out ways to turn gardening and cooking into forms of rewarding recreation, and ended up surprising herself with the amount of pleasure as well as profit she got from the exercise.

As she told me, 'If you grow your own food, it changes how you think about it.' Shuddering at the thought of some of the processed foods she used to eat, such as macaroni cheese from a packet, she is now of the view that the best way to stop worrying about what is in food and whether it is on the label is not to eat labelled food at all. Before she grew her own food she wasn't much of a cook. She bought in expensive luxury foods for her dinner parties and ate out a lot. Now that she is focused on thinking up delicious ways to serve her own produce she enjoys cooking so much that she looks back on her boring 'food as fuel' days with a sense of disbelief. Cooking home-grown fresh food for herself has also been good for her waistline and great for her bank balance. One has gone down while the other has gone up.

Like Bronwen with her bananas, Lynda doesn't accept that living on a small city section should cramp one's food-growing style. A firm believer that the edible is also beautiful, she used feijoas, not pittosporums, for her hedge, and the 'shady grove' part of her garden was planted with olive trees. Her mantra is, 'If you only have room for one tree, make it a fruit tree.' Living at the time on a section that was smaller than the footprint of some of the McMansion investment houses that are now covering the good growing soils on the outskirts of Auckland, Lynda also sees social benefits in making home a place where there is food in the ground. 'People might stop thinking about houses as a place to make money and start seeing them as a place to live.'

A place to live well for a very small investment in plants. From $20 worth of strawberry plants Lynda was able to pick a bowl of strawberries worth the same amount *per day* in summer. During summer around 30kg of fresh food came from the garden every week, and even in winter there was about 10kg there for the harvesting. This is more than she would have bought in her food-buying days – and now it's all free. Since she couldn't eat it all, she started selling her surplus down at the City Farmers' Market, or swapping it for luxury items she couldn't afford on her $10 budget, such as organic chicken or artisan cheese. She also preserved as much as she could, and even experimented with transforming some of her surpluses into alcoholic beverages. She ruefully turned over the cushions on her sofa to show me the stains made by a bottle of home-brewed cider that exploded, showering the room with fizz, but apart from this setback her brewing went pretty well. The wine critics at *Cuisine* magazine said her elderberry wine was weak and anaemic and suggested matching it with your worst enemy, but they commented favourably on her elderflower bubbly and walnut liqueur.

Lynda is a largely self-taught cook and gardener. The web is her saviour when it comes to finding recipes for whatever she has a glut of and of course it also provides lots of plant-growing information. Her gardening and garden-writer colleagues are helpful sources of information too, but ultimately there is no substitute for learning by doing. Lynda cooks and gardens by a principle I also subscribe to – MEME. It stands for Minimum Effort, Maximum Effect. No time-consuming and back-breaking double digging or even scientific composting for us, when leaving the pulled weeds around in heaps or rows to decompose works just as well for returning organic matter to the soil, stimulating earthworm activity and mulching the ground. Similarly, saving seed is a good and thrifty thing to do, but letting things go to seed and sow themselves is easier and almost as reliable. Self-sown greens can often be left where they are; self-sown tomatoes and pumpkins usually need to be shifted to where they can be staked, or ramble. This is still easier and/or cheaper than the alternatives of raising them oneself in pots or buying them in.

Lynda doesn't care one scrap if this means that her food garden does not resemble a designer potager. She is much more interested in plants and the people who grow them than in designs and designers, finding greater variety and stimulation in the match between particular individuals, what they grow, and how they grow it in their home patches. She wants food gardening to be fundamental, not fashionable. Why shouldn't it be when, as she says, there is no downside to gardening? It's great for personal health and well-being to be out in the fresh air, working up a sweat to produce the best fresh food there is, but also taking time to sit back and relax in the garden, enjoying the scent and colour of the plants and the song of the birds. It has economic benefits for the household, saving money that would have been spent on inferior food. It has social benefits, bringing one into positive contact with neighbours, fellow gardeners and other real food lovers. It has significant environmental benefits, which could grow to planet-saving proportions if the majority of us could grow as much fresh produce as possible as close to home as possible, without using toxic and/or unsustainable fertilisers and pesticides, and without producing wastes that cannot be put back into the nutrient cycle on the site where they were produced.

All these benefits can be quantified and measured, and it would be good and useful if economists started measuring them. For this is the true bottom line, the correct measure of our actual standard of living and our quality of life in real health and welfare terms. It usually has little correlation with the commonly used and quite misleading figure derived by dividing the gross domestic product (which includes all the expenditure on health and welfare negatives such as illegal drugs, gambling, waste dumps, pesticides and junk food) by the number of people in the country to get an average dollar figure per person. There are many reasons, such as inequality of wealth distribution and big expenditures on weaponry rather than food, why it can never be claimed that everyone in a country is 'better off' just because the cash economy as a whole has grown.[2]

On the two occasions in world history when home growing has been deemed worthy of the attention of policy-makers – during both world wars in Britain and the US and to a lesser extent in New Zealand, Australia and other Allied countries – it was quickly realised that it made an essential contribution to provisioning the home front, thus releasing commercially farmed food for the troops. So those still at home were encouraged to 'Dig for Victory!' What they produced was never less than 10 per cent of the produce consumed in Britain during World War Two, and in the third quarter of each war year (the harvest season in Britain) it was as high as 25 per cent. Studies done on wartime food production in Britain, which were continued into the 1950s, also showed that home gardeners were more efficient food producers than farmers, growing 7.1 tons of food per acre to the farmers' 6.3 tons.[3]

Now that industrial food production and consumption is damaging the health of Britons and their environment so badly, there is a revival of interest in Victory Gardens, although the slogan should probably be changed to 'Dig for Survival!'[4] It is known both from the British World War Two experience, and the experience of Cubans during their 'special period' in the 1990s after oil supplies from Russia stopped coming, that growing one's own food and eating a lot more fresh organic produce and a lot less meat has a very positive effect on health. In Cuba obesity rates halved and deaths from all causes dropped by 20 per cent.[5] If any country were truly serious about improving the overall health and nutritional status of its population it seems obvious that ensuring each household has enough land, whether at home or nearby, to grow some of the fresh produce it consumes, and that everyone has access to knowledge about gardening, are the first and most important steps it should take.

It is crazy that the only time this has happened in the past 100 years is during world wars. Do we not have good enough reasons for living in a healthy, sustainable and more satisfying way the rest of the time? Ways that are measurably better for our health and the health of the land?

Grown with aroha

As the saying goes, 'Not everything that matters can be measured, and not everything that is measured matters.' While talking to Auckland academic and writer Paul Moon, Tuhoe tohunga Hohepa Kereopa offered him a piece of raw carrot and asked him what he thought of it. Paul replied: 'All the normal tastes I had come to associate with a carrot were there, but they were heightened. Every aspect of the flavour was more intense and more pleasurable.' He told Hohepa it was one of the best carrots he had ever eaten, and Hohepa then quizzed him as to why that might be. Paul guessed that it was something to do with the rich organic soil the carrot was grown in, but while Hohepa agreed that this helped, he said it was not the main reason.

> When you place a value on what you grow, it becomes full of energy because of the energy you put into it when planting it and watering it and all the stuff that goes into looking after it. So that when you eat it, or somebody else eats it, all that energy, and all the value you placed on the food as it was growing, goes back into it, and so it is more tasty, and it is also more healthy for you. So when all these big shops and supermarkets … grow their vegetables and fruits in huge orchards, there's no energy of the person going into the planting and caring. And there's no value placed on it, apart from the money value – which really is useless. So soil and watering, and all those other things we do to protect the plant, is important but the most important thing is valuing the gardening you are doing... that carrot was grown with lots of care, and the person who grew it looked after it and put all their energy into it, and you can taste that when you eat it.[6]

These words made a lot of sense to me when I read them, because I have plenty of experience of eating food grown with such caring energy and I know how different it tastes from shop food. Most of the vegetables I ate as a child, and a lot of the fruit, came from the backyard garden tended by my father. He fed the soil with compost and green manures and gradually built it up so that it was thick, dark and rich with humus. As Hohepa Kereopa says, that is important for creating flavour, as is freshness: a carrot that travels only 10 metres and 10 minutes from garden to plate is always going to beat out one that travels hundreds of hours and kilometres, let alone globe-trotting produce. It is going to be – and hence taste – more alive, bursting with the flavour compounds and nutrients that steadily diminish the longer it has been out of the ground or off the bush. As Lynda Hallinan says, 'Ask yourself this: have you ever stepped off a long-haul flight in cattle class feeling crisp, juicy and succulent?'[7]

Home-grown vegetables will also have more nutrients in them to start with, because home gardeners producing for their families have more motivation and more time to put into creating good rich soils that grow highly nutritious crops, and to ensure that each plant has the soil and water requirements it needs to grow best. Such gardeners tend to care for their veges as carefully, and as energetically, as my father's father, who fed 10 children from his patch. He was out there every morning with a watering can, giving each plant exactly what it needed – he also insisted that it was wrong to put cold water on warm earth. He returned all spent crops, and weeds before they flowered, to the soil, digging them in lightly on the spot, and whenever a patch was cleared of a food crop he planted a green manure crop in that space to keep the soil covered and to provide more organic material to dig in.

This level of care is just not possible in large-scale market gardens and orchards that grow for profit. In any case, the main varieties of commercial fruit and vegetables available today are grown for their high yields and cosmetic appearance, and for their ability to withstand long-distance travel without bruising or rotting. The people who tend them are focused on achieving these three goals, not on nourishing people they know and love. Not surprisingly, their food does not taste as good and is not as good for us.

Grown at work

But in these days of urban sprawl and urban intensification, leading to a loss of good food-growing soils within and next to cities, where can we garden? Many urban New Zealanders no longer have a garden big enough to feed a family, even if they have the skills to do so.

Does that mean it is time to throw in the trowel? Or can we make the concrete bloom again? This was a challenge taken up by some Wellington posties a few years ago. A conversation at smoko time in the mail-sorting centre in Khandallah, about a father-in-law who proposed to grow potatoes inside an old tyre, led long-time postie and home gardener John Maynard to start a demonstration of just how much can be grown in containers.

He brought a large pot to work, put it against the wall of the small carpark behind the centre, filled it with soil and planted one spud. The site was sunny and sheltered – always a challenge to find in Wellington – and soon other pots and plants – tomatoes, lettuces, silverbeet, cucumbers, broad beans, carrots, rhubarb, courgettes, red onions, spring onions, radishes, celery, strawberries, beans – joined the additional potatoes that were planted. Culinary herbs joined the line-up, and all are now well used by three of the posties who are trained chefs (having found that job too stressful, they now focus on making good food for their families and friends, rather than strangers). After three months of keeping the pots well fed and watered there was enough produce for a 'first fruits' feast, which was based on a potato, green bean, red onion and spring onion salad for 14, supplemented with bread rolls, ham and a home-baked chocolate cake.

Three or four of the posties do most of the gardening work, but the produce is shared out among all the workmates according to need and preference. Some of them have home gardens, one with some unusual crops, puha and dandelions, which are fed to pet rabbits. One postie calls himself an accidental gardener. He makes a rough compost, throws it on the garden and sees what grows out of it. Vege seedlings as well as plants are raised behind the mail centre. Some of them end up being grown there, while others might become a special delivery in the mailbox of a postie's relative. While John was away overseas for a month one summer his colleagues kept him in the gardening loop by sending him cellphone photos of them watering and harvesting the veges.

Grown in boxes

The posties' vege production system demonstrates that not only do you not need to own a garden to produce home-grown produce, you don't even need to own a home. Lots of worksites could be good growing places – some preschools, schools and universities provide such places already – and even a temporary home can have a garden. It could be in pots, or it could be in durable and attractive raised beds of the type provided by the Auckland business Patch from Scratch. Sarah Davies created Patch from Scratch[8] in 2007 as a way to meet the needs of time-poor, cash-rich Aucklanders who want to grow their own fresh organic vegetables but don't have the space, time or inclination for a full-blown garden, or the gardening skills needed to create and maintain one.

Sarah provides them with a viable alternative by installing raised beds made from untreated, durable macrocarpa timber, filling them with compost layered with pea straw, and planting them up with organic seeds and seedlings. The client then receives two consultations three months apart on how to manage the mini-garden – an excellent personal education service that also includes a half-day workshop on organic growing, a weekly email news and tip sheet, an organic growing booklet Sarah wrote especially for raised-bed growing, and (I think this idea is especially clever) laminated information sheets, including a month-by-month planting calendar, a pest and disease control chart and a crop rotation chart. I so wish I had had these when I was a beginner gardener. It would have saved my gardening books from muddy smears and crumpled pages, and my floors from getting dirty every time I went inside to consult them.

Patch from Scratch's customers are mostly professional people leading busy lives, but the raised-bed method also suits retired people whose digging days are over, and parents of young children who find the beds a congenial way to have their kids gardening alongside them. Enabling everyone to produce fresh food sustainably is one of Sarah's goals in life, and to this end she already volunteers at one community garden that has been established for mental health patients, and makes Patch from Scratch personnel available pro bono to advise schools, rest-homes and other not-for-profit groups wanting to develop a garden.

A Patch from Scratch raised bed is a beautiful feature for a garden, but raised beds can be made to suit any budget, from any materials that will hold soil. I have seen them made from recycled bricks, river stones, cement and clay mixes, recycled timber and even the offcuts of corrugated perspex roofing sheets. Old tyres can be stacked to any height desired, and old sinks and bath-tubs can also become garden beds. Small moveable 'beds' that can be raised to any height are easily constructed by creating square frames from boards 50cm long and 10cm wide and stacking them to the desired height before filling them with soil. Cover the tops of these boxes with glass or plastic to make a warm environment for the plants. The only limiting factor on growing in these outsize containers is the volume and quality of soil in the box, which must meet the nutrient requirements of the plants to be grown in them.

Growing in raised beds and other types of boxes is becoming popular even in gardens where there is enough room and good soil to plant straight into the ground. Many people find it easier to tend plots that are raised off the ground. Vegetable beds can become front-garden features rather than being banished to the back yard. Feeding the soil and managing weeds is easier, and raised beds and boxes are more easily covered with glass, plastic or netting. It is nice to have plants closer to eye and nose level, and raised beds and boxes can be put in places that otherwise would be hard to garden, such as the strip of ground between the driveway and the house wall that gets lots of sun, but has poor, stony soil. Finally, a raised bed or big box is a good place to start for someone who is new to the ways of seeds, seedlings and growing plants. It's easier to see what's going on and make adjustments.

Grown close to town: sustainable smallholders

Looking at what can be produced from such limited growing spaces makes me wonder why anyone needs a quarter acre, let alone more, to be self-sufficient in fresh greens and well supplied with other veges. What do people with more space *do* with it all? How much land is actually needed to provide everyone in New Zealand with at least 400g of fresh produce every day?

When I visited Wyenova Farm, a smallholding just south of Christchurch, I discovered that by using careful organic methods a huge amount can be produced from a relatively small area. In the 1960s Ivan and Vanya Maw bought 30ha and gradually transformed the land into one of New Zealand's first Biogro organic-certified properties, growing linseed, peas and carrots. Today Wyenova is just 9ha, which is more manageable for Vanya by herself. It is also a perfect size for her to realise her twin dreams of growing a Noah's Ark of food and restoring nature.

Vanya's farming is focused on food. She has been a student of nutrition for over 30 years, and was especially motivated by the death of a relative from bowel cancer at the early age of 51. Vanya optimises the nutritive value of the food she produces both by growing it organically and by growing a great variety of it. She uses surprisingly little space for growing vegetables – barely 1000 square metres – considering that she sells them, and soup made from them, at a weekly market. This is mainly because her kitchen garden is constantly enriched with compost and her market gardens are created in different places every year, in paddocks that have been fertilised by grazing sheep and/or by the red clover in the mixed-species hay crop produced the year before. Soil thus enriched produces heavy crops on a small space.

A large part of Wyenova is devoted to fruit and nut trees and Vanya's collection is impressive. It can also be hard to spot, because as well as growing edible species in the usual orchard formation, Vanya has created hedgerows of mixed species. The edible trees in the hedge that protects her from the southerly wind include hazels, elderberries and birches.

I didn't know there was anything edible about birch trees, but Vanya plans to try her hand at extracting a syrup from them, like maples. I was also surprised when she took me to see her collection of cacti and succulents, until the prickly pear cactus was pointed out to me. Vanya is eagerly awaiting its first fruiting. (One can also eat the green parts of this cactus, once the spines have been removed. I have eaten it in Mexico, where it is a popular vegetable and goes by the name of nopales.) Her vegetables also push the boundaries for most people: she is keen on 'wild' greens such as chickweed, comfrey, nettle, puha, dandelion and marshmallow. There's no doubt that these are more nutritious than most 'tame' greens, especially the ones that have been beaten into submission by industrial production and distribution systems. However, don't expect to see these weeds on sale any time soon – even on Vanya's stall, as she knows most people won't know how (or why) they are good to eat.

They will come up in your vege patch anyway, if you let them, and it's your choice whether to save them for salad (or soup, pesto, stir-fry or boil-up) or pull them for composting. Vanya lets them contribute to the greenery in her kitchen garden, which also produces a lot of self-sown vegetables and even fruit trees from stones thrown onto the rich soil. A lot of her orchard trees, especially the peaches and plums, came from self-sown seedlings. Such trees do not come true from seed, so sometimes the resulting fruit will be unsuccessful, while other times it will be better than the original. If, like Vanya, you have the land and time to find out which is which, this is a great way to grow fruit trees.

Self-sowing is also a good way to get the trees she is currently concentrating on planting, namely a half-hectare block of native trees as part of a restoration project that will eventually become a protected reserve. Over 1000 trees and shrubs have already gone in, and there will be plenty more yet. As with the farmed part of her property, Vanya finds multiple values in her reserve. In addition to encouraging native birds by providing them with food and shelter, and enjoying the reserve's contribution to the beauty and privacy of her property, she has plans for making herbal medicines from some of the native plants. The next step in her plans includes constructing a building for storing, drying and processing her harvests, with a commercial kitchen. I am hoping she'll go back to producing gherkin relish on a commercial scale there, as she used to make a beauty.

When I put this to her she laughed it off, saying that she started making it only as a way of using the gherkins that were too small, misshapen or old to sell fresh, as she hates waste. Living lightly on the earth is all part of Vanya's philosophy of life. She detests the throwaway lifestyle that comes with industrial over-production. She points out that far from reassuring us that there is enough for all, it actually prevents us from seeing, appreciating and respecting the abundance of nature. No matter how many cans and packets there are on the supermarket shelves, they can't and won't reproduce themselves. By contrast, just one small tomato contains the seeds for dozens more, and just one potato tuber can also produce an abundance.

Indeed, international experience of urban agriculture – farming within cities and on the peri-urban fringe[9] – shows that one of the best ways a country can ensure that its citizens are well fed and healthy is by protecting smallholdings within and close to towns and cities. This is the most effective way of protecting both the fresh food supply and the environment. Wyenova Farm is one example, and there are literally thousands of others throughout New Zealand. The ones close to urban areas are critically important, because it is these places that used to, and still could, cut the many links in the industrial food supply chain that are degrading food and environment.

The valley where I grew up is only 15 minutes by bike from the centre of Christchurch. Until the 1980s, when the trend toward covering good urban growing land with concrete really gathered momentum, the valley had three big market gardens on its warm slopes, growing a range of vegetables, from sweetcorn to cabbages. There were also glasshouses full of tomatoes, a raspberry farm, a chrysanthemum grower, a rose grower and a plum orchard. None of these productive enterprises was more than a hectare in size and most were less. All of them were just 4km from the auction markets in the centre of town, so that produce could get from the farm to the market to the greengrocer in 24 hours or less. In addition to the health and energy conservation benefits of getting food from producer to consumer so easily and quickly (and more cheaply because of the lack of middlemen and large-scale infrastructure), the arrangements for growing the food were also a lot less energy-intensive, as well as more socially positive.

Most of the labour on smallholdings is done by the family that lives there. When they need extra labour, as at planting and harvest time, it comes from neighbours, or at least from the same region. I got to my casual jobs of picking raspberries and planting cabbages on my bike, along with other teenagers who lived in the valley and some mothers-at-home who were also available for this work. Smallholdings have smaller labour requirements, which fit in nicely with the needs of locals for part-time and casual work.

Nadene Hall, the editor of the smallholders' magazine *Lifestyle Block* (formerly *Growing Today*), knows what it's all about because she grew up this way. Her parents kept poultry and grew telegraph cucumbers in glasshouses. In the 1980s it was still possible to make a living from cucumbers grown in 1800 square metres of glasshouse, but today that glasshouse is leased out to a grower who has 10 or more other houses of a similar size – and still has to have another job. Up the road from Nadene's old place there is a smallholding (4ha) that has gone monocultural. It is completely covered in glasshouses, in which the feeding and watering of the plants is automated, and no real soil is used to grow them. Glasshouse growers are like other large-scale produce growers, with contracts to supply supermarkets with a set product at a set price. While conditions are certainly not as socially and environmentally ugly as they are in European glasshouse-growing operations that use exploited immigrant labour,[10] they are certainly not as pretty and functional as on smallholdings devoted to a variety of crops and animals, where the owners live and produce for the home as well as the market.

Like the products of kitchen gardens in urban areas, the production from smallholdings is of no interest to those in charge of national accounting and national economic planning. Very little of the produce from smallholdings is exported or sent to food processing factories, so small farmers are not taken seriously by the financial and political elites. To my ears the usual term employed to describe smallholders and their land – 'lifestyle' farming or 'lifestyle' block – suggests that what happens there is different from what 'real' farmers are doing.

The reality, to which Nadene and her magazine can attest, is that most smallholders work harder than most people to get food for the home and for the market from their land. The reason most of them can't make a living at it is the same reason that a lot of bigger farms now also rely on some off-farm income: the market has been rigged against them by corporate concentration, supported by government policies that favour such concentration and discriminate against smaller producers. Unless smallholders specialise in producing something that goes into a genuinely free and open market, like farmers' markets, rather than a monopolistic, concentrated one like supermarkets, they cannot make a living off the same amount of land that, up until the 1980s, was plenty for market gardeners, fruit-growers, free-range egg and poultry producers and small dairy farmers to do well on.

As the English historian, writer, grape breeder and self-sufficient gardener Edward Hyams expressed it in 1970:

> There is a widely accepted delusion that very large-scale agriculture is more
> 'efficient' than small-scale cottage or peasant agriculture. This persists in the face
> of the evidence, even scientific evidence … The truth is that by 'industrializing'
> agriculture and horticulture, big money profits can be made, but only at the
> expense of food production; to the best of my knowledge it is impossible to stay
> alive by eating dollar bills or one-pound notes, or even ten-pound notes.[11]

Making socially and environmentally friendly farming economically viable again will require public policy shifts and private purchasing shifts. This is discussed in more detail in Chapter 8. It will also require recovering gardening knowledge, which is discussed below.

Growing good gardeners

Whether you grow veges on 4ha, a quarter acre or in a box, it helps to know what you are doing. For almost 30 years, between the late 1970s and mid-2000s, New Zealand had world-class, tertiary-level education courses, and research, in organic growing and farming, and was thus in a strong position to host the tenth biennial conference of the International Federation of Organic Agriculture Movements (IFOAM) at Lincoln University in 1994, and showcase New Zealand organic research and practice. This is no longer the case. The last of the dedicated organic teaching and research departments, at Unitec in Auckland, closed at the end of 2008. For those wanting to make a career in organic growing the only options now are to do a part-time correspondence course, or to enrol in a training course much reduced in time and content, supplied by a private provider or industry group. There are no opportunities for dedicated higher study or graduate research in organic growing or farming at university level, although some general degree courses sometimes offer optional papers in organics, and some graduate research may have organic applications, such as research into non-toxic forms of pest control.

This lack of investment in organics study and research, and thus in growers and farmers who know how to combine best economic *and* ecological practice, and scientists who can help them lift their game, seems remarkably short-sighted given the huge environmental and nutritional challenges our nation faces. Without proper public investment in expanding the sustainable production knowledge base, it is much harder for organic producers to be commercially successful, since they cannot fund much research and education for themselves. It also retards the spread of sustainable gardening knowledge in the public at large. The graduates of the university and polytechnic courses offered until 2008 have gone on to use their education in a variety of ways, including setting up small businesses that include education as well as growing. These people, fully educated themselves, are some of the few now offering education in sustainable gardening theory and practice.

Sarah Davies of Patch from Scratch, for example, is a graduate of the courses run at Unitec's Hortecology unit. An important feature of her business is the provision of educational resources in organic gardening. This service is also provided by Rachel Knight, who gardens and teaches right at the end of the Ohariu Valley Road in Wellington. Rachel was tutored in organic growing by Bill Martin of Christchurch Polytech, before its organics course was cut in 2006. She has developed a vege box scheme and plant sale business and has also become part of the informal education sector by running workshops in organic gardening for small groups. Rachel's productive gardens are the site of hands-on learning. They also serve as a source of sustainable design ideas, incorporating different ways of fitting plants to places, and making best use of nature's services. Students from the workshops are given notes to take away, and can keep up to date with a fortnightly e-newsletter containing gardening articles and recipes.[12]

With so few formal education opportunities in good gardening now available, anyone wanting to move beyond the basics is going to have to put together their own informal course of study, and be prepared to travel to where the best teachers and practitioners are. One such unofficial 'college' is run by Charmaine Pountney and Tanya Cumberland of Earth Talk, on the Awhitu Peninsula, south of Auckland. They have an example of most aspects of sustainable living and growing on their 11ha property. Half of their land is being restored to its original native forest and wetland vegetation, while the rest is in productive use growing food plants and timber trees. There is also a special collection of heritage weaving flaxes, grown in partnership with the local hapu, Ngati Te Ata. This amazingly abundant and diverse haven for people, and birds, looks and feels quite different from the surrounding farming landscape, with its monocultures of grass and shelterbelts and too many buildings with very few gardens.

Because such well-loved land speaks for itself, Tanya and Charmaine's preferred form of teaching is to take guided tours, or to let visitors do their own thing in their own time with a self-guiding leaflet. Charmaine has plenty of experience in education – she was formerly principal of Auckland Girls' Grammar School – and it has led her to the realisation that unless people *ask* to learn something, they won't learn. Even with the guided tours she believes that the people who learn the most are those who 'know what they need to know'. Such tours may not cover the whole property, but rather focus on the aspects in which the students want to become proficient, from subtropical fruit growing to worm farming.

Tanya and Charmaine offer workshops on and off the property, helping women in particular on the road to sustainability. Their 'Food for Thought' workshop series starts, like all their teaching, with a grounding in the 'Treats of the Treaty', for they are convinced that nurturing the land and nurturing relationships are indivisible. As they say on their website:

> We … have a passionate commitment to good relationships – with each other, with Ngati Te Ata, the mana whenua of our area, with our neighbours and the wider community. Together, in our different ways, we continue to work towards sustainable development and social justice in Aotearoa.[13]

Demonstration and display gardens where expert tutoring in sustainability can take place are an extremely valuable educational resource. Community gardens, and private initiatives like The Kitchen Garden and Earth Talk, have begun meeting this need, but it is vital that developing such educational gardens on public land becomes a priority for towns and cities. Every city should be promoting sustainable gardening as a solution to the increasingly pressing urban problems of organic waste disposal, air and water pollution, water shortages and really fresh and accessible food supplies. The best place for such gardens is in existing civic gardens and parks.

Hamiltonians are especially blessed in this regard. The Hamilton Gardens devote quite a lot of land to productive gardening activities and involve amateur and trainee professional gardeners in establishing and working them. There is a large kitchen garden, which is worked by horticulture students as part of their studies, a big herb garden and also, the epitome of sustainable gardening, a demonstration permaculture garden. This 'Sustainable Backyard' garden was established by Hamilton Permaculture Trust volunteers in 2000 and opened in 2001. In 2006 the Hamilton City Council, via its gardens staff, took over responsibility for the daily maintenance of the Sustainable Backyard for the next 10 years, but trust members are still actively involved in running workshops and other educational events in the garden.[14]

The trust's project co-ordinator and educator, Cheryl Noble, took me on a tour of the Sustainable Backyard and I was impressed by how much had been fitted into such a small space. This is possible when one follows permaculture principles, which include designing for multiple functions and turning potential problems into positive solutions. (The 12 permaculture principles, with detailed explanations of how they work, can be found on the Permaculture in New Zealand website (www.permaculture.org.nz), along with lots of other information on permaculture groups, properties and educational events in New Zealand.)

Every distinctive element in the Sustainable Backyard has a sign that shows you how it works, with enough information for you to work out how to do it for yourself. I carefully studied the signs showing how to set up a small aquaculture system and grow azolla (a nitrogen-rich water weed that makes a great mulch) and water chestnuts – it looked so easy! The Sustainable Backyard is also a great place to see unusual vegetables and fruits growing and to visualise the potential of vertical gardening: growing food crops on fences, arches, pergolas and the like. This makes a lot of sense if you have limited ground space.

There is an increasing demand for the workshops and classes Cheryl runs here and at community gardens, schools and on urban marae. There was a big surge of interest in 2008 (no doubt fuelled by rising food and petrol prices) and Cheryl now has waiting lists for her workshops. Kindergarten, kohanga reo and primary school pupils also come to the Sustainable Backyard for ideas on what could be done at their place, and Cheryl is an adviser to preschools. Although this is demonstrably educational work, and requires teaching as well as gardening skills, most of the public funding for Cheryl's work comes from the employment and health budgets.

This is not the case at the Auckland Regional Gardens, where trained teachers are funded by the Ministry of Education to teach the sustainability theme of the national curriculum. This includes edible gardening, and the educators at the gardens have a 'Create Your Own Garden' programme that involves teaching the basics of organic gardening on-site, and providing printed resources to take away. This programme is increasing in popularity and the food-garden beds beside the Children's Garden, which has demonstration beds of food plants, are to treble in size to allow for more hands-on gardening by visiting classes. The gardens also have a huge Edible Garden, enabling people of all ages to learn more about food plants, either on self-guided walks or with an expert. It is designed to showcase what will grow easily in the Auckland region, without sprays or special care. I was fascinated to encounter the ice-cream bean tree and disappointed to find it was too late in the year to sample any, and that they won't grow much further south.[15] Apparently this tree is very popular with young visitors when it is fruiting!

The persimmon tree in the Children's Garden would also be popular, but they have a dilemma there between sustainable food gardening and nature conservation. The pukeko that roam the gardens flap into the tree and peck at the fruit. Sad for fruit fanciers, but a good lesson in how it sometimes isn't easy being green. Yet sustainability and conservation educators and advocates are increasingly coming to see how providing safe, fresh, local food for humans plays a vital role in ensuring a safe, clean environment with abundant food resources for other species. The Enviroschools programme[16] and the World Wide Fund for Nature have both been supporting organic gardening in schools by providing a mixture of expert personnel, gardening and teaching resources and funding.

At this point these programmes are only available for a few schools and children, and not necessarily the ones that have the greatest need. It's a step in the right direction, but it is still a long way from Charmaine Poutney's vision of *all* schools becoming SEED schools, where SEED stands for Sustainable Learning, Ethical Behaviour, Environmental Responsibility and Democratic Participation. It is also a long way from where New Zealand was 50 years ago, in terms of the natural integration of growing food at home into the best of daily household activities. To return to that, we need to work out how to grow together again, in more ways than one. Let's take a look at how this is starting to happen.

Dill mayonnaise

(enough for two or three potato salads or coleslaws)

Ingredients

1 cup of fresh dill sprigs

1 egg

½ tsp salt

½ tsp Dijon mustard

2 tbsp cider vinegar OR

lemon juice

about 1 cup light oil

Method

Chop the dill finely.

Put the dill, egg, salt, mustard and vinegar into a food processor and whizz to combine well.

With the motor running, drip and then drizzle in the oil until the mayonnaise is thick and creamy. (If it gets too thick, it can be thinned with a little water just before use.)

If not using at once, store in the fridge in a covered glass jar for up to two weeks.

Variations

Use other soft green herbs, singly or in combination – coriander, parsley, chervil, chives, mint. For potato salads, add chopped garlic with the herb(s) – up to half a bulb. (This much garlic does not taste as strongly garlicky as one would expect and is delicious in combination with coriander.)

Auckland Botanic Gardens - even in May the Edible Garden has peas in flower and loads of other veges ready to eat.

Auckland Central - five storeys up. No garden? No problem. Glenys Casci, senior lecturer in culinary arts at the Auckland University of Technology, grows food on her office balcony.

Khandallah, Wellington - postie John Maynard shows me the garden at the back of the mail sorting centre.

Hamilton Gardens - detail on a raised herb bed in the Sustainable
Backyard Garden.

Hamilton Gardens - a healthy taro plant grows beside the pond in
the Sustainable Backyard Garden.

Hamilton Gardens - aquaculture can be part of a sustainable backyard garden.

Ohariu Valley, Wellington - vege seedlings in a cold frame in The Kitchen Garden.

CHAPTER THREE

Community@Garden

Maara Maori

These days we can learn a lot about gardening from books, magazines and the internet, but the best garden teachers will always be those who know our local soils and climate, who have years of experience in choosing and nurturing plants, and who are able to show – not tell – us what to do. When you work alongside such teachers in the garden, or relax with them after work, the knowledge – and respect for the knowledge – sinks in.

For hundreds of years this on-the-job education was the only form of gardening education in Aotearoa, and it clearly worked well. Clever methods were developed for extending the growing range and times of introduced subtropical crops like taro and kumara, and equally ingenious techniques were devised for extracting the food value from rather unpromising indigenous plants such as cabbage trees.[1] Traditional gardening was a communal activity, with whanau and hapu working large areas of ground together. Well-worked Maori gardens thus became prime sites for establishing Pakeha homes and gardens in the 19th century. Antonio Te Maioha, one of the presenters of the *Kiwi Maara* gardening programme on Maori Television, makes a wry reference to this when he says that to describe his birthplace in a Maori or indigenous context would be to say, 'I was born next to the massive gardens that used to stretch across the old Paa site at the foot of Te Totara I a Hua – now known as Maunga Kiekie. In a non-Maori context that just means I was born in National Women's Hospital.'[2] Food producing, gathering and preparation in pre-colonial New Zealand was a collective enterprise, and even when horses, ploughs, private housing, grocery shops and other technological and social innovations arrived, the communal gardening model did not die, but took new forms.

Horses and ploughs enabled the garden area to be extended more easily and rapidly and new crops, such as potatoes and wheat, to be grown. Any surplus found a ready market in the settlements the British colonists were creating in New Zealand, and even as far away as Australia, which took much longer than New Zealand to become self-sufficient in the British diet. Until the 1950s and 1960s most Maori in rural areas continued to have large gardens, which were ploughed each spring. These gardens, although often attached to private dwellings, were worked communally.[3] By the 1970s a combination of factors – migration to the cities, increased access to cheap industrial food, increased paid employment opportunities for women as well as men, smaller families – meant that food gardening by Maori went into the same sort of decline as its Pakeha counterpart. Maori, however, have paid a greater health toll than Pakeha for this loss of ready access to fresh, whole, low-cost plant foods. Lower incomes, limited residential choices and lack of transport options mean that their access to good food has been heavily constrained. Thus diet-related disease rates are higher for Maori than for Pakeha.

That's the bad news. The good news is that home and community gardening by Maori is undergoing a renaissance that is possibly even bigger and brighter than the one happening among non-Maori. In kohanga reo kindergartens and kura kaupapa schools, on marae, in back yards and on Maori-owned commercial farming and market-gardening land, a new form of growing is being developed and applied. It combines traditional tikanga with complementary and supportive approaches from Western sources, such as biodynamics and permaculture. The new synthesis can be seen on *Kiwi Maara*,[4] where the presenters bring together fluency in tikanga and te reo with training and expertise in organic, bio-intensive, biodynamic and permaculture gardening methods.

Grounding the production of food in traditional tikanga while making good use of new knowledge and methods is also the focus of Te Waka Kai Ora, the national Maori Organics Authority of Aotearoa (New Zealand). Te Waka Kai Ora has created a Maori organic certification standard, Hua Parakore. Launched in July 2011, the Hua Parakore standard incorporates traditional Maori ways of growing that are consistent with contemporary definitions of organic production, and also includes the traditional cultural dimension, such as the karakia appropriate to planting and harvesting. Te Waka Kai Ora's kaupapa is to 'promote the use of traditional Maori values and ethics of organic food production. Ecological and cultural sustainability are central to our mission. We are committed to responsible economic development in a manner that is consistent with our guiding principles ...'[5]

Promoting Maori economic and cultural development and sustainability through growing food is also the kaupapa of Tahuri Whenua, the National Maori Vegetable Growers Collective, a non-profit organisation that represents Maori interests in the horticulture sector. As well as running a dedicated scientific research programme into better varieties and production methods for traditional Maori vegetables, especially taewa (potatoes), Tahuri Whenua has a programme called Spud in a Bucket, which provides participating primary schools with everything they need to grow – and to learn about growing – the humble but so important spud. The programme also puts potato growing within its wider cultural and horticultural context.[6]

In addition to these national initiatives some iwi are engaging in sustainable growing research and development. One example of this is He Whenua Whakatipu, established in 2004 to assist Ngai Tahu landholders in Te Waipounamu (the South Island) to generate sustainable livelihoods from the land, and also to create positive environmental and social outcomes from their farming. He Whenua Whakatipu is a collaboration between the iwi and the Agricultural Research Group on Sustainability (ARGOS), which has an ongoing programme of research into sustainable farming practices, including economic and social sustainability as well as sustainable agronomy.[7]

The social and economic context is especially relevant to regenerating Maori farming. The climatic and ecological differences between the north of the North Island and the south of the South Island led to different traditional foods and different ways of procuring them. The colonial land purchases of the early 19th century deprived Ngai Tahu hapu of good farming land, and also access to their mahinga kai (traditional food gathering and hunting sites). The Ngai Tahu settlement of Treaty of Waitangi claims in 1998 provided money and processes, as appropriate, for getting back land and also access to mahinga kai, but this is not enough to rebuild a sustainable and healthy food system based on ancestral lands and practices. The Whenua Whakatipu programme seeks to rebuild communities who have the knowledge and skills needed to make a living from growing and wild-harvesting of food in and around the old village sites that were largely abandoned when their inhabitants went off to work in the market economy.

John Reid and Gianni Prencipe, who work for He Whenua Whakatipu, believe that the process of regenerating land and people is a complex one, involving as much work on nourishing relationships and motivations, and balancing effort and results, as on acquiring knowledge of plants and how to cultivate them. Yet that side of the programme, which also involves rescuing old varieties and foods, trialling new ones and finding suitable markets for them all, is obviously vital to its success. Gianni's training and experience as a chef in Belgium is helpful when it comes to identifying what will find favour with professional chefs and anyone else looking for something to give their cooking an edge. Yet he is just as focused on the inherent quality of common foods when they are grown and prepared in the right way. Echoing Hohepa Kereopa, he says, 'The intention with which food is made has an effect on the body.'

So does the wider environmental context within which food is produced, and here the work of He Whenua Whakatipu draws on the traditional Maori understanding of kaitiakitanga, meaning responsibility for and relationship with the whole environment in which food is produced and found. Turning on an irrigating machine to water grass for dairy cows may be good for the farmer's profits, but what does it do to the rivers that are drained and dammed to provide the water and the power, and the other species that live in and from them? If the rivers and streams no longer run free and pure to fill the lakes, what will happen to the lakes' wildlife?

This sense of the connectedness between humans and nature is cultivated in Maori gardening just as surely as the plants. Some Maori schools have full teaching programmes devoted to transmitting the knowledge and experience of kaitiakitanga. Te Kura Toitu o Te Whaiti Nui-a-Toi is one of them, and the record of a student field trip to Whaingaroa (Raglan) is a delight to read. They visited the Kaiwhenua Organics Trust, which started by growing vegetables on a small patch of land and now supplies the local shops with everything they grow. The students say:

> They do not use chemicals on their land and they experimented and listened to nature for the best ways to grow things. It must work because we all thought the strawberries were deliciously sweet! ... We asked Uncle Malibu (a lifetime surfie) what Kaitiakitanga meant. He said it is a rich concept that governments can never define at an official level and that it was not just about the land but also embraces people. He told us that it was something that must start first within ourselves.[8]

From little things, big things grow

The sooner it starts the better. The benefits of learning by doing things with others can begin at a very early age. Lily White, the co-ordinator of the Kids' Edible Gardens programme in Christchurch, told me a remarkable story. At one of the schools where she gardens with the children she was especially impressed by one boy who was always eager to garden and was very well behaved. He quickly became knowledgeable about the plants and how to grow them successfully. When she was asked by another teacher what she thought of the behaviour of this student, the teacher concerned thought they were talking about a different boy. In his regular classes his behaviour and abilities were considered so problematic that he had a special needs teacher permanently assigned to him.

For most children, gardening won't make such a big difference, but it will perform more everyday miracles. Schools that make the commitment to having a food garden find that this has multiple benefits. Lily has been teaching children to garden ever since her own children had a friend to stay over one weekend. The little guest was offered a special Sunday breakfast made from eggs collected from the bantam hens in Lily's garden, but refused to eat the 'dirty' eggs that came from the hens' bottoms, and held out for 'clean' ones from the supermarket. At that time Lily was on the Parent Teacher Association of her children's school. The egg incident was the trigger for her suggesting to the PTA that she teach gardening. She was given their blessing, and $30 for expenses.

Lily's philosophy is to reuse good materials and recycle everything possible. She starts off each group of new young gardeners by showing them where and how to find the seeds in the autumn garden, how to clean, dry and store them, and how to grow them on to be planted out in spring. This is the best possible way to teach where life – and food – begins. Now that horticulture is no longer part of the core curriculum, school gardens can have an important role in community-building. Putting together a successful school garden is certainly an exercise in nourishing relationships: the activity is voluntary, and makes use of public resources – the part of the school grounds used for the garden, the time of school staff who liaise with the garden facilitator, money from school funds to pay the garden facilitator and buy tools and so on for the garden, as well as private good will – the time and materials donated by supportive parents, other community members and local businesses, grants from charitable organisations.

Lily has learned the hard way that there is no point in responding to the regular requests she gets to come and set up a garden in yet another school unless she gets real commitment from all the adults involved. This starts with bringing together the school principal, at least two teachers with an interest in gardening, the groundsman and some parents for a preliminary workshop that covers exactly what is involved in having a school garden and whether they can commit to it. If the commitment is there then the garden can go ahead, although if the adults get too enthusiastic about it that can cause problems too. At one school some parents came in over the holidays and re-landscaped the garden to what they thought was a better arrangement. Lily was not happy. What the parents thought was prettier was not as functional, and it gave an unwelcome message to the children: they were downcast because they thought it meant that what they had done was not good enough. Once everyone gets to understand what a school garden can and should be, however, things go as well as they do in other community gardens, where people learn to work with each other and with nature to produce food in environmentally friendly ways.

Community gardens are now happening at every level of education, from pre-schools to university level, and all the ones I have seen are doing a nice job of mixing students, parents and the wider community to extend the influence of the garden beyond the small patch in the school grounds. Kate Hewson, who was Sustainability Advocate at the University of Canterbury and co-ordinator of the community garden there from 2006 to 2010, showed me around the garden and said that one of the pupils at the pre-school next door had a morning routine of walking around the garden and stroking all the sculpted chickens before she would go in to school.

Canterbury University is not the obvious university for setting up a food garden, since it does not teach agriculture, horticulture, landscape architecture or the culinary arts. What it does have, however, is a very active student environmental club, Kakariki, and it was members of this club who saw what the Organic Garden City Trust was developing by way of community and school gardens in the rest of Christchurch, and started pushing to have one at the university. A steering group of students, staff and members of their families was set up, and finding a suitable site and co-ordinating the development of the garden became part of Kate's responsibilities as Sustainability Advocate. A lovely secluded stream-side site was found and working-bees began to construct and plant the garden. Student interest in the garden crosses all faculties and disciplines, including Fine Arts. This last is especially noticeable in the garden, with sculpted chickens, a mosaic birdbath, iron flax stalks at the entranceway, brightly painted stones instead of boring plastic for plant labels, and flower paintings on the noticeboard. Some engineering students have constructed a clay pizza oven that gets fired up for social gatherings in the garden.

Recycling and composting are as central to this garden as they are to other community gardens. The beds are edged, and slightly raised, with very old and lovely recycled tiles. Food waste deposited in dedicated outdoor containers around campus goes into the garden's compost bins, as does waste from some of the university's departments. Kakariki and other student clubs with a green bent hold their meetings in a small building in the garden, and workshops are run there for the university and the wider community. Kate feels that the garden has a lot more potential to feed into research and teaching programmes in the university, especially in the areas of ecology and sustainability. Maybe that will come, but for now the garden is definitely a prime site for informal learning. It is also a haven for relaxing in a setting that is more private, vibrant and interesting as well as more sustainable than much of the rest of the university landscape with its energy- and water-hungry expanses of lawn.

Growing together: community gardens

Although it is based on a university campus, and has the potential to be used for formal education, the Canterbury University garden also reaches out to engage with the wider community, and you don't have to be a staff member or student to garden there. For most community gardens, involving the widest possible range of people in the garden is a priority. Different gardens do this in different ways, as I discovered when I began visiting them.

My first stop was the Grey Lynn Community Gardens in the grounds of St Columba's Anglican church, Auckland, where I was welcomed by two of the founding gardeners, Andrea Higginson and Peter Wham. Andrea and Peter were part of the group involved with Auckland City's first community garden, St Benedict's Urban Farm (later Basque Gardens), which was set up on public land in Basque Park in Newton in 1993. Initially the garden was welcomed by the city authorities as a way to solve some waste and water problems associated with a hitherto neglected site, and to increase the amenity of inner-city dwellers living in garden-less flats. But when it came under pressure from big business, in the form of real estate interests and building contractors, who claimed that it would reduce the value of their brutalist concrete tower blocks if they overlooked a 'messy' productive garden, the city council gave the Basque Park gardeners their marching orders. Some of them went to a smaller and even more obscure council site on Bond Street, which has no views into or out of it. Others who lived near St Columba's asked the vicar and his wife if they really needed a back lawn, and whether they wouldn't rather have a garden there instead. The St Columba's complex of church, vicarage and hall already had a lovely ornamental garden wrapped around it, and the couple were not averse to having their back lawn dug up and turned into several small but highly productive beds.

This pattern of lots of beds, often raised ones, with paths winding around them, is typical of community gardens. Form follows function, and having several small beds rather than a few big ones allows for a more socially and environmentally efficient use of the space. Some beds can be allotted to individuals or families to work, while others can be kept for group efforts. Crops can be rotated more easily. Beds accessible from pathways on at least two sides can be worked without compacting the soil. Further, as we have seen, they are more easily managed by gardeners with a disability, children, and those getting on in years. Small raised beds also facilitate vertical gardening. This is important when overall garden space is limited.

Another common feature of community gardens is a larger and more sophisticated composting operation than most home gardens can boast. As well as material produced on site – weeds, grass clippings, fine prunings, chicken manure and so on – gardeners bring their kitchen and other organic wastes from homes. They may also encourage their neighbours to do the same. Now if you are thinking that nothing could be more pathetic and less likely to save your suburb, city and country from being swamped with waste, and running out of good soil, than lugging a bucket or two of kitchen scraps down to the local community garden for composting each week, please think again. An experiment run at the Christchurch South Community Garden in Strickland Street, where neighbours voluntarily bring their scraps for composting, showed that over the course of a year the manager and volunteers on the 1200m^2 site could effectively process more than 30 tonnes of organic waste and turn it into good compost. This is waste that would otherwise have gone to a landfill – expensive and not environmentally friendly – or perhaps to a municipal composting operation. These are better than landfill, but they are still much more energy- and machinery-intensive than the neighbourhood composting solution, and hence less sustainable in the long run.

Composting at the community garden scale certainly requires careful management of the waste stream as it comes in, to ensure that there is no pest or smell nuisance created, and that unsuitable materials such as noxious weeds, bones and meat are excluded. Once a well-managed system is established, however, this is easily achievable. Everything proceeds just as it would at home, only on a larger scale. Most community gardens also have a worm farm to process kitchen scraps into especially nutritious vermicast and 'worm-wee', which is the leachate from worm farms. The Grey Lynn Community Gardens worm farm has an ingenious arrangement of five old bathtubs full of worms set on a slight slope, with pipes connecting all the plug holes. The drain hole of the lowest tub is connected to a container for collecting the leachate from all the tubs.

By paying such careful attention to feeding the soil and plants, the Grey Lynn Community Gardens make a big contribution to producing nourishing food for the gardeners. They make a contribution to their social needs as well. As Andrea Higginson says, 'Nourishing relationships is the key to nourishing the land.' This also makes sense if you put it the other way around. Gardening with others requires you to relate to them, paying attention to their various needs and abilities, caring that gardening is positive for everyone. From this strong base every person can look after their patch of garden, or work with others on the communal patch. Yet wanting to do the best by the land also means wanting to do the best by the people who live from it, so there is a happy synergy that can happen when those who work the land are also those who eat from it, whether that land is a community garden or a family farm.

There is some American research showing the strong and measurable positive social effects from community gardens. For example, a study of over 60 community gardens in upstate New York found, unsurprisingly, that the gardeners ate better and got more exercise than they did before they started gardening. There were other benefits too. These included improving residents' attitude toward the neighbourhood, improved maintenance on neighbouring properties, reduced litter and greater neighbourhood pride. Community gardens also spurred tree planting and mural painting in the neighbourhood, the formation of neighbourhood associations and crime-watch efforts. Best of all, this 'garden effect' was four times more likely to occur in low-income neighbourhoods, precisely where the need is greatest.[9] Similar benefits have been noted anecdotally for New Zealand community gardens. Community gardens promote social inclusion by engaging people on four key dimensions: production, political participation, consumption and social interaction. Christine Blance, manager of the Christchurch South Community Garden, says all this is happening in Christchurch through the community gardens. 'From working with local organisations through to eating high-quality organic produce, the shared goal of the gardens is to provide an environment that both values and encourages respect for all members of the community.'[10]

Some community gardens in New Zealand also play an additional social role. They are places where those who are unable to participate fully in everyday life because they suffer from a mental or physical illness or disability can take part in a useful activity that allows them to work and to interact with others, at whatever level is comfortable and appropriate for them. This can include preparing for mainstream employment. The Framework Trust, an Auckland community-based mental health and intellectual disability services organisation,[11] operates two community gardens for its clients, Kelmarna Organic City Farm in Herne Bay and Devonport Organic City Farm. Both offer specialist training in organic horticulture and sustainable development as well as individualised learning and support in horticulture, sustainable living and life skills, personal development and pre-vocational skills and further education. The gardening education is carried out through practical experience in the gardens themselves and visits to other organic gardens, and through a series of training modules covering compost making, worm farms and companion planting. The trust staff who work at the gardens are a talented bunch, combining gardening skills with social work and psychology qualifications. 'Sometimes,' says Linda Christianson, the senior co-ordinator of the trust's gardens, 'the most one of my clients can manage is to get out of bed in the morning, get to the garden, and sit beside me while I do some gardening.' At the other end of the achievement scale, some clients go on to do New Zealand Qualifications Authority (NZQA) qualifications in horticulture, although the trust is focused on improving general life and employment skills, rather than turning out professional gardeners.

The spirit of growing sustainably

The vicar of St Columba's and his wife understood the potential of a community garden on church land straight away, and gave up not only their back lawn but also their carport for conversion into a quaint little clubhouse that gives no hint of its utilitarian origins. None of the gardeners were churchgoers, until the day they made a special slide and music presentation about the life of the garden – and brought tears to the eyes of some of the parishioners.

A church congregation is one kind of community of interest, and a Roman Catholic religious order is even more so, since its members dedicate themselves to communal living as an alternative to family life. No surprises then that the sisters of the Home of Compassion, in Island Bay, Wellington, were very open to the idea of having a communal garden on their property. They also have a special gardening asset in the form of Sister Loyola Galvin, who has been the head gardener for the extensive grounds of the home since her late retirement from her profession of nursing and caring for children. When the readers of *New Zealand Gardener* magazine named her Gardener of the Year in 2008, Sister Loyola was 86 years old, and clearly an inspiration to many. When I met her for the first time I came away hoping that I might be as full of life, love and gardening knowledge at her age.

She has some help to keep the ornamental gardens at the Home of Compassion in order, but she works her own raised-bed organic vegetable garden, with associated propagating shed, by herself. She is also 'consultant grandmother' to the community gardeners who have established a permaculture garden called Common Ground in a prime spot in the grounds of the Home of Compassion. About 20 people come regularly from their flats in neighbouring suburbs to work their own plots and the communal plot. Sister Loyola pays $10 per year to be a member of the group, just like the other members. She doesn't work a personal plot in Common Ground herself, but she joins in communal activities and supports the work in many other ways, such as making up notices about what should and should not go in the row of compost bins. Her own garden also serves as an excellent example. Its neatly clipped internal hedges of hebes grown from cuttings serve to baffle the fierce southerly gales that come this way. Between the beds are soft, weed-free paths made of heavy cardboard covered with a thick layer of pine needles, which thwarts slugs and snails, while the raised beds are bursting with edible greenery. Most important are what Sister Loyola calls the 'engine' of her garden: the compost bins.

An ardent conservationist, Sister Loyola has propagated thousands of native plants for revegetation projects in the Wellington area, including the hills that link the Home of Compassion and the Tapu Te Ranga marae, and were once part of a farm owned by the Sisters of Compassion. They are slowly being replanted in the trees that would have once held the soil and tempered the wind. The latter will not come soon enough for Sister Loyola – she has already been blown off a bank and into a carpark at the home, sustaining serious injuries that prevented her from walking for a while. This did not keep her from gardening, though. She had railings put on either side of the steps up to her garden, drove up to them in a battery-powered wheelchair, and then hauled herself up to the garden. Incredibly determined, incredibly knowledgeable about gardening and its contribution to sustainability (I came away with pages of excellent tips), yet also humble and eager to learn from others and from nature, Sister Loyola is an ideal mentor for beginner gardeners. The founder of her order, Suzanne Aubert, was a remarkable plantswoman herself – she formulated herbal medicines based on native plants – but primarily she was someone who was dedicated to compassionate action.[12] Sister Loyola carries on in her spirit, having moved on from her 'first career', nursing and caring for children, to her 'second career' of nursing and caring for the earth.

Growing greener cities

Starting a community garden in a place where you are wanted and loved and the value of nourishing relationships is understood is a breeze compared with fighting – and educating – City Hall. Community is a word open to many interpretations, from neighbourhoods where people live in close proximity up to whole towns and cities. It also applies to communities of interest – students, golfers, nurses, Chinese people, Muslims, musicians, you name it – within those cities and within the whole country. Most communities, even long-established neighbourhoods and professional interest groups, experience a certain amount of flux as people move in and out, and in some, such as schools, the turnover can be quite rapid.

A theme already apparent in New Zealand's short history of community gardening is that self-defined communities of interest are more sympathetic than geographical communities toward providing sites and in some cases paid personnel for community gardens. This seems to be because towns and cities are subject to a politics of land and resource management that is either ignorant of, or deliberately divorced from, a philosophy and practice of nourishing relationships and connections with healthy food sources. The fight over the use of part of Basque Park for a productive garden is a good example.

The lack of care and respect for public space that has turned many cities into concrete jungles has led to various levels of support for 'guerrilla gardening'. It is currently practised most enthusiastically in Britain, encouraged and promoted by Richard Reynolds via a website[13] and a book, *On Guerrilla Gardening*, but also has many passionate supporters in the US, Canada and Germany, and a few in other parts of the world, including New Zealand.[14] Most guerrilla gardening plantings are of hardy or come-again ornamentals, and a few stunning annuals (small shrubs, ornamental grasses, bulbs, sunflowers) rather than food crops, but the Basque Park garden probably qualifies as a guerrilla gardening initiative, since it also involved planting and tending neglected public space.

When you consider the rules and regulations with which most councils in New Zealand surround the use of public space, and the entrenched 'can't do' attitudes in some local bodies, guerrilla gardening starts to seem the most rational way to get some food grown on public land that is not being used for any other good purpose. In discussion with a senior open space planner at Auckland City Council, which after the Basque Park debacle developed a policy on community gardens that went into operation in 2002,[15] he and I canvassed the apparent contradiction between the possible need for community gardens to have some sort of fence or other protection, and the city rule that public space cannot be 'privatised' by restricting access. The contradiction is more apparent than real, since almost all the city's public sportsgrounds and other playgrounds have restricted access clubrooms or other buildings on them, and even playing areas that are fenced off. So how about a level playing field for those whose recreation is team gardening, not team games?

Auckland has also adopted the policy that providing 'open space' is the primary function of public parks and other sites suitable for community gardens, and therefore community gardens should be allowed only if they are tucked into corners and do not 'dominate the primary useable area of neighbourhood parks'. In applying for a lease to use some city land for a garden the would-be gardeners must incorporate themselves into a trust or other legal entity to be eligible. Then they have to prove that their proposed site is effectively out of sight – hence probably out of sun. Should any group manage to jump through all these hoops successfully and actually get to put some potatoes in the ground, in four years they are going to have to start hoop-jumping all over again, because leases are for a maximum of five years. So why wouldn't someone who was keen to get fresh food on the table this month rather than next year, and to nourish relationships not bureaucracy, go looking for a friendly church, school or other possible provider of garden space without all this palaver?

In 2007, prior to the Auckland super-city amalgamation, Waitakere City made land available for the Ranui Community Garden in a small park by a creek at the end of a dead-end street, opposite a primary school. The first plots created were immediately taken up by a range of gardeners, reflecting the diversity in the Ranui community. The school took some plots, so there is a young cohort coming on, while the elders of the garden include a Maori nanny, a Rwandan man in his seventies and a Samoan couple. One of the gardeners is also a nurse who teaches cooking at the community house. The choice of vegetable plants grown reflects the variety of the gardeners, and their size and health is a testament to everyone's gardening skills.[16] Workshops on worm farming, pruning, seed saving and other relevant topics are held at the garden. Council workers also received a crash course in organic gardening after being stopped just in time from spraying the comfrey under the fruit trees.

Celebrations of the seasons, such as Matariki, are also popular at the garden.

Yet although the garden is clearly providing positive social, environmental and educational benefits for the community, the development of its infrastructure and its programmes has proceeded slowly because it depends on the success of continual ad hoc funding applications. Educating councils to see community gardens as much more than 'hobby space', and agree to long-term funding, will probably take a while. As the experiment at the Strickland Street gardens in Christchurch shows, community gardens have a huge capacity to process the urban organic waste stream close to source, whether it is done using traditional bins and methods, or with the latest in small-space, labour-saving composting technology, such as the super-efficient solar-powered Vertical Composting Unit used at Unitec.[17] This ability to process waste close to source may be even more important than the production of high-quality and almost-free food within walking distance of consumers who do not have their own gardens. Both composting and car-free food consumption make a big contribution to minimising environmental damage, especially in regard to reducing greenhouse gas emissions.

Community gardens can also provide flexible part-time jobs close to home, and effectively supplement the income of individuals and the community by allowing cheap or free access to quality food. Working in the gardens also contributes to the health of the gardeners, while the connections made with other members of the community provide immeasurable benefits to social health and wealth. So much so that I found that while many of the gardeners I met in community gardens do actually have a garden at home (some of them quite large and productive), all were enthusiastic about community gardening precisely because it grows relationships as well as plants.

A favourite way of building those relationships is over a communal meal based on produce from the garden. Community gardeners are great recipe swappers and food sharers. The more diverse the community, the more diverse the recipes, and so new ways of cooking and eating as well as new ways of growing are evolving in New Zealand. In the next chapter I take a look at what's new on the dinner table Down Under and how it got there.

Ranui Community Garden
Mexican spiced kumara soup

(serves six)

Ingredients

1 onion, diced

2 tbsp butter or oil

1 tbsp ground cumin

½ tsp turmeric

¼ tsp chilli powder

1kg kumara, peeled and sliced

1 litre water

½ tsp salt

200ml cream OR creamy plain yoghurt

1 avocado, mashed

1 large clove garlic, crushed

juice of 1 lime

corn chips

Method

Gently fry the onion in the butter or oil until soft and golden.

Add the cumin, turmeric and chilli powder and fry gently for 2–3 minutes.

Add the sliced kumara and roll in the spice mix.

Add the water, mix well, bring the soup to a simmer.

Simmer 20 minutes, or until kumara is soft. Turn off the heat.

Make a salsa by mixing the avocado, garlic and lime juice.

Purée the soup or mash the kumara with a potato masher.

Add the salt to the soup, then the cream or yoghurt.

Reheat the soup gently.

Serve in bowls garnished with the avocado salsa and some corn chips.

(Recipe from the June 2010 issue of the *Ranui Community Garden Newsletter*, p. 2)

Student gardens at the Unitec Hortecology Unit.

Tomatoes growing up kanuka stakes at Bluegums homestead, Purau.

Grey Lynn community garden.

Kelmarna Gardens bring food close to many homes.

Sister Loyola's garden in Island Bay.

A sustainable backyard garden in Hamilton.

Autumn in the biodynamic garden at the Rudolf Steiner School in Christchurch.

The University of Canterbury community garden occupies a lovely stream-side site.

CHAPTER FOUR

Dining@Home

Our home dining heritage

Most New Zealanders have an ancestor or ancestors who immigrated here in the 19th century. What did they eat at home? Someone reading this could be a descendant of one of the men who had the Reverend Alexander Don to dinner on the Otago goldfields in 1889 and served up roast fowl and cress, dry oysters and dolichos root, roast pork and onions, Japanese dried fish and white nuts, pig's paunch and peas. This was accompanied by bowls of rice and tiny, but frequently refilled, cups of brandy.[1] The range and size of this meal becomes even more astonishing when we learn that the cooks were not professionals with a proper kitchen, but three goldminers on a claim at Horse's Flat, a long way by packhorse from city suppliers and amenities.

As James Ng's history of 19th-century Chinese migration to New Zealand shows, rice, pork and tea were as much the basic staples of the Chinese miners as bread, mutton and beer were for those of European descent.[2] However, the Chinese brought in and cooked a much greater variety of foods than were commonly consumed by Europeans. At the height of the gold-digging era in Otago there were 27 Chinese market gardeners supplying vegetables to miners of all national origins, as well as 96 Chinese storekeepers who stocked Chinese as well as European provisions. (Some European storekeepers also stocked Chinese foods.) The Chinese miners were good customers, too, of non-Chinese stores, farms and gardens, and it was estimated that they spent 10–50 per cent more on their food than the European miners. This was partly because imported rice was more expensive than locally produced bread and potatoes, but mainly because they ate a greater variety of foods, both local and imported. Perhaps they also fed more people well, since anyone passing by at mealtime was freely invited to partake. Reverend Don recalled one occasion when he and three other passers-by dropped in for dinner and ate their fill. Then the three strangers departed without their hosts even knowing who they were.

In the southernmost Chinese gold diggings in the world, at Round Hill in Southland, there were tea shops and general stores selling Chinese groceries and vegetables, including all the usual Chinese bakery treats such as moon cakes, pork and sugar dumplings, bean-curd cakes and bean-jam pies. In the settlement and nearby there were gardens producing fruit and vegetables in abundance. There was also some hunting and gathering of wild food going on – mainly woodpigeon, whitebait (which was dried), eels, trout, seaweed, manuka flowers for tea and even the leaves of the exotic boxthorn.

Every miner's hut, no matter how humble – and many were very humble indeed – had its chop block for preparing meals. It was in one such hut that Reverend Don was served some very fast food made from scratch. A chicken from the yard was killed, plucked, cut up and cooked, onions and celery were also quickly sliced and no doubt stir-fried, and the whole was served with rice – all in only 45 minutes from catching the chook. There would have been soy sauce for flavouring, and perhaps other condiments or pickles.

Looking around the hut where he was eating, Reverend Don may well have seen decorations in the form of gold characters on red paper slips, carrying mottoes that showed how much the inhabitants valued good food and how they associated it with good fortune. In one hut he noted that he saw over the meat safe the words 'Herein are edibles', 'Fine-flavoured and various', and over the chop block, 'The rules for carving are subtle'. On the rice chest were the words, 'We beckon wealth and valuables come forward'.

Who were these labouring men who knew how to cook and eat so well? Most of them came from villages in Guangdong Province in southern China, where peasant agriculture was thriving. Raising and cooking a great variety of foods in a great variety of ways had been practised there for centuries. Men as well as women were involved in food preparation. The miners brought these skills to their new home, and worked out how to grow produce and raise pigs and poultry in a very different climate. They also established an effective supply chain for bringing in the staples and the delicacies of home that they could not produce themselves. They had a great culinary tradition to draw on, and the ability to recreate it in a strange land.

Those from Britain and Ireland were not so fortunate. In both countries a self-provisioning peasantry had been largely driven off land they owned and used in common by the great aristocratic enclosures (privatisations) of land that took place from the 17th to the 19th centuries. These enclosures enabled large-scale, mono-cultural, industrial agriculture, to the detriment of the land and the people living on it. Hundreds of thousands of families were driven into cities, or across the world, to find alternative employment. Those left in the country might be little better off than those in the cities, for the land stolen from them by sleight of law often included the area around their houses, so they could not even grow food for themselves when paid work was scarce.

Whether in the city or the country, the poor ate very badly. Normal daily fare was bread, sometimes with potatoes, porridge or gruel. Small amounts of butter, lard, suet, milk, tea, sugar and treacle provided a little extra taste but precious little nourishment. Flour was made into stodgy filling foods such as dumplings and boiled puddings. Cheap forms of meat, such as neck of mutton or sausages, were eaten as often as the family could afford them and in preference to vegetables and fruit, which were seldom consumed.[3] In good times more meat would be eaten, and some vegetables and fruit, but in bad times there are records of people eating chaff and other animal fodder. Or starving to death, as around one million people in Ireland did during the famine in the 1840s and 1850s, after the potato crops failed. There was plentiful wheat and other good food being produced in Ireland at the time, but it was exported to England at a profit, since there was no political will to share it with the poor or give them the means to buy it.[4]

For those who were well off, food was so rich and plentiful that the contrast with what the majority ate can only be described as obscene. A typical middle-class Victorian dinner party would consist of two or more soups, several fish dishes, even more meat dishes, plus an assortment of pies, puddings, tarts, custards, ices and other sweet dishes to finish. An ordinary family dinner for those with money would have at least two different kinds of meat dishes, such as roast beef and a boiled chicken with sauce, plus soup or fish to start with and more than one sweet dish to finish.[5]

Two features of this well-to-do 19th-century English style of eating came to influence food preferences in New Zealand and to be favoured by all who could afford it (as many more could in the new colony). They were the predominance of meat as the mainstay of all meals – even breakfast, with fried meats, such as mutton chops, bacon and sausages being common – and the fondness for sweet things, both at the end of a meal and with cups of tea at any time of the day. Sadly, neither of these categories of food is the basis of a healthy diet. Both were easily and quickly turned into even less healthy industrial versions. On the plus side of the diet ledger, however, the arriving colonists had easy access to something that most of them had been deprived of in England: that was enough land around their houses to produce food. This was indeed one of the reasons why many of them emigrated, and for the first decades of colonisation fruit and vegetable growing was enthusiastically pursued by most households, rich and poor.[6]

By the 1880s, however, there were signs that the abundance of cheap meat, and the British heritage of lack of enthusiasm (and recipes) for eating vegetables, were again leading to a dull and unhealthy diet. As Michael Murphy wrote in the preface to his 1885 *Handbook of Gardening for New Zealand*, it was 'unfortunately a notable fact that vegetable growing is much neglected by the majority of small farmers. Cheap bread and cheap meat, with an abundance of potatoes, seem to satisfy most of those engaged in rural pursuits.' He went on to point out that a diet consisting mainly of animal foods was not good for anyone's health, and especially that of children. He advocated planting a quarter acre with vegetables; if well managed it would keep a large family all year round with 'an ample supply of wholesome vegetables'.[7] Perhaps his book (which went into three editions) helped more people get into home vege growing. Perhaps the depressed economic times of the 1880s and 1890s were also an incentive. (Sound familiar?) Since no one has ever studied home gardening in New Zealand with a view to assessing its contribution to national health and wealth, we have no way of knowing whether the almost two-thirds of households that were growing vegetables by 1956 represents a high point, a low point or somewhere in between for New Zealanders having easy access to really fresh plant foods.

What we do know, however, since there are lots of cookbooks from the 19th and 20th centuries to study, including plenty compiled by home cooks to raise funds for good causes, is that vegetable cookery remained at a low point, while meat, butter and sweet things dominated the average Kiwi table. Early New Zealand cookbooks contained much more information on rendering all parts of a wide variety of animals edible (even pukeko) than they did on creating equally varied dishes from a greater variety of vegetables. In *First Catch Your Weka*, David Veart notes that the 1869 revised edition of Mrs Beeton's famous cookbook had 287 pages of meat recipes and only 65 for vegetables, and that 'this pattern, inherited from British antecedents, would be repeated in New Zealand cookbooks for the next 100 years'.[8]

No books on vegetable or vegetarian cookery were written or published in New Zealand in the 19th century, and only three were produced during the first half of the 20th century. The 'meats and sweets' diet was what New Zealand girls were taught to cook, eat and feed to others both at home (in the 19th century) and at school (from the 1900s to the 1970s). The *Home Science Recipe Book* compiled by 'Homecraft Teachers' for the Canterbury Education Board, which was in use in the 1960s when I went to 'manual training' classes, has six recipes for meat dishes, but no vegetable recipes whatsoever. There are only instructions for preparing and cooking them by boiling, steaming, baking or roasting. (Although at least this book does not say, like Mrs Miller's much reprinted *Economic Technical Cookery Book*, used in schools and technical colleges from 1889 until the 1920s, that '[a]ll vegetables, with three or four exceptions, require to be *thrown* into boiling water'. Emphasis added.)[9]

The *Home Science Recipe Book* does have two pages of 'salad suggestions', but most of them bear little resemblance to what would be served as a salad today. The most extraordinary one is the Candle Salad, which consists of half a banana stuck into a canned-pineapple ring with a 'cherry flame' on top. There is a recipe for a jellied-vegetable salad (these have long been popular in the US but have thankfully never caught on in New Zealand), and recipes for cooked and uncooked salad dressings, the latter being that Kiwi classic Highlander condensed-milk mayonnaise. French dressing is mentioned twice but no recipe is given. I am not surprised since making this dressing, which is a variously bastardised Anglo version of the classic French vinaigrette, does at least require an edible vegetable oil, preferably olive oil. I know from rancid experience, having tried this at home at the age of 14 in 1966, that olive oil bought from the chemist's shop – the only place I could find it in Christchurch in those days – makes a truly nauseating dressing. It was to be some years before I encountered real olive oil and realised how it is meant to taste. Until then I did not know what to make of the enthusiasm for the stuff in foreign cookbooks, including health-food cookbooks.[10]

A short shift in home dining

I was only one of many home cooks, although perhaps one of the younger ones, who started experimenting with new foods and new ways of cooking in the 1960s. Before the explosion of fancy restaurants and cosmopolitan cafés in the 1980s made sampling of a range of cuisines possible, it was the only way for most New Zealand-born diners to recreate the dishes they had eaten on trips to Europe or Asia, or to experience them without travelling.

There were a lot of changes in New Zealand society after World War Two that promoted a move to more delicious and nutritious home cooking. These included more migrants from continental Europe and from Asia, bringing new foods and recipes with them; the arrival of television and with it the first television cooking shows; and the significant increase in young New Zealanders gaining access to both tertiary and 'overseas' education. This often meant leaving home at a young age, much younger than previous generations, for study or job training, and with that came a need to cook for themselves. This was often in communal flatting situations, which further increased exposure to different ways of cooking and eating. During my seven years of student flatting in the 1970s various flatmates introduced me to Chinese-style Malaysian and Singaporean cooking, bourgeois Swiss cuisine and vegetarian cookery. During that time I also visited China and ate my way appreciatively from Guangzhou to Beijing, noting the changes in cuisine as I went. I started picking up the little fundraising cookbooks being produced by New Zealand's ethnic communities and cooking dishes from them, as well as from the more comprehensive cookbooks of foreign cuisines, which became more readily available in New Zealand at that time, along with much better vegetarian cookbooks.

Meal-based entertaining at home also increased in popularity in New Zealand during this time. In the 1960s New Zealand's first television chef, Graham Kerr, was an enthusiastic advocate for culinary home entertaining with his TV series and book of the same name, *Entertaining with Kerr*.[11] A decade later Tui Flower's *Modern Hostess Cookbook*[12] covered every possible type of meal-based entertaining at home, from breakfast through lunch and dinner parties to after-theatre suppers. She also included informal eating entertainments such as picnics and barbecues. By the 1970s the backyard barbecue had successfully established itself as a very Kiwi form of home entertaining, while the fondue party flourished briefly and then faded away. Progressive dinners (which require several households to co-operate in providing a different course in each house, with the diners moving from one house to the next) were popular for a while, but seem to be rare now. So do home dinner parties of any kind. With the proliferation of restaurants and cafés, cooking as entertainment has been professionalised and fewer people enjoy entertaining at home.

And fewer people seem to know what is good to eat. While one can overhear conversations about good ingredients and how to cook them at farmers' markets, you never hear them at the supermarket. Sometimes I feel like an ingredients ambassador when I go through the checkout with an eggplant or other attractive vegetable and I'm asked 'What is this?' and sometimes, 'How do you cook it?' Once I was really taken aback to be asked, 'How do you eat this?' when buying a loaf of bread. It was recognisably a loaf of bread, but it was a dense whole-grain organic loaf, unsliced and wrapped in clear cellophane, not fluffy white slices in a brightly patterned plastic bag.

Even more unsettling was a conversation I heard at the hairdresser. If I hadn't been so close to sharp scissors I would have jumped in shock at hearing one woman tell another that there were apple pies on special at the supermarket, four to a pack, and that she had looked up all the additives in them on the internet and they were okay ('not the bad ones'). I was amazed that someone was so keen to buy fake food, but even more astounded that she would do so only if she had received reassurance that the fakery was 'safe'. If she was going to resort to the internet for food information, why not look up recipes for real apple pies, with no questionable ingredients at all? Given that real apple pies are so easy to make, and much more delicious, and that nutritious real bread can be toasted and made into sandwiches just as easily as faked bread, why are people ignorant of the real? Or even prepared to go to some effort to seek out excuses for it?

Crisis in home dining – crisis in health

Just as New Zealanders were opening up to more interesting, varied and healthy home cooking and dining, and there seemed to be a small window of opportunity for men as well as women to develop the skills and inclination to cook well for others at home on a regular basis, a number of economic and social factors began to work against this trend. Perhaps the most important of these was the increased paid employment of women, particularly mothers of young children. Very few men stepped up to take an equal share in the home cooking when women went out to work, so something had to give. Usually it was the time spent preparing and eating meals at home, whether ordinary family meals or culinary entertainments.

Women pressed for time to cook family meals found an industrial, commercial solution for this state of affairs: the convenience of supermarket shopping for convenience (prepared) foods. Yet much of this supposed convenience is really an illusion. Such foods may take less time to cook, but acquiring them usually requires driving to and from a supermarket, and then walking up and down the aisles making a selection. This kind of shopping takes much longer than when food vendors regularly came to the door or sold from street barrows, and fresh-food stores were within easy walking distance. As a result there has been no net gain in leisure time for home cooks, and the satisfying exercise of creativity has been replaced by an activity that is dull and uncreative.[13]

There is also something ironic about being subjected to endless television advertisements that proclaim that today's busy worker/parent has 'no time' to prepare family meals when a majority of New Zealand adults watch three or more hours of television per day. If just one of those hours was spent preparing dinner, rather than watching ads saying that we have 'no time' to cook, how might the physical and mental health of the nation improve? We have never actually had a lack of time problem, we have only had a 'sharing out the food work fairly' problem, so that it isn't always Mum's job to cook dinner after she has worked an eight-hour day outside the home.

If food shopping now takes as much time as food cooking used to, and 'saving' time is seen as more important than eating healthy food every evening, then the industrial food system has another answer: why not pick up takeaways on the way home from work, or go to a fast-food restaurant or food court? Such 'convenience cafés' began to proliferate in New Zealand in the late 1970s, at the same time as the big supermarket chains started to supplant greengrocers, fishmongers, butchers and bakeries, which began to decline dramatically in numbers. For example, in Christchurch at the end of the 1960s there were more than three times as many greengrocers' shops as there were at the end of the 1990s. It was the same for butchers' shops. The situation for grocers' shops, which sold fresh as well as dry goods, was even worse. Three-quarters of them disappeared between 1968 and 1998. Since the population of Christchurch kept increasing during this time, this means that more and more people had less and less access to fresh food within walking distance.

There was an even more dramatic pattern for the increase in fast-food outlets. By 1988 there were six times as many takeaway food stores in Christchurch as there were in 1968.[14] The same trends are observable in other New Zealand cities. By the late 1990s fresh-food stores had pretty much been replaced, on every city high street, by a range of fast-food outlets, and easy access to a variety of fresh, unprepared foods has been replaced by easy access to a limited range of prepared, high-fat, high-salt, high-sugar foods.

The end result of eating more and more of this energy-dense and nutritionally deficient 'convenience' food, and less and less nutritionally balanced home-cooked food, has been the increase in the severity and type of non-communicable diet-related diseases: cancer, ischaemeic heart disease and cerebrovascular diseases. These are already the top three causes of early death and illness in New Zealand, as they are in all the other countries that have switched to the 'industrial diet'.[15] These three diseases alone cause almost 60 per cent of deaths in New Zealand. Now Type II diabetes is creeping up to join them, and it is steadily becoming a major problem as it afflicts younger and younger people.

We clearly need to return to using mainly fresh, unprocessed plant foods. But how on earth can it be done when almost everyone in New Zealand under 40 has received little to no instruction at school or at home in how to grow and cook food for nutritious and interesting family meals? On top of that, they are constantly being told by the food industry, and by the state education authorities (who have no excuse for this), that such skills are not necessary or worthwhile.

Furthermore, there is the huge imbalance of the effort put into promoting junk food. During 2007, for example, the fast-food industry in New Zealand spent $12.94 on television advertising for every man, woman and child – something over $55 million in total. Add to that the $20.16 million spent with television companies advertising chocolate in all its forms and $17.75 million on fizzy drinks. This compared sadly with $1.44 per New Zealander spent on the television advertising of fruit and vegetables during 2007 – 11 times less than the junk-food spend.[16] This in 2007 was over $30 million more than what was spent in 2003 – a 33 per cent increase in just three years. Unsurprisingly, then, the '5 + A Day' fruit and vegetables promotion campaign has had no impact on reducing obesity and diet-related diseases.[17] Most New Zealand households not only continue to eat less than the recommended daily amounts of fresh fruit and vegetables, but spend more on confectionery than on fresh fruit each week.[18]

Our national diet is so out of whack that getting it into balance is one of the biggest challenges we face as a nation. What are the best ways to take up this challenge and win? First, what *not* to do. It seems pretty clear that increasing the spend of public money on healthy food promotion to counter the industrial food industry's advertising is just not possible, even if it were likely to be effective – and there is no evidence that it would. State interventions in food promotion would be better targeted at regulations to remove junk-food advertising from television altogether, or at least relegate it to the wee small hours, when children are in bed. This should go hand in hand with maximising the opportunities for children to produce, prepare and eat healthy food at school, since such opportunities are no longer guaranteed to occur at home.

Preaching the healthy food message doesn't work, but experience of healthy food does. If any public money is to be spent on improving the national diet then it needs to go toward supporting and multiplying the sorts of grassroots initiatives that are already working to achieve this end. These are aimed at providing opportunities and support for experiential learning in producing, preparing and sharing good food at home, at school and in community settings. In Chapter 8, I consider the role that the state could play in helping to multiply, diversify and democratise those initiatives, but first let's take a look at what they are. They start with new ways of *thinking* about food.

Three principles for good food

It would seem to be a totally non-controversial statement that we eat to live, and therefore that eating food that makes us sick and kills us in slow and unpleasant ways, like diabetes, is a stupid thing to do. It is individually stupid and also collectively stupid, since there are huge economic and social costs and no benefits to providing long-term medical care for people suffering from diet-related diseases. It will be a test of our collective intelligence and political strength to see if the food industry can be reined in before it imposes even greater costs on public health and the public purse.

Yet when, if and most especially *before* it is, something better has to step up to take its place, and that something better cannot and will not be simply a return to the way we used to produce, prepare and share food 50 years ago. A series of intermediate steps will be taken to develop a healthier food culture in Aotearoa, and those steps will involve a re-examination and reconfiguration of how and where we produce food, what we produce, how we prepare it and how we share it.

As well as taking into account health concerns, our new foodways will also factor in

- **sustainability**: can we keep producing healthy food this way *forever*, without damaging the natural resource base on which food production depends?
- **equity**: does *everyone* have access to sufficient healthy food, and the skills and means to prepare it?
- **pleasure**: is this food not only good for health, the environment and society, but also *delicious* and delightful to eat in convivial settings?

All these characteristics of truly good food were only vaguely in the back of the minds of the post-World War Two generation of New Zealanders who began experimenting with organic gardening, communal gardening, communal cooking and eating, wholefood vegetarian cookery, foreign cookery, food co-ops, dining clubs, wine clubs, cheesemaking, winemaking and other new ways of extending the range and variety of their knowledge about food and beverages, and their access to new foods and new ways of enjoying them. A lot of us learned by leaping into these new ventures.

One of my more spectacular learning curves involved selling some of the surplus of the Ponsonby People's Union food co-op on Ponsonby Road one Saturday morning in 1978. First, I finally found out how to eat avocados from an upwardly mobile young couple who bought them from me. At least I did not do what a Dutch friend my age did when she first tried avocado: she threw a hard one into a pot of water and boiled it to make it soft! Second, I found out that Indian families use a lot of fresh ginger in their cookery, after one Indian man returned three times to buy up all we had for sale, as word got around his extended family. Third, when a policeman came by I found out that what I was doing was illegal. I needed some sort of street-trader's licence to sell there.

What was news to me and my generation in New Zealand, when it came to learning about food from the sustainability, equity and pleasure perspective, was more familiar to our counterparts in Germany and France, Italy and Greece. Yet by the late 1970s they were also starting to become aware that traditional European ways of producing and consuming food were under threat from industrial food. By the late 1980s, as the garish arches of McDonald's began despoiling ancient city centres across Western Europe, a cultural counter-attack was launched from Italy. It took the form of the Slow Food Movement, which describes itself as a

> non-profit, eco-gastronomic member-supported organization … founded in 1989 to counteract fast food and fast life, the disappearance of local food traditions and people's dwindling interest in the food they eat, where it comes from, how it tastes and how our food choices affect the rest of the world. To do that, Slow Food brings together pleasure and responsibility, and makes them inseparable. Today, we have over 100,000 members in 132 countries.[19]

That includes New Zealand. The Slow Food International Manifesto, drawn up in 1989 and endorsed by delegates from 20 countries at the first international Slow Food conference, states that the 20th century 'invented the machine and then took it as its life model'. This has led to humans being enslaved by speed and the 'fast life'. This machine-dominated fast life has changed our way of being, our environment and our landscapes, and threatens us with extinction. To these threats, 'Slow Food is now the only truly progressive answer.'

The Slow Food Movement differs from all previous food reform movements in several ways. First, it posits pleasure rather than health as the central reason why the food system needs reforming. Second, it links gastronomic pleasure to environmentally sustainable and naturally diverse forms of production. These are not novel ideas in Italy, but they are certainly novel in New Zealand, where even professional cooks have only recently started to think about and discuss gastronomy as opposed to cooking techniques, and *sustainable* gastronomy is still a niche concept. (Chapter 7 looks at some early adopters of this trend.)

New Zealand is also not just a geographical antipodes to Italy, it is gastronomically upside-down as well. Unlike Italy, New Zealand did not have a rich diversity of traditional food and drink producers who began to be threatened by the expanding industrial food system in the 1980s. On the contrary, that was when New Zealand took its very first steps toward creating ecologically and economically sustainable forms of gastronomic diversity. Any such diversity we did have was either imported, or produced at the margins of the industrial system.

We have had to invent what Italy took for granted, and our 'tradition' in this regard is not even half a century old. Yet we are fast learners, and have achieved a lot in a short time. The late 20th-century growth in types of cheese production illustrates this perfectly.

A cheese (dis)course

Until the 1980s, cheese production and consumption in New Zealand were dominated by the dairy export industry. Domestic consumers were offered only what was produced in large factories for export, which was mainly a uniform and rather bland cheddar-style cheese, plus a little bit of colby-style ditto. In the 1960s these were joined by processed cheese, a basic cheddar processed with additives to make it smoother, softer and long-lasting.

In 1952 the Eltham dairy factory in Taranaki daringly produced New Zealand's first commercial blue vein cheese, but it didn't really catch on. Twenty-seven years later, when over 400 Christchurch households were surveyed on their cheese-buying preferences, only 12 per cent of the sample had bought blue vein cheese in the past month and 73 per cent had never bought it, or had bought it more than two years ago and not since.[20] There was even less demand for other 'speciality cheeses', as they were called then. Only Parmesan had been bought in the past month by more than 5 per cent of those surveyed, and over 90 per cent of the sample were not acquainted with Camembert,

Cheshire, Danbo, Edam, Erbo, Feta, Gouda, Havarti and Romano. Almost 90 per cent were not familiar with Gruyère. Most of these cheeses were being produced in New Zealand by then and some were being imported. However, the quality was variable, and truly fresh (or properly matured) indigenous artisanal cheeses had yet to be created.

Processed cheese, on the other hand, was quite popular, with over a third of households buying it. It was especially popular with children, probably because the cheese was packaged in small foil-wrapped triangles, ideal for school lunches. It may also have been due to the great popularity of the Chesdale Cheese advertisement on television, which became one of the best-known ditties in the land, and inspired parodies, including this late-1960s effort from some young cynics (or possibly gourmets) at a Papakura school:

> *We are the boys from down on the farm*
> *We really know our fleas*
> *There's no better value in Chesdale*
> *It always fails to please.*
> *Chesdale slices thickly,*
> *always crumbles, has no taste,*
> *and boy is it a bloody waste*
> *Chesdale Cheese*
> *The Poms all buy it – don't try it.*[21]

Writing about the range and quality of cheese available in New Zealand in the mid-1980s, local gourmet Tony Simpson compared it very unfavourably with the French cheese scene, which he had been lucky enough to experience.[22] The only local cheese for which he evinced any great enthusiasm was New Zealand's first 20th-century artisanal cheese, the Evansdale Farmhouse Brie. This cheese was first produced in 1980, in a converted shed in the yard of cheesemaker Colin Dennison in Evansdale, just north of Dunedin. The first Evansdale cheeses were made from the milk of a house cow, but as demand for the product grew, a 'milk tanker', which consisted of a large stainless steel box on the back of an ordinary trailer, was needed. What began as a part-time hobby for Dennison and his family grew first into a local and mail-order cheese business, and then expanded again into its current dairy factory with a salesroom and café on State Highway 1 just south of Waikouaiti.[23]

Evansdale was followed by a number of other small independent cheese-makers producing an interesting range of classic and original cheeses. A few larger dairy factories also took the opportunity to reinvent themselves as quality cheesemakers rather than bulk cheddar producers. The Barry's Bay cheese factory at the head of Akaroa Harbour on Banks Peninsula is a good example of this. In the 1970s it made only cheddar cheese in a rather bland mild version and a rather vicious tasty version. (At least my flatmates considered it so when it was purchased in error.) After reinventing itself in the 1990s, Barry's Bay now makes a range of excellent cheddars, including the only cloth-rinded cheddars in New Zealand, plus some traditional European cheeses.

The milk for Barry's Bay cheeses comes from small local dairy farms around the harbour and in this regard it is typical of all the smaller cheesemakers, which source their milk locally or run their own dairy farm as the sole or main supplier to their business. Examples of farm-based award-winning cheesemakers include Mahoe Farmhouse Cheese in Northland and Karikaas in Canterbury. The biggest market for such cheeses is also the local one. In this way the artisan cheesemakers have a much smaller ecological footprint than the export giants like Fonterra. There is, however, another irony in this tale of New Zealand's journey toward making real cheese sustainably. Fonterra capitalises on the taste trend that has been set by the artisan cheesemakers by owning some gourmet brands, such as Kapiti and Ferndale, which are for New Zealand consumption only. SOLE food buyers beware.

Cultivating taste

Gourmet cheeses produced by industrial giants to capture market share are but one of the traps that the would-be sustainable gastronome has to watch out for. Yet ignorance of the marketing wiles of corporate agri-business becomes a problem only when one is ignorant of more fundamental knowledge still – what good food really is, and what it tastes like.

This is knowledge that can only ever be properly taught at home. The best people to provide food and teach about food are parents and grandparents, uncles, aunts, older siblings and cousins, for only they are motivated by a heartfelt wish to nurture the next generation with healthy food, and to please them with tasty food. Laura Shapiro, whose book *Something from the Oven: Reinventing dinner in 1950s America* looks at how Americans came to lose cooking skills and eat so badly, sums up the case for learning to cook real food at home:

> Today our staggering rates of obesity and diabetes are testimony to the faith we put in corporations to feed us well. But the food industry is a business, not a parent; it doesn't care what we eat as long as we're willing to pay for it. Although

some people think of cooking as a choice now, no more necessary to learn than sewing or shoemaking, that perspective holds up poorly when we gaze around a mall or an airport at Americans en masse. Home cooking these days has far more than sentimental value; it's a survival skill.[24]

The bad news is that we have lost a generation of home experts on food as a result of outsourcing our diet to the food industry, and dumbing down the education of the post-1970s generation by depriving them of opportunities to learn to cook and to understand food. The good news is that so far it is only one generation; the previous generation is still alive and knowledgeable; and opportunities for the next generation to learn to produce and cook food for themselves and their families are increasing.

Parents and other caregivers are no longer staring at defeat when it comes to battling the food industry for control of their children's tastes and consumption. Useful advice on how to get off the industrial food grid and back to enjoying home-cooked food has now almost become an industry in itself. There is a proliferation of books and blogs by parents who have chosen the real-food route and taken their kids with them. One of the more amusing ones is the Fresh Mouth blog, where American parents Eileen and Dirk document their family mission 'to eat only fresh food or processed food with five ingredients or less for 30 days' – and how they kept going.[25]

This is a more realistic goal for most families than a complete opt-out from industrial food, but accounts by families who have conducted experiments into being locavores (eating only locally sourced foods) or even self-sufficient in food can also be great for inspiration, if not total emulation. Barbara Kingsolver's *Animal Vegetable Miracle* self-sufficiency experiment in Virginia is a good example, while a bit closer to home is Linda Cockburn's *Living the Good Life*, the story of an enterprising Kiwi who fed her family from a half-acre section in Queensland for a year. Both books also contain useful extra information on the environmental reasons that motivated the authors and their families to try this experiment.[26]

Having read a fair bit of the literature on how to change young people from junk-food addicts and vegetable refuseniks into eager junior gourmets and kitchen helpers – and save the planet at the same time – I can report that the two most important pieces of advice they contain are:

1. Eat well yourself and feed your children exactly what you eat, at the same time and place.
2. Introduce new foods to children slowly, in small amounts, and don't

accept that a child really does not like a particular food until it has been rejected more than 10 times.

Note that this is advice about *how* to eat, not what to eat. The industrial food system has profited mightily from creating special foods for children to be eaten at separate places and separate times from adults. This practice, like industrial food itself, is worst in English-speaking countries, mainly as a result of the bad precedent set by the middle and upper classes in England in the 19th century, who confined children in nursery wings at home, and sent them to boarding schools. In both places they were fed different food from adults. It was even higher in starch, fat and sugar and lower in fresh fruit and vegetables.[27] At Hogwarts, that fantasy epitome of the English boarding school, they are still eating a version of this diet, and the fact that they are not so obese that they break their broomsticks when they sit on them can only be due to magical means.[28] Fast-food and other cheap restaurants in English-speaking countries commonly offer a children's menu, which generally consists of fatty fried things and sugary stuff. Recognising that New Zealand families are becoming victims of this trend to feed children the least healthy, least delicious part of the adult diet, and relearning to eat the same things at the same time as them are probably the most important steps we can take toward culinary and dietary recovery.

This is going to require regaining confidence in home-cooked food as not only the most healthy but also the most *delicious* food that children are likely to eat, and it should be presented to them in this way. They should be encouraged to try new tastes and to give a considered opinion on what they are tasting. Is it like …? Is it better than …? Would it be better with … ? Was it cooked for too long/not long enough/just right?

With this approach to food, even quite young children can form sophisticated opinions. I got a lesson in this from my niece Aleksandra, whose cheese-tasting skills at the tender age of six really rocked me. In a tasting session she sampled three award-winning but quite different cheeses. They were a firm white sheep's cheese, an aged Gouda and a creamy blue cheese. She nodded her approval of the first two, but when she got to the third and I asked her opinion she pronounced the blue to be 'quite an ordinary cheese'. I had to agree with her, and so did the cheesemonger. The first two were at the top of their class, whereas the blue was not quite so special. Aleks was too young to teach the theory of tasting cheeses, but she was not too young to learn the practice, because learning comes through paying attention and through caring. I cared enough for her to buy her good cheese, and set up a sampling session, and she cared enough for cheese to give it her best attention.

Paying attention is the most important thing we can do with food, whether eating it, cooking it or buying it. If we want to know what good food really is, we need to truly *taste* it, and then we need to *talk* about it. This shows respect for the food, for the cook, for our fellow diners and for the producers of the food. This education in taste and discernment can begin at an early age and can be a life-long resource, both useful and pleasurable. If New Zealanders are to learn just one thing from Italians about the pleasures and virtues of sustainable gastronomy, let it be the most important thing: to take cooking and eating seriously, and to devote to them the time and attention required to do them well.

Fortunately, doing this is not only healthier than slumping in front of New Zealand's biggest time-waster and bad-food booster, it is also a lot more interesting. In the next chapter we look at where and how New Zealanders who don't have a member of the older generation handy to pass on their skills can still get the knowledge they need to transform their home-grown produce into delicious home-cooked food.

Anna Thomas's Caesar salad

(for two)

Ingredients

half a loaf of ciabatta, or
half a baguette
2–3 tbsp olive oil
2 cloves garlic, crushed
1 free-range egg
juice of 1 large lemon
¼–½ cup extra-virgin olive oil
⅓ cup freshly grated
Parmesan cheese
1 head of cos lettuce (or
equivalent)
dash of Worcestershire sauce
salt and freshly ground black
pepper, to taste

Method

Cut the bread into bite-sized croutons, place them on an oven tray and dry them in a medium-heat oven for about 20 minutes.

Heat the first measure of olive oil in a frying pan, add the garlic and toss the croutons in the garlic oil over a low heat for 5–10 minutes. Remove to a bowl.

Bring a small pot of water to the boil, add the egg and boil it for exactly 1 minute. Drain the pot, run cold water over the egg briefly, then set it aside in a small bowl.

Squeeze the lemon, and put the juice in a small jug. Measure the extra virgin olive oil into another small jug.

Wash and dry the lettuce leaves thoroughly, tear them into bite-sized pieces, and put them in the salad bowl.

Grate the Parmesan cheese and put it in a bowl.

Assemble the salad in the following order:

(1)   Pour half the extra-virgin oil over the lettuce leaves and toss gently.

(2)   Break the egg over the lettuce and toss again.

(3)   Add more oil and toss.

(4)   Add the lemon juice and toss.

(5)   Add a dash or two of Worcestershire sauce and toss.

(6)   Add salt and pepper to taste. (To my taste, neither is necessary.)

(7)   Add the Parmesan cheese and toss.

(8)   Add the croutons, toss, taste and add more oil and seasonings if desired.

Some of the 66kg of kiwifruit harvested from my home vines in 2009.

Sugarsnap peas are easy to grow and delicious to eat raw or cooked.

Bay of Plenty plenty - stopping at farm shops en route to Katikati brought forth this delicious selection of fruit, cheese and preserves.

Wild-harvested blackberries, home-grown strawberries and creamy organic yoghurt make a delicious breakfast.

A traditional willow trug full of baby vege and herb plants about to go to their new home.

Let the bottling begin - tomatoes and herbs ready to be made into tasty puree.

Persimmon trees are long-lived and can get very big – this old tree on a farm near Bulls was planted by the picker's grandparents and is still producing well.

CHAPTER FIVE

Cooking@Home

Recovering Kitchen skills

When my nephew Michael was 10 years old I took him on a special tour of my garden, giving him samples of all the edible fruit, vegetables, flowers and herbs to touch, smell and taste. He enjoyed the sweet black berries of the shadbush, the furry leaves and strong smell of peppermint-scented geranium and the scent of the aptly named chocolate cosmos. He tasted a fresh young leaf of the native wild spinach that I had been growing both as an ornamental groundcover and as a vegetable and declared that it tasted like a pea pod, which indeed it does. Later I heard that he had given a school talk about his weird aunt and her unusual garden.

Today Michael is a university-educated scientist, able to distinguish native plant and animal species from each other. He is also a home-educated cook, able to distinguish and combine flavours in a skilful way. Encouraged and taught to cook at home, he became so good at it that he financed his studies by working in cafés and as a private cook. On his Christmas holiday visits home I enjoy cooking with him. One year we made spanakopita, the classic Greek spinach and cheese pie, with my home-grown silverbeet substituted for spinach. As we worked we swapped recipes and cooking methods, tastes and techniques. We had to make a decision on which of our two slightly different ewe's milk feta cheeses was best for the pie, and which was better kept for eating straight. After sampling each one we agreed instantly on which was which. Maybe it was a genetic preference, but I doubt it. It is more likely to be born of our interest in good food – an interest that involves constant tasting, and constant *thinking* about tastes.

The ability to taste is the first essential for becoming a good cook – and then come all the other necessary skills, including the techniques of cooking, the ability to follow a recipe correctly, the knowledge of ingredients and many others that can be summed up by the term 'kitchen literacy'. American historian Ann Vileisis has written a whole book about how the kitchen literacy that most American women, and a lot of men, possessed in the 18th century – which for farm women included growing vegetables and keeping chickens for eggs and meat and cows for milk – was slowly eroded as America urbanised and the industrial food system developed.[1] This happened even though the consequences of food illiteracy are dire, while the pleasures of kitchen literacy are many, just as they are with reading and writing literacy.

When we learn to read we don't start with Shakespeare, and becoming kitchen literate has to start with mastering the basics first as well. But just what are those basics, and how do we acquire them in a world that seems designed to keep us ignorant about good food? This chapter looks at how to make the garden–kitchen connection most effectively, and then at what it means to be literate in cooking skills, recipes and ingredients.

Getting it from the garden
1: Planning

Learning how to grow food at home, or close to it, is the first step toward much fresher, healthier and more delicious meals, but there is no point in having a patch of fat cabbages if you don't know how to make coleslaw, sauerkraut, stuffed cabbage leaves, spicy coconut cabbage, sweet and sour cabbage … It is also a bit pointless having a big patch of fat cabbages and nothing else in the garden to team with them – no carrots, apples, celery or spring onions to slice into the coleslaw, no beetroot to make borscht, no dill or parsley for cabbage salad dressings and garnishes.

So cooking from the garden is not just a matter of being able to grow the food, it also involves planning to have a sufficient variety of vegetables available when they are needed. Almost anyone can produce a surplus of silverbeet in January, but few are interested in eating it then, and most would rather have ripe tomatoes instead. This part of gardening is a bit like doing a vegetable form of Sudoku, getting everything lined up in the right time squares. It is much more of an intellectual challenge than Sudoku, however, since vegetables all have their special characteristics, which must be planned and catered for.

I wish I could give a simple formula for planning a vegetable garden so that you, the cook, always had the right number of vegetables available at the right time for the meals favoured by your family. Unfortunately this can't be done, since I don't know where you live, how big your family is or what vegetables your family especially likes or dislikes. A two-person family in Northland that loves leeks and hates broccoli is going to have very different winter vegetable requirements from a four-person family in Southland that loves broccoli and hates leeks, and each family will have its particular challenges in producing what it likes exactly when it is wanted.

Given such variations there is no one-size-fits-all, garden-to-kitchen plan. Every household needs to evolve its own plan for what to grow when, and how much of it. Sorting out which vegetables you want and don't want is the easy part. Working out how much seed and how many plants you need, and when to plant them so that they will be ready when you need them is more complicated, and for this you need to refer to a guide that gives both quantities and times. I have prepared one for this book, which you will find in Appendix I: A New Zealand Kitchen Garden Planning Guide.

Getting it from the garden 2: Harvesting and keeping

The next point on the garden-to-kitchen knowledge curve, if all those well-grown vegetables are going to be eaten at the peak of perfection, is knowing when and how to harvest crops, and the best ways to process or store them if they are not to be eaten immediately. This is another puzzle involving doing the right thing at the right time with a range of plants that have differing requirements.

Since supermarkets began making raw fruit and vegetables from all over the world available all day, every day, the knowledge of how to look after food properly in the home has largely been lost, along with how to tell when things are just right for picking. Regaining it takes time and effort, because there is a lot to learn. A good kitchen gardening book will tell you, vegetable by vegetable, the best times and ways to harvest the crop, and the best ways to store them.

But the only New Zealand home vegetable garden book I have seen that provides a quick reference guide to harvesting and storing vegetables in tabular form was last printed in 1958.[2] I have yet to see even a dated tabular guide to fruit storage. So to save you – and myself – the bother of flicking through the pages of several books to find out what to do, and then having to do it all again next year, I have compiled a ready reference guide. See Appendix II: A Guide to Harvesting and Keeping Home-grown Fruit and Vegetables.

Kitchen literacy 1: Cooking skills

The freshly harvested cabbage, carrots, celery, spring onions, dill and parsley are sitting on your kitchen bench – now what? Are they going to be turned into one dish or several? Soup or salad, main dish or side dish? How should they be cut? Should they be steamed, boiled, stir-fried, roasted, baked – and for how long? How should they be seasoned and flavoured? Just with salt, or with soy sauce, ginger, garlic, mayonnaise, sesame oil, sunflower oil, cider vinegar, lemon juice …?

These are just some of the very basic things that need to be learned before good ingredients can become delicious meals. They can all be found in books, but unless the student is very motivated, it is better to learn from a good teacher. Such teachers are no longer provided as a matter of course in New Zealand schools and most of today's young parents have received little or no training in domestic cookery. This makes it harder for them to teach their own children to cook. At this point in New Zealand's food evolution it is necessary to look outside the formal education system to learn cooking from an expert.

For adults in daytime employment the best option is to enrol in a night class. High schools and polytechnics with continuing education programmes often run cooking classes, usually once a week for a full term, or sometimes at weekends. A large city will have a choice of schools running a range of cooking classes, from basic skills to vegetarian cookery, ethnic cuisines, baking or other specialised forms. There are also classes for new migrants, featuring New Zealand ingredients and ways to use them, and cooking classes just for men. The easiest way to find out about these classes is to ask at your local public library. Until recently they were run on a not-for-profit basis and sometimes received government funding. However, in its 2009 budget the National–Act government slashed $13 million from adult community education, causing almost half the schools offering it to stop doing so, and the remainder to charge higher fees.[3]

This is a terrible shame. Watching an experienced cook at work – in person, not on a TV screen – is the best way to pick up simple but important techniques such as the fastest and neatest way to peel and slice an onion. This may seem trivial, but as almost every soup, stew, casserole, curry, pasta sauce and you-name-it recipe starts with 'Slice an onion', being good at it really saves time – and tears. Other useful things taught in classes but not on most TV cooking shows include kitchen hygiene and safety, safe food-storage methods, creative use of leftovers, food budgeting, knowledge of the ingredients and how to use kitchen tools and equipment safely.

During the day there is a range of informal opportunities run as part of the outreach and support programmes of community centres, churches and other community groups. Often these are free classes, or are very cheap. It is also possible to have one-to-one teaching in places where there is a SuperGrans branch. SuperGrans volunteers help their clients develop their abilities and confidence in a range of domestic and life-skill areas, including basic cooking skills and menu creation, making the dollar stretch when buying food for the household and food gardening.[4]

For those who have mastered the basics, discovered that they really like cooking and have time and money to invest in becoming a really good cook, there are any number of specialist classes all over the country, plus tours led by top Kiwi cooks to France, Italy and other gourmet destinations.[5] These are good places to learn the finer points of traditional cuisines and the latest in contemporary foodways, but if you want to learn how to prepare everyday healthy foods in the most delicious ways you'll need to ask around. I uncovered only three New Zealand cooking schools/classes that explicitly emphasised 'nutritious and delicious' in one package.[6] All use predominantly organic ingredients and provide instruction in using nutritious but unfamiliar foods like pulses, amaranth, millet and sprouts. In these classes nutritional as well as culinary advice is part of the package offered, and there may be additional extras – The Healthy Kitchen, for example, offers lunchbox and weight-loss classes. Some yoga centres, gyms and other health-oriented places also offer healthy cooking classes or advice as part of their regular programme.

Kitchen literacy 2: Recipes

Once basic cooking skills have been acquired the next thing the home cook needs is recipes – lots and lots of them – for all those fresh-from-the-garden vegetables and fruit. But not just any recipes. While it is a lot easier than it used to be to find recipes based on fresh produce, not all of them will be useful to cooks who grow their own dinner, or buy only local, seasonal food. Such cooks cannot use recipes that have asparagus and eggplants in one dish, or require fresh basil to be added to a purée of parsnips, or fresh figs to be teamed with fresh raspberries, no matter how delicious these combinations may be.

The average home gardener will not be able to produce these ingredients at the same time, and nor will any honest farmers' market. Recipes that contain such combinations are not only anti-seasonal, they are also uneconomical, for even if the out-of-season ingredient is obtainable, it is bound to be pricey. It is also probably imported, which means it won't be fresh. This sort of cooking is fine for the professionals, who tend to develop these sorts of recipes, but won't do for the home cook who wants to eat from the garden. Home cooks don't need to know how to put together a lot of fabulous things from the shop, but rather how to put together a meal from what is at its best in the garden right now – and make it taste fabulous. This also prevents miserable dining experiences brought on by eating the same thing cooked in the same way over and over again for a month or more.

These days finding such recipes is no problem for any New Zealander with an e-mail address. Simply subscribe to *New Zealand Gardener*'s free e-list 'Get Growing with NZ Gardener'[7] and every Friday you will receive recipes for whatever is in season, along with planting, harvesting and plant-care advice for that season. Plus you can have your gardening queries answered, and you can share your own recipes and gardening tips. It's an amazing service, useful for beginner gardener/cooks and experienced ones alike.

It is still worth investing in good cookbooks. For ready reference in the kitchen my New Zealand fresh food standby for nearly 30 years has been Digby Law's *A Vegetable Cookbook*, still in print and now a classic.[8] It has lots of recipes for all the common vegetables, and a few of the rarer ones. It is organised alphabetically by the name of each vegetable, which makes it easy to see how to turn that broad bean surplus, for example, into a soup, salad, side dish or substantial main dish, with just a few extra, common ingredients. My own *A Cottage Garden Cookbook* is organised by type of dish rather than vegetable, but it is based on the vegetables and fruits that are easily grown in New Zealand back yards.[9]

For gardening and cooking advice in the same volume, *The Cook's Garden* and *More from the Cook's Garden,* by the talented trio of sisters Mary Browne, Helen Leach and Nancy Tichborne, are the classic local works.[10] They cover growing as well as preparing vegetables and fruit, and have plenty of easy and tasty recipes for fresh produce. Just recently, thanks to the renaissance of interest in cooking from the garden and eating locally and seasonally, more books that make the growing/eating connection have come out. They include *The Grower's Cookbook* by Dennis Greville and Jill Brewis,[11] *Grow It Cook It* by Sally Cameron[12] and the *Homegrown* series published by *New Zealand Gardener.*

Looking overseas for further inspiration, I find it hard to go past Rosalind Creasy's *Cooking From the Garden*.[13] This is a truly wonderful resource covering the full geographic range and cultural depth of American vegetable gardening and cookery. It includes examples of traditional gardens and cookery, immigrant gardens and cookery, and the new wave of food gardens (edible flowers, gourmet salads etc), along with an 'encyclopedia of superior vegetables' section that gives growing instructions. There is plenty in this book to keep non-Americans growing and eating with success and enjoyment, and for those who like to have some historical depth to their understanding of what there is to eat, and how it came to be prepared the way it is, it is essential reading.

Across the Atlantic the chef and farmers' market patron Hugh Fearnley-Whittingstall has been promoting sustainable growing and delicious dining since the mid-1990s, in a series of books and TV programmes.[14] At the same time Nigel Slater – who has never written a recipe that was less than delicious and easy – was cultivating his own garden, and cooking from it. He recently shared his gardening knowledge and recipes in two books, both entitled *Tender*.[15]

Cooking from the garden means cooking seasonally, but you don't have to know how to grow really fresh food to appreciate eating it. Local cookbooks that showcase fresh seasonal produce are *At Its Best* by Margaret Brooker,[16] *Fresh* by Julie Biuso[17] and *A Good Year* by Lois Daish.[18] Any books by these writer-cooks are worth having. They all contain easy-to-follow recipes for simple but delicious food, made with inexpensive fresh ingredients. These are recipes that the family will like to eat often and guests will receive with pleasure.

Once your garden starts producing too much to be eaten up at mealtimes, or you realise what bargains are to be had at farmers' markets, books on preserving are also handy. Again, preferably local ones, since foreign ones tend not to have recipes for tamarillos, feijoas and a few other things that New Zealanders take for granted. Digby Law's pickle and chutney recipe book, another classic that is still in print, is invaluable,[19] while Gilian Painter has given us a great selection of produce cookbooks with an emphasis on preserving. *A New Zealand Country Harvest Cookbook*[20] is gorgeous as well as practical. There are lots of recipes for preserves in the *Homegrown* series, while Marlborough chef and farmer's market organiser Chris Fortune's book *Pick, Preserve, Serve: Enjoying local and home-grown produce year round* is about just what its subtitle suggests.[21]

Vegetarian and 'health food', 'wholefood' or 'natural foods' cookbooks are the next most obvious place to find good recipes for fresh produce, and for information on how to prepare the full range of whole grains, pulses and other nutritious foods that New Zealanders were missing out on until recently. Such books were rare in New Zealand before the 1970s – when processed foods and fast-food outlets began to dominate food stores and high streets. Reading these books today is rather shocking. Whole books are now devoted to the critiques of the industrial food system contained in their introduction. Who would have guessed in 1970 that in 30 to 40 years humans would be dying from new and ghastly diseases caused by keeping food animals in confinement and/or feeding them the remains of other animals, that plants genetically engineered to resist chemicals would be widely released into the human food chain, that industrial methods of food production and distribution would be making a major contribution to climate change, and that genetically engineered sheep and cows would be dying young, cruel deaths in Waikato paddocks?[22]

A classic example of the new health cooking genre is *The New York Times Natural Foods Cookbook*, first published in the US in 1971 and republished in New Zealand in 1979.[23] The book's introduction rings alarm bells about the industrial food system that have only grown louder in the intervening years – chemical residues in meat and produce, additives in processed food, the health and environmental impacts of industrial-scale production and consumption. The same remedies are proposed – organic production methods, eating only fresh wholefoods, eating like a peasant. There is also the 'Pollan solution',[24] which advocates a return to pre-industrial foods, or what grandmother (or great-grandmother) used to eat. The common but utterly specious 'my grandmother didn't eat tofu' objection is addressed head on: 'A special advantage to this book is that many ingredients used in the recipes were unknown to our grandmothers.' These include Asian ingredients like tofu and seaweed, but also sprouted seeds, yoghurt, sunflower seeds and plenty of other things that are easily sourced in New Zealand today.

I keep a few of these wholefood cookbooks handy for turning quinoa, amaranth or something else unusual and highly nutritious into a tasty dish, but I wouldn't recommend them as the starting place for improving your diet from a delicious as well as nutritious perspective. For that you need a cookbook with recipes that even confirmed carnivores will relish. I was lucky that Anna Thomas's books *The Vegetarian Epicure* and *The Vegetarian Epicure Book Two*[25] came out when I was teaching myself vegetarian cuisine. Until then the vegetarian cookbooks in English tended to be either dull, or strange. The dull ones were based on the Anglo diet model, with plain, boiled vegetables accompanying mock meat and fish dishes constructed from TVP or other synthetic substances. (If you don't know what TVP is, you don't want to.) The strange ones were a bit wacky, heavily influenced by the hippie lifestyle and eclectic Asian ingredients. Not that I have anything against hippies, or eclectic Asians, but some of the dishes created by Americans under these influences are just not edible.

Anna Thomas is different. Her only interest is good food, and how to cook it. She points out that many of the world's great dishes are vegetarian by design, not default. In her own Polish culinary tradition one of the most important meals of the year, the Christmas Eve supper, is intentionally vegetarian and features a great composed salad (a salad that is arranged, rather than tossed). Hindus and Buddhists, working from ingredients as different as those found in Sri Lanka and Japan, also produce exquisite vegetarian food. My copy of *The Vegetarian Epicure* is now falling to pieces, while *The Vegetarian Epicure Book Two* is horribly stained with tomato sauce, olive oil, pesto, soy sauce and other key ingredients. It was from Anna Thomas that I learned that a salad could be a main dish. She also set me off on a masochistic path of ordering Caesar salads in restaurants to see if any of them were as good as mine, when made according to her method, with lettuce fresh from the garden, organic free-range eggs, lemons straight from the tree and extra virgin olive oil. Of course they aren't![26] To get a salad made this way from the very freshest and finest ingredients at a restaurant would be very expensive, whereas made at home from largely backyard ingredients it is affordable as well as delicious.

Other vegetarian cooks whose books can be relied on for good recipes for garden produce include Colin Spencer, Deborah Maddison and Mollie Katzen, of the famous Moosewood Restaurant. There are now vegetarian cookbooks available for almost every cuisine as well. I find it very easy to create Mediterranean vegetarian meals, using simple recipes drawn from Italian, Greek, Turkish, Lebanese and North African traditions, which are all rich in delicious vegetable-based dishes. A favourite quick, healthy, tasty meal at our place is falafel burgers, where wholemeal organic pita bread slit almost in two replaces the white-flour bun, falafels (fried patties or balls made from ground chickpeas and assorted flavourings) replace meatballs or meat chunks, and torn lettuce leaves, slices of tomato and sometimes avocado are popped into the pita bread along with the patties. A sauce of plain yoghurt, grated cucumber and crushed garlic completes the contents of the pita pocket. Chilli sauce or spicy tomato sauce are optional, non-traditional extras.

The theme of my favourite everyday recipes is slow food, fast. English cook Nigel Slater calls this 'real fast food', and his book of the same name is a superb source of recipes for excellent food that can be made in half an hour or less.[27] From Slater's book and many other sources I have built up a collection of recipes for main dishes and side dishes based on fresh produce that can all be prepared in around 30 minutes. That's at least as long as it takes to order a pizza and have it delivered, or to go to the nearest high-fat/-salt/-sugar fast-food place, wait for the order to be assembled and packaged and take it home. So the 'no time to cook good food' argument doesn't wash with me. With the right recipes, the right ingredients and a few basic skills and tools, dozens of delicious and nutritious dishes can be prepared with very little time and effort.

More ambitious meals that take longer to prepare can be saved for weekends and holidays, when there is more time to cook, and perhaps extra family and/or friends to cook for. There is not even any need to learn to cook lots and lots of 'real fast food' main dish recipes, unless you really want to. It saves time and effort to have just a dozen favourites for each season, and rotate them. If everyone in your household likes asparagus quiche, say, or eggplant curry, they will be happy to have it three or four times a month when these vegetables are in season, before moving on to the next season's delicacies. It is also useful to have some any-season recipes memorised, using dried vegetables like peas, beans and lentils, for the times when your fresh-produce supply runs a bit short, or you just feel like it. These can be as elaborate as a moussaka where brown lentils replace the more traditional minced lamb, or as simple as a can of mixed beans, drained and rinsed and tossed through hot pasta shapes flavoured with fried onion and garlic, fresh herbs, balsamic vinegar and finely grated Parmesan cheese.

Simple recipes are going to taste good because the ingredients came straight from the garden. If you have planted the right varieties of fruit and vegetables, picked them at the right time, and stored them properly, they will have a huge flavour and nutrition advantage over the varieties that suit the industrial food system's requirements for tough produce that can be picked early and look good no matter how tired it is. After 30 years of export-oriented growing and import-oriented eating, New Zealand has suffered a huge drop in nutritional quality and taste variety in fruit and vegetables. But some of us are working hard to get it back, to make sure that the apples in our pie and the potatoes in our pot are the best they can be. For no matter how good your cooking skills or your recipes, if the ingredients are no good the meal will be bad as well.

Kitchen literacy 3: Ingredients

During the 19th century New Zealand imported and bred literally thousands of vegetable and fruit varieties. Before then, Maori were already at work breeding new varieties of kumara and other food plants. At New Zealand's first, and so far only, ethnobotany conference, held at Rehua Marae in Christchurch in 1988, we heard of the breaking up and overseas sale of a kumara varieties collection painstakingly assembled by scientist Doug Yen for the Department of Scientific and Industrial Research. When the DSIR decided it no longer wanted the trouble and expense of storing and growing the heritage kumara, they were disposed of, thus depriving all New Zealanders, and Maori in particular, of access to kumara well adapted to New Zealand conditions. (Later research on one of those pre-European-bred varieties showed that it performed well – possibly better than modern varieties – in extreme drought conditions.)[28] Dr Yen went to work in Australia, where public-good research into traditional food plants was still being funded. At the ethnobotany hui he remarked on the irony that the reason he left New Zealand in the first place was the reason he had been invited back to attend the hui.

As a result of Dr Yen telling his story at the hui, some of the kumara varieties were brought back. As former DSIR scientist Dr Oliver Sutherland recalled: On hearing from Doug Yen at Rehua of the fate of the collection and its dispersal to nga hau e wha (the four winds), Dell Wihongi of the Pu Hao Rangi Trust decided to retrieve the nine varieties most significant to Maori. With some encouragement (but not money) from DSIR, and derision rather than support from the government of the day, Dell eventually caught the attention of the world-famous botanist Dr David Bellamy, who funded the travel to Japan for Dell and other kaumatua … where they were given tubers of the valued varieties …[29]

Dell Wihongi put in another 20 years of voluntary work on biodiversity conservation before she died in July 2008. Her work included organising the WAI 262 claim to the Waitangi Tribunal, on protecting traditional rights to indigenous plants and their uses.[30] While she was having to rely on charity from a foreigner to restore significant food plant varieties to their homeland, the DSIR was being restructured into a series of Crown Research Institutes (CRIs) with a more commercial focus. Senior scientists who specialised in expanding our knowledge of nature, such as taxonomists, mostly lost their jobs. Technologists are replacing them, as I found when on a tour of the genetic engineering unit of the CRI Crop and Food Research laboratory at Lincoln. There I met a science student who was engaged in a project to find and engineer a gene into broccoli that would make it look greener for longer after harvest. The 'demand' for such broccoli is not, of course, from consumers who are clamouring to eat tired old broccoli dressed up as fresh young sprigs, but from a large supermarket chain, which was part-funding this project and would obviously benefit financially from keeping food looking edible on the shelves for longer. When I asked the scientist whether she knew what effect such artificially prolonged greening might have on the nutritional value of the broccoli, her answer was 'No'.

While funding is available for producing food plants that are neither nutritious nor delicious, and may even be dangerous to the health of humans and the environment, most of the conservers and breeders of tasty, healthy varieties work more for love than money. One such person was the late Graham Harris, an Open Polytech lecturer in horticulture. In 2000 Harris received an award from the Slow Food Foundation that recognised his conservation work on traditional Maori white potato varieties, and provided some funding for him to continue that work and to move on to traditional kumara cultivars.

Sadly, Harris died in 2006 before this good work could be completed, but it is being carried on by others.[31] When I visited Koanga Gardens (now Kaiwaka Gardens) in Northland on an autumn day in 2008 I saw sacks and sacks of heritage seed potatoes that had just been delivered from a grower in the Hokianga. They included the traditional Maori varieties in various shades of purple, pink and yellow, as well as the white kinds we are more familiar with. Maori potatoes or taewa are more varied and interesting than the standard commercial varieties because they have a different source and method of breeding. It is believed that their original seed source came directly from the homeland of potatoes, South America, and were brought to New Zealand by the first whalers and sealers in the late 18th century. They certainly look closer to those Andean ancestors – and the spuds on sale today in markets in Peru, where all colours, shapes and sizes are available – than they do to the white potatoes that came from Europe in the 19th century. In Aotearoa the potatoes adapted to local growing conditions, and the best adaptations were selected and grown on. Today they are being developed still further as a prize crop for Maori and other organic growers. These gardeners are also growing traditional European-bred varieties that have qualities the popular commercial varieties lack, including disease resistance and, more importantly for the home gardener/cook, superior flavour, cooking and keeping qualities.

One such variety that has been making a comeback in New Zealand recently is the Pink Fir Apple potato. Skinny, knobbly, pink on the outside and creamy yellow on the inside, the Pink Fir Apple is a perfect salad potato as it keeps its shape when cooked and sliced. It also has so much flavour that whenever I make salad from it some slices do not make it into the bowl. Pink Fir Apples, and other heritage potatoes that are full of flavour even when simply boiled, are very different from the large white starchy potatoes destined to be processed into commercial chips, crisps, wedges, flakes, hash browns and other artificial-flavour-added forms. They are worth seeking out in order to understand that even this most basic, common and usually unexciting vegetable can be a treat, if a good variety is selected.

Finding those good old varieties is a bit of a challenge for home gardeners at present, as they are not standard garden centre stock. As far as I can ascertain only Kaiwaka Gardens has some for sale by mail order, along with other heritage vegetable seeds and fruit trees.[32] Farmers' markets are a good place to look for them. They can certainly be found in coastal Otago markets, where grower Roger Blok keeps up a good supply.[33] You might even be able to find them on Trade Me, where I found a gardener/cook auctioning organic heirloom seed potatoes – Urenika, Pink Fir Apple, Karuparera and MoeMoe. The seller noted: 'I do not have to cook as many for my family of five. I usually have to cook about 1kg of any store bought variety with a roast dinner. My family only ate 600g of these potatoes because they are more substantial and nutritious.'

As with potatoes, so with every other kind of fruit and vegetable you can think of, especially common ones such as the apple. At Treedimensions orchard near Motueka, 127 varieties of organically grown apples are picked and despatched to mail-order customers between December and May every year.[34] Only three of the varieties available – Gala, Granny Smith and Fuji – are likely to be sold in your local supermarket. Several varieties – Gravenstein, Cox's Orange, Kidd's Orange, Jonathan – were commonly grown and sold on the local market until the 1980s. Then apple production in New Zealand became primarily export-oriented and these tender and delicious varieties were axed – literally. The other varieties supplied by Treedimensions come from all over the apple-growing world. Some of them have irresistible names, like Cornish Aromatic, Beauty of Bath, Peasgood Nonesuch, Reinette Marbree d'Auvergne or Altländer Pfannkuchenapfel. I haven't eaten my way through all of them yet, but I am growing some of them and can report that the Altländer Pfannkuchenapfel ('old country pancake apple') is one of the best cooking apples I have ever met. Stewed with just a couple of slices of lemon (no sugar needed), sprinkled with cinnamon and topped with a spoon of creamy natural yoghurt, this apple makes a great winter dessert.

Some of these old apples are much more nutritious than modern varieties that have been bred for sweetness, colour and transportability. Research commissioned by the Central Tree Crops Research Trust of New Zealand found that one old New Zealand apple variety, Monty's Surprise, was exceptionally high in the phytonutrients that help prevent cancer.[35] One of these apples a day really could keep the doctor away! So could Hetlina, Fuero Rous, and any number of other uncommon old varieties that have been neglected.

In Appendix II you will find information on where to source some of these special varieties of apple. The nurseries that propagate heirloom apple trees also tend to have other heritage fruit varieties available, including many varieties that have not been sold by the big garden centres for a long time, if ever. If you want to taste the fruit before you commit to buying a tree, the best place to go looking for a taste is the nearest farmers' market or organic store. There you are likely to find a range of fruit and vegetables that never make it into supermarkets.

Farmers' markets and organic shops are also the best places to find packets of seeds for old and unusual varieties. Stella Christofferson of Running Brook Seeds specialises in heirloom vegetable and flower seeds, which she sells at the Clevedon farmers' market, just south of Auckland. She is a very knowledge-able teacher on the subject of seeds and how to grow them, and is equally informative on the subject of what seeds can teach us, if we pay attention to how they grow – adapting themselves to new and different growing conditions and subtly altering their genetic make-up so that the next generation will cope better. Traditional farmer-breeders understood this phenomenon and how to make it work for them very well, even if they did not know the science behind it. It is the basis of all the landrace[36] breeding that has gone on for millennia, providing the huge variety of potatoes, apples, wheat, rice, corn and every other staple food that has nourished and delighted the human race during that time.

I have been growing Stella's seeds in my own gardens on Banks Peninsula for several years, and we have had interesting conversations about how envi-ronment as well as genes have a big impact on the plant. A case in point was the Red Kuri and Australian Butter pumpkins I grew from seed that she sup-plied. I asked her if the Red Kuris were meant to grow only as big as softballs, and was told that they should be as big as soccer balls. Stella advised me to save seed from the Red Kuris, and sow it again the next year, predicting that the plant would have 'learned' from the environment what it needed to grow better. She had seen this happen with a bean variety that produced a few miserable plants from new seed one year, and a bumper crop from seed saved from those plants the next year. See 'Super seed sources' (next page) if you want to experi-ment for yourself with growing more delicious and nutritious vegetables.

Kaiwaka Gardens manager Romi Curl told me that in New Zealand we have retained only 3 per cent of all the edible plant varieties that were intro-duced to the country in the 19th century. That's a terrible loss of agricultural and culinary diversity. It seems that it is mostly up to home gardeners and cooks to care that they are growing the best in order to eat the best. Fortunately they have some help from the new breed of retailers of fresh produce who are also committed to quality and variety, and who are the subject of the next chapter.

Super seed sources

Among the many, many great things about growing your own food is that you get to choose your favourite varieties of vegetable. When the supermarket has nothing but soccer ball-sized iceberg lettuces, tough on the outside and pale and watery in the centre, you have a choice of the soft yellow-green leaves and hearts of buttercrunch, the super-crisp green leaves of cos, the tasty frills of red oakleaf and all the other looseleaf lettuces that don't fit the supermarket philosophy of 'buy 'em cheap and pile 'em high'.

To add to your salad, instead of uniformly round, red and tasteless tomatoes, you can sample the delights of Yellow Pear, Black Krim, Tigerella, Brandywine Pink and dozens and dozens of other interesting and tasty varieties. Then there are herbs that are seldom, if ever, commercially available – chervil, Greek oregano and pizza thyme are three I like to use a lot but have never seen for sale.

You could try your local garden centre seeking interesting herb and vegetable plants. In my experience, if they are there at all, they sell out pretty fast. Curiously, the garden centre owners never take this as a message to grow or order in more. After years of being able to buy buttercrunch lettuce plants in spring, but being offered only iceberg plants as the year goes on, I have concluded that the only way to get delicious diversity into one's diet year round is to grow from seed.

This means knowing where to source the seeds. If you want to buy them over the counter, the best place to go is usually an organic food shop rather than a regular garden centre. Organic food shops often stock organically grown seeds as well, and these seeds tend to be varieties selected for good home garden results rather than chemically assisted commercial production. Organically grown seeds can also be obtained from specialist retailers such as Kaiwaka Organics Heritage Garden Centre, which has an online seed catalogue: www.kaiwakaorganics.co.nz, and Eco-Seeds, which also sells online: www.ecoseeds.co.nz. So does New Zealand's biggest specialist seed retailer, Kings Seeds (www.kingsseeds.co.nz). The selection from Kings gets bigger and better every year, and now includes organic seeds, seeds for sprouting, micro-greens, medicinal and culinary herbs, and gourmet and ornamental vegetables.

You will find Kings Seeds at good garden centres, and you may also find the Niche range, imported from the US. This is a great range of seeds, with very tempting packaging – but be aware that even the cheaper packets cost almost twice as much as a standard New Zealand seed packet, and may not contain as much seed.

Foreign seed firms, such as Chiltern Seeds in Britain (www.chilternseeds.co.uk/chilternseeds/index), are also a great source of interesting seeds. However, before you cheerily type in your credit card number and confirm your order, check with the nearest Ministry of Agriculture and Forestry office to see if any of your choices are banned imports.

Buying seed from overseas is the expensive way to get unusual vegetable seeds. The cheap way is to join a Seed Savers group (www.seedsavers.org.nz) and swap seeds with other keen growers. This method has the advantage of ensuring that you will get seed from plants that are well adapted to local conditions – like those sold by Stella Christofferson, proprietor of Running Brook Seeds, at the Clevedon market every week, and by catalogue – send $5 for the catalogue to 34 Cooper Road, RD 4, Waiuku 2684.

Digby Law's carrot cake with cream cheese icing

Ingredients

1 ½ cups peanut oil (or other light-flavoured oil)

2 cups raw sugar

4 eggs

1 tsp vanilla essence

2 cups wholemeal flour

1 ½ tsp ground cinnamon

1 scant tsp salt

3 cups grated carrot

1 cup chopped walnuts

2 tsp baking soda

Method

Grease and flour a cake tin (22cm diameter or more).

Heat the oven to 160°C.

Whisk together the oil and sugar.

Beat the eggs lightly, and beat in the vanilla essence.

Add the eggs and vanilla to the oil and sugar and whisk together.

Sift the flour, cinnamon and salt together into a large bowl.

Add the grated carrot and walnuts.

Add the wet ingredients to the dry ingredients and mix together.

At the last minute mix in the baking soda.

Pour the mixture into the tin and bake for 55 minutes or until cooked. It is a very moist cake, so it will be soft, but a skewer should come out clean.

When the cake is cool, ice it with cream-cheese icing.

Cream cheese icing

Beat together until smooth:

1 large (250g) container of regular cream cheese

¾ cup sifted icing sugar

1 tsp vanilla essence

¼ cup melted butter

(The original recipe for this cake is in *Digby Law's Vegetable Cookbook*, see endnote 8.)

One simple basic recipe; two very different afternoon tea treats – herb scones and raspberry scones.

Tropical flavours in home baking with all vegetable ingredients – lime & coconut vegan cupcakes.

A pair of bandicoots check a kumara bed to see if the crop is ready to harvest. (The slang term for taking the first fruits is 'bandicooting'.)

Koanga (Kaiwaka) Gardens.

The compleat gherkin — plant, flower, fruit and pickles.

Heritage seed source - Koanga Gardens (now Kaiwaka Gardens and the Koanga Institute) have been saving and growing on heritage seed varieties for two decades.

Mezze are superior snacks and light meals from the Middle East - great recipes to make fresh from the garden.

Quinces are beautiful as whole fruit and gorgeous as jelly.

Soba noodles are made from buckwheat and are a fine base for a salad of roasted garden vegetables flavoured with Asian sauces and oils.

Too many zucchinis? Make a tasty and inexpensive relish.

CHAPTER SIX

Almost@Home

Reclaiming real markets

'It's a congregational thing, the market,' sheep farmer and charcuterie producer Chris Wilkinson said to me when I met her at the Napier market. Chris has been selling her products at Hawke's Bay markets for several years. As well as highlighting the social benefits of farmers' markets, she suggested that they have built-in health benefits, referring to one man with severe health problems who comes to the market every week just to surround himself with positive people. The really fresh, nutritious and affordable fruit and vegetables he buys there probably help too.

In 1998 there was only one farmers' market in New Zealand, the Whangarei Growers' Market. When the Farmers' Market New Zealand Association (FMNZA) held its inaugural conference in 2006 there were 21 markets that met the authentic farmers' market standards of selling only food produced locally. Two years later there were over 40 markets listed on the FMNZA website and more were in the pipeline.[1] Now every weekend thousands of people visit farmers' markets, either doing the weekly big spend they used to do at a supermarket, or just adding value to their diets with fresh seasonal produce and artisan breads, oils, cheeses and the like. Thousands more are also getting farm-fresh produce and artisan-prepared foods directly from other markets that are not strictly farmers' markets, but that have a fresh-food component.

When you compare farmers' markets with supermarkets it's easy to see why they have taken off. For starters, the environmental and social ambience is so different. Farmers' markets are usually held outdoors, or are only lightly covered, so the air around the stalls is fresh and the light is natural. If there is music, it is live and fresh too, not canned Musak. There is space for children to play, and, blessed relief, there are no industrial foods familiar from advertising to children to pester their parents into buying. Adding to the social pleasure, there is a much better chance of running into friends and neighbours and having a good catch-up at a four-hours-a-week market than at an open-all-hours supermarket.

But the main reason people are flocking to the markets is of course the reason why they exist, which is to transfer really fresh, healthy, locally grown food directly from producer to consumer. There's not a can or carton covered in deceptive claims to be seen. Most of the food sold is raw, unprocessed and unlabelled. Even when a product comes in a glass jar or bottle, you can have confidence that the person selling it to you made it herself from this season's local harvest. There's also a good chance she grew some of the ingredients herself. You can always ask, because she's right there and able to answer your questions about what's in it, when it was made, and how she made it. Plus she'll usually let you taste before you buy, and can give you advice on how to use the product to best advantage in a recipe. After all, she made the product with the very hands that take your money for it. That's the shortest food chain there is, and the one in which you can have most confidence.

Consumer trust and confidence are key components of farmers' markets, but it's not the reason why they began in the first place. They were started in New Zealand – and in Australia at about the same time, and in the US before that – by growers who were sick of the indifference of supermarkets to the freshness and quality of their produce. Supermarket chains were only interested in piling it high and selling it cheap. They didn't care where it came from or whether it had any nutrients left by the time it reached them. After squeezing the local auction markets out of the supply line, they then started squeezing the growers to deliver more product at a lower cost. To many small-scale growers it seemed they had only two, equally unpleasant options, both of which were going to cost them: to get big or to get out.

At about the same time the new players on the local produce-growing scene, the organic growers, who weren't interested in growing on an export scale, were having even bigger problems trying to get their produce into local supermarkets. Cutting out the problematic and greedy middleman and selling directly made a lot more sense. So did joining forces with a range of other producers to create a market that had all the fresh-food options and none of the downsides of the supermarket. It was clearly the way to maximise sales at a fair price. Thus the Whangarei Growers' Market got going in 1998, followed by Hawke's Bay in 1999, and all the rest since then, making farmers' markets the biggest food retailing phenomenon to hit New Zealand since the supermarkets began their rise to dominance in the 1960s.

Most cities in New Zealand now have at least one weekly farmers' market, and many smaller places have them too. There are very big markets with over 50 stalls – like the Otago market, which takes place every Saturday at the historic Dunedin railway station and has thousands of customers – and there are very small markets, like the tiny one-stall Purau Valley Produce market that takes place fortnightly in summer and monthly in winter on the sunny side of Lyttelton Harbour. There may be only one stall, but it carries the bounty of up to 15 producers who live locally, including most of the things that can be bought at the much bigger Lyttelton Market across the water – vegetables, fruit, eggs, honey, nuts, olive oil, preserves, plants, home baking. Sometimes there are *very* local delicacies, like rabbit pasty.

Sales at the Purau Valley Produce market only supplement the regular employment or retirement incomes of the producers involved, but for stall-holders at the bigger markets this is where they make most of their income. Marlborough organic fruit grower Bob Crum explained to me the importance of the market to the viability of the orchard he runs with his wife Jennie, where they grow top-quality blueberries and plums. The organic shops in Wellington would take all they can grow, but they want to do the green thing and sell locally. However, most of the local supermarket managers are not interested in their product or capable of selling it properly. The last straw came when a new produce manager at Bob's local supermarket expressed real interest in taking blueberries direct from Bob and selling them very fresh and very fast. Bob gave a silent cheer. Alas, it turned into a groan when the produce manager was overruled by the accounts manager: the fruit would have to be trucked to the company's giant warehouse near Christchurch first, and held there for however many days it took for invoicing and despatch to be sorted out, before being put on a truck again to come back to the supermarket less than a kilometre from Bob's orchard.[2]

Bob and Jennie were appalled at the idea of adding all these unnecessary carbon emissions to their food, and also at the loss of nutrition and flavour all this long-distance travelling and warehouse-holding would entail. So when the idea of a farmers' market in Marlborough was mooted by local chef Chris Fortune – who was fed up with living in a province producing top-quality fresh food and not being able to get it straight into his kitchen – they enthusiastically joined the organising committee. These days they sell around 600kg of plums a week at the Marlborough and Nelson markets, and 70 per cent of their income comes from market and gate sales of their fruit. They sell big punnets of organic blueberries at the market for the same price as the supermarket charges for small punnets of chemically grown ones, which is a win/win situation for producers and customers. Bob has grafted over the plum orchard so that it now produces over 20 varieties of plum, which ripen between early December and mid-April. This means that at any one time four to five quite different varieties are for sale. Most of them are varieties you will never see in the supermarket, where tasteless Californian plums are sold for less than the price of home-grown ones. Not only are Bob's plums much fresher and more nutritious, they are also full of flavour because they are picked when they are perfectly ripe – a nerve-wracking business for Bob at times, holding on for that optimum point of ripeness, but getting in before birds or bad weather strike. Down at the market on Sunday morning customers don't have to guess if he got it right, because free slices of fruit to taste are on offer at the Crums' stall.

The stalls and surrounds of the popular Matakana Farmers Market in Northland were purpose-built in a rustic style.[3] There is a good range of top-quality products and a permanently installed kitchen turning out a tasty selection of brunch food. Rainbow Valley Farm, New Zealand's premier permaculture farm, has a versatile stall there, selling vege plants, vermicast liquid fertiliser and hot buckwheat pancakes, as well as fruit and veges. On the Rainbow Valley Farm stall I found a vegetable I'd never seen before, a yacon, and I got another unfamiliar one, a super-sized round radish with a rough black skin, from the Pak Thai stall. They were grown in a local garden run by a Thai/Kiwi couple who produce Asian veges as well as the familiar Kiwi ones.

Several of the stallholders have photos on display of their farms and I was gazing at the pictures of ducks behind the Mahurangi Pekin Ducks stall when the stallholder asked me, rather plaintively, if I'd like to buy some eggs from a 'poor old duck farmer'. I did, and we got into conversation about the difficult economics of duck farming in these times, with the price of duck food jumping a whopping 75 per cent in one year.[4] Most of the duck farmer's business is with Asian restaurants, bakeries and on-sellers in Auckland. Hard bargaining is the cultural norm there, so the farmers' market makes a nice change. It's also the best place to sell his duck-manure-based compost. I didn't have room in my luggage for that, but there was room for another novelty from the market – a bunch of gorgeous waterlilies. Who knew that they can have such long stems, and smell so sweet?

In sharp contrast to the rustic chic of Matakana, the City Farmers' Market at Britomart, right at the harbour edge of the Auckland CBD, feels like urban grunge.[5] Held in a carpark surrounded by multi-storey concrete buildings, with no paddocks or farm animals for miles, it is nevertheless a weekly oasis of real food for the increasing numbers of CBD dwellers. There are around 20,000 people living in the Auckland central business district today, 10 times as many as there were in 1990. I visited early on a chilly autumn morning and began the day nibbling on a freshly baked French pastry, washing it down with coffee. Suitably refreshed, I was then in a position to start sampling the goods for sale and was delighted to be able to find my favourite honey variety, rewarewa, along with other native flower varietal honeys produced on the islands near Auckland.

Although the environs are not beautiful, from a sustainability point of view it is a great location, right next to the Britomart transport centre. For farmers' markets to be a really sustainable replacement for supermarkets we also have to change the unsustainable pattern of driving to do our shopping. It should be easy for city people to get their fresh food without having to pay for fuel and carparks.

Or if it's necessary to drive to buy food, why not make it a family outing? A country market close to a big city, like Clevedon, provides that sort of opportunity.[6] As befits horsey country, pony rides are part of the attraction of the market, with tiny people being led about on tiny horses. There are other animals to view in the paddocks right next to the rural market, and some surprises among the stalls, including traditional Hungarian pastries, and the quintessential Latin American meat pie, the empanada, made by an Argentinian pasta maker. There is a good choice of organic produce, and also organic meat. The stall that kept me the longest, though, was the one encapsulating where all this productivity starts. The Running Brook Seeds stall, run by Stella Christofferson, is a treasure trove of open-source (non-hybridised) seeds. These are tried and true heritage varieties that perform well and taste good (see box on page 99).

It wasn't market day when I arrived in Hamilton, but I spoke to outgoing market manager Gail Brown about what's involved in putting a market together.[7] In summer 30 stallholders must be in place and ready to trade when the market bell rings at 8am, and there is all the infrastructure – toilets, rubbish bins etc – to take care of, so it could be chaos. But it always comes together on time, says Gail, because of a common goal and community spirit. Like other markets that are run by a not-for-profit trust, the Hamilton market has a community table where amateur gardeners with a small amount of produce can sell their surplus. But only three times a year – they are encouraged to take up a regular stall when they are able to grow more. Meanwhile larger stallholders may find there is such demand for their product from regular retail outlets or restaurants that they can no longer supply the market as well. Gail thinks this is usually a good thing: the market works as a business incubator, giving producers a place to get their fundamentals right – helped by lots of direct customer feedback – before going on to bigger things.

This view is seconded by Cherry de Negri of Napier, one of New Zealand's most experienced market managers. She doesn't want the market to be just a 'camping ground', with the same stallholders from year to year, but rather a place where new food businesses can get a foot on the ladder and move on up to full-time retail or wholesale. She says it's important to look after small food businesses, especially as individuals able to grow good food are rare. 'We have to protect them or there will be nothing left,' she says. Cherry talked to me over a cappuccino made by her Italian husband Carlo at the Napier Farmers' Market. Carlo dispenses coffee and his handmade gelato ice-creams in a dozen flavours at the market, while at the stall next to him Cherry sells her extensive range of preserves. The Napier market is small, never more than a dozen stalls, unlike the big Hawke's Bay market, which Cherry used to manage as well, but it has everything the Saturday morning shopper needs to stock up for the week ahead – fresh produce, meat, cheese, bread, plus a few treats as well.[8]

Cherry estimates that no stallholder travels more than 30 minutes to bring their goods right into the heart of Napier. Cherry herself gets some of the raw ingredients for her preserves straight from her town garden. Just that week she had dug the horseradish to make the very seasonal horseradish cream she sells. Being genuinely local is an important point of difference for authentic farmers' markets. The members of the Farmers' Market Association are strict on policing local boundaries, with 'local' usually defined as the province in which the market is located. Even then, they will give preference to the producers closest to the market, although this needs to be balanced with getting a good range of products. Cherry made an exception by going just outside the Hawke's Bay boundary to get a sheep milk cheese producer who could sell at the Hawke's Bay market, but has refused offers of stalls from Taranaki. Most markets operate on an '80 per cent local' rule, to get around the issue of foods and ingredients that have to be sourced outside the province in order to offer the full range of produce that one would find in a supermarket. Customers have cottoned on to this rule pretty fast, and generally support it, which is why there were rumblings about bananas being sold on the big organic produce stall at the Lyttelton Farmers' Market: is this is a compromise too far? It not only breaks the 'should be local' rule, it also contravenes another principle inherent in buying straight from the grower, which is seasonality. However, since bananas are not grown commercially anywhere in New Zealand, maybe the principle is irrelevant in this case, with the justification that the market should be a one-stop shop because it saves energy to do the big weekly shop in one place. Perhaps what is important is that the *intention* of the local rule is honoured: never to buy anything from far away if something the same, and/or of comparable quality, can be found closer to home.

For the rest of the goods on offer at the Lyttelton market this is certainly the case.[9] I love being able to get to this market from my home by a special kind of public transport, a ferry ride across the harbour, although I always underestimate how much I will buy and end up with aching arms carrying heavy bags back to the boat. I also enjoy being able to supplement my market shopping with bulk-bin staples like oats and rice from the organic store on Lyttelton's main shopping street, and treats from Ground, an excellent deli-café that used to be a little further along the road before the February 2011 earthquake, and will, I hope, be back on the main street one day. The Lyttelton Farmers' Market was conceived by the community-minded people of Project Lyttelton as one of several ways to revitalise the little port township by attracting more businesses and more custom to the main street, and it has certainly been a success. It also wants to incubate new food businesses, and Ground is one of its success stories, since the owners started by selling herb and spice mixes at the market.[10] The market has also succeeded in providing fresh local food at affordable prices to port residents, and decent returns to local growers and other food producers.

The multiple and often synergistic roles of farmers' markets are what differentiate them from the one-track, one-size-fits-all supermarket system. The keynote speakers at the 2008 FMNZA conference, Jane Adams from Australia and Bernadine Prince from the US, shared examples of how markets in their countries had found more ways of boosting environmental sustainability and social equity, including 'gleaning' after each market. This means gathering up unsold food that won't keep and distributing it to local food banks or community kitchens. Fresh Farm Markets, which runs eight farmers' markets in the Chesapeake Bay Watershed area, is set up as a charitable trust. This enables it to run other not-for-profit programmes, such as the FoodPrints education programme in local primary schools, and the five gleaning partners it supports. These provide hot meals and in some cases culinary education to homeless and/or at-risk clients.[11]

In Australia some farmers' markets have set up programmes of working with growers to enhance the sustainability of their farming. These can lead to market growers and customers going on to Community Supported Agriculture (CSA) and other forms of the 'box scheme' (more on these below), whereby customers connect directly with farmers and in some cases invest some 'sweat equity' in the farm by helping with weeding, harvesting, packing and so on. Customers can also invest in organic dairy herds by buying their own cow. This not only helps the farmer expand sustainably, but is also the only legal way in Australia and New Zealand to get access to raw milk. (If it's your cow you can drink the milk any way you like.)

Other ways in which farmers' markets can help build local and sustainable food connections include gates sales and local food trails, regional/co-operative farm shops, community and school gardens (some of which sell their surplus at the market), providore vans, which sell a range of market products between the market days, and community tables at markets where home gardeners sell their surplus produce. Gastronomy and good nutrition also get a hand-up, with top chefs doing cooking-from-the-market demonstrations – there are even two New Zealand cooking-from-the-market cookbooks.[12]

Many nutritionists find farmers' markets the best place to take clients to educate them about what is worth eating, and how to prepare it. Informal education of young consumers and cooks is also a big plus of farmers' markets. Cherry de Negri notes that a generation of market kids is starting to appear. Even those barely able to see over the stalls are stepping up to survey the wares and put their money down, keen to taste new things and to advise their parents on good buys. Knowing that at least some of the next generation will be able to pick the best in unprocessed foods based on their inherent qualities of taste and nutrition, rather than being the victims of TV advertising, has to give us some hope for a better food future.

That brighter future will be based on restoring the direct, unmediated *relationship* between food producers and consumers that the industrial food system has destroyed. By keeping things local farmers' markets show that there is no necessary contradiction between doing good business and making a positive contribution to community health and wealth. Back in the 18th century the doyen of free-market economists, Adam Smith, told us that the two should go hand in hand (the 'invisible hand'). But that was when small local markets were the main game in town, buyers and sellers had a face-to-face relationship, and comparing quality and price was as easy as stepping from one stall to the next and giving the product and the producer a good once-over. Big national and transnational corporations, producing and distributing food on an industrial scale using sophisticated marketing techniques, changed that game out of all recognition until we reached today's situation, where big food business is usually destructive of community, both in the farmlands and in the city. Taking our food system back to the local level and reconnecting producers and consumers therefore works as a solution to more problems than the painfully obvious ones of poor nutrition and unsustainable greenhouse gas emissions. It is also a route to greater local prosperity, better public health and stronger community cohesion.

Super-special shopping

There are a variety of other ways in which Kiwis are now bypassing the supermarket and seeking out fresh food sources that they can trust. These may not be quite as convenient as the farmers' market, but they can still be a good part of one's personal food web, depending on where one lives. As we saw in Chapter 4, there has been a dramatic drop in the number of food outlets in towns and cities that are easily accessible by foot or bicycle. However, more and more people are now twigging to the fact that once you factor in the price of buying a car and putting fuel in it to get to the supermarket, maybe the food there isn't really cheaper at all, even if one could trust the quality. The standard New Zealand IRD mileage rate for private-vehicle work-related travel up to 3000km is 62 cents a kilometre. So travelling just 20km a week by car to shop for food costs nearly $650 per year in running costs alone. Are you going to save this much shopping at the supermarket?

My guess is that you won't, because only the processed food at the supermarket is cheap. The fresh food costs as much as or more than the same food from a local market or independent greengrocer. Fresh food pricing is different from processed food pricing, because it depends on seasonal supply. So when apples are cheap at the supermarket they will be the same price or less at the greengrocer. Out-of-season apples that have been shipped in from the northern hemisphere are going to be more expensive wherever you buy them. People think that because supermarkets *say* they are cheaper, and carry a few loss-leaders, that they are cheaper overall. If they did some comparison shopping they might be shocked at how much more expensive the supermarket really is. In October 2000 Wellington-based cook and food writer Lois Daish looked at how savings could be made by buying from independent produce retailers, when she went shopping for fresh ingredients for a hearty vegetable soup. She found a big difference between the cost of supermarket fresh vegetables and those from her local greengrocer. At $10.94 the supermarket veges were almost twice as expensive as the greengrocer's ($5.90). Bought from the Sunday market they were a little cheaper again ($5.55).[13]

That would be an interesting experiment to do for yourself, if you are lucky enough to have a local greengrocer and market. It seems that not only would you save on the costs of getting to and from the supermarket, you would also save on the produce itself. When I lived in Mt Eden in inner-city Auckland in 1978 I used to enjoy strolling down to the high street on Friday evenings to do essential shopping for the weekend. There were four greengrocers, three butcher's shops, two or three bakeries (including an excellent German one), two fishmongers and a delicatessen, plus a couple of general grocery stores. I used to check them all out and note the best deals before making my purchases and popping them into my backpack. Today on the same stretch of Mt Eden Road there are lots of trendy cafés and a bookshop that specialises in cookbooks – but hardly anywhere to buy fresh food to cook. In April 2011 I spoke with a shopkeeper at the last remaining greengrocers in Mt Eden Village. When her family bought the business in 1989 there were three other greengrocers on the high street; now theirs is the last one left and she says it only keeps going because it is a family business that employs only relatives. Independent greengrocers have been effectively forced out of business by the supermarket stranglehold on produce markets, which has seen the end of the auction markets and the rise of wholesalers offering discounts to supermarkets that buy in bulk, but not to independent stores buying smaller quantities.

Having a variety of small fresh-food stores in every neighbourhood provides environmental, social and health benefits that are well worth the extra few cents one might have to pay for a bun or a banana. Luckily the trend toward eating more organic food has meant more options for one-stop environmentally friendly shopping. Organic green/grocery shops are becoming more common. Christchurch now has four such stores, whereas 10 years ago there was only one. There is now an organic version of most of the things you can buy in the supermarket, and certainly of all the things worth eating. The downside is that a lot of them are imported, as they are not yet made or grown in sufficient quantities in New Zealand. That's the case for wholesome basic foods such as rolled oats, lentils, pasta, tomato paste and also for unwholesome frivolous foods, although in my view the world has no need for organic versions of industrial biscuits. As far as fresh produce goes, though, the supply is usually good. Thanks to their connections with local growers and with organic produce wholesalers, all organic shops in New Zealand are pretty well stocked with genuinely local or at least New Zealand-grown produce. The price will be good as well, sometimes lower than the supermarket, if seasonality is respected. Apples are always cheap in April and pricey in January. Since that's when the berries and stonefruit are at their peak, who needs apples?

Good deals on organic produce can also be had at the organic produce stalls and vans that set up in suburbs or come to workplaces. I don't know how many there are in New Zealand or if there is one near you, but they are worth looking out for and encouraging.

If you can't access fresh food close to your workplace then another alternative is to buy direct from the farm. Unless you live on the edge of the city, or in a country town, I'm not suggesting this as an everyday or sustainable mode of stocking your pantry. However, it is good to do once in a while, taking children if possible, to reconnect with where food comes from, how it is produced, and who is producing it. It's also starting to be seen as a desirable form of leisure travel, and food trails are being developed to complement existing wine trails. The Food Hawke's Bay organisation has led the way in this regard by developing a 'Wine Country Food Trail' that covers most of Hawke's Bay, and is divided into sections to allow for genuinely leisurely exploration. A sixth edition of the trail's map and brochure came out in 2008, with 50,000 copies printed, indicating the size of the demand for this experience.[14] Northland's Food and Wine Trail[15] includes artisan food producers, speciality shops, cafés and restaurants, wineries, farmers' markets and stalls and special events and excursions. Among the last category is one that is surely an 'only in New

10 reasons to shop at your local farmers' market
(from the Waikato Farmers' Market website)

1. Know where your food comes from.
2. Connect with the seasons through flavourful fresh produce.
3. Support local farmers and artisan producers.
4. Help promote responsible land use and preserve our cultural heritage.
5. Do the environment a favour, reduce food miles.
6. Enjoy the regional bounty brought to you with love and care.
7. Contribute to the local economy.
8. Give your body a hug with healthy food – and the occasional treat.
9. Get to know the best farmers, growers and food makers in the Waikato.
10. Meet friends, enjoy the music and market fanfare.

Zealand' experience. As the website blurb puts it: 'The Kumara Box presents "Ernie" and his Live Kumara Show. Allow an hour to relax in Ernie's kumara shed/converted theatre to experience his unique story and DVD presentation. Phone first to check if Ernie's around.' A Coromandel Homegrown Food Trail was launched in 2007 along with the first Coromandel Homegrown Food Festival, which is a whole month of celebrating 'Coro' food and Kiwi music.[16] The latest kid on the Kiwi food-trail block is the North Canterbury Food and Wine Trail, which covers the Waimakariri, Hurunui and Kaikoura districts.[17]

The development of food tourism in New Zealand is an interesting and welcome outcome of the move towards local, quality food production. But can it really help to raise the sustainability stakes? Further, can it make a positive contribution to ensuring that *all* New Zealanders, not just those with the leisure time and money to explore a food trail, have access to good fresh food at a reasonable price? In Australia a group of community entrepreneurs have created an initiative to deal with this issue.

Hawkesbury Harvest[18] was started in 2000 when 12 people representing all facets of food production, consumption, governance and administration in the Hawkesbury catchment area, which includes a lot of the north Sydney region, got together to work on addressing environmental sustainability, food security and local economic development issues. Agriculture in the region makes a vital contribution to the fresh food eaten in Sydney – 90 per cent of the green leafy vegetables eaten in the city are produced within or next to its boundaries, and 12 per cent of New South Wales' agricultural production comes from the 1 per cent of land used for growing food around Sydney. How it is produced not only affects the nutritional quality of the food, but also has a huge impact on how much water there is for the city, and how clean that water is. It affects employment as well, with some 11,500 people employed full time in primary production around Sydney. Planning for sustainable farming in and around the city is therefore one of the most pressing economic and environmental challenges for the city councils in the region, and for the state authorities of New South Wales. They are all involved with Hawkesbury Harvest, along with producers, workers and public issue groups of all kinds, from wildlife protectors to food bank providers.

I visited an orange grove in the Penrith City Council region in the west of Sydney where I learned first hand from the grower what a difference his council's policy shift has meant to his livelihood. Promoting gate sales is part of an overall programme designed to keep small local producers viable in order to boost employment and sales in the region, and also to mitigate the environmental impacts of food production by keeping things at a sustainable scale. Before this change, the grower produced only one variety of orange, and the whole crop went to an industrial juice company. Then he waited for up to six months for that company to pay him, making it a struggle to keep afloat. Once gate sales were approved, he started selling cases of juicing oranges to local customers, and also growing a greater variety of oranges and other citrus fruits for eating. When we spoke he was looking at converting to organic production – for his own health, the health of his family and his workers, and in line with the healthy environment goals of the council.

The importance of developing and applying policies and practices of sustainable urban agriculture if we are all to eat well is revisited in Chapter 8. Gate sales and farm-gate trails are definitely part of the solution to the problem of our dysfunctional food system, but realising their potential to provide maximum sustainability gains still needs a lot of work. For most people, going out to the farm regularly is not going to be an option. The Hawkesbury district has come up with another model for those who need good food cheaply and conveniently – the not-for-profit co-operative shop. The Food Barn co-operative store is a church initiative, set up as part of the Hawkesbury Food for All Project to provide cheaper, better food for those living on welfare benefits.[19] The prices are on average 12 per cent cheaper than local supermarkets, and the fresh produce is really fresh, since it comes straight from local growers. There are further discounts available for pensioners and health-card holders, and a food voucher scheme as well. These semi-private stores can also reduce waste in the industrial system by being an outlet for seconds that are perfectly good to eat, but are deemed not large, regular or pretty enough for the commercial system. These foods would otherwise be dumped or not picked at all.

Fresh food to your door

The bulk food-buying co-op is another way of getting the best food cheaply. Popular in the 1970s, these were run by groups of neighbours – often student households – or by community organisations like the Ponsonby People's Union. They are being reborn in an organic form, with neighbours and/or workmates banding together to buy bulk organic dry goods and fresh produce wholesale, then getting together once a week or so to divvy it all up for the participating households. Food co-ops certainly save money, and help make organic food more affordable. They may also save carbon emissions if they are workplace- or neighbourhood-based. Their main cost is in the time to organise them, and to do the weekly pack-out.

This may not suit people with full-time jobs, who seem to be the ones signing up for the organic produce box schemes that are starting to proliferate. In the simplest box schemes, customers contract with a local organic grower to pay a set price for a box of veges, and sometimes fruit, each week or fortnight, and the grower fills that box with a range of produce in its prime, to the agreed value. This makes life easier for the grower, as s/he has a guaranteed income, can avoid having to sell cheap when crops are plentiful, and has some protection against crop failures. It benefits the customer because the food is generally delivered to the door, and is good value for money. The possible downsides for the customer are that the range of produce available may not cover all that was wanted that week, small-scale growers may not be able to supply a sufficiently varied box in the colder months of the year, or at all, and some of the produce may be unfamiliar and require learning new recipes.

These issues can be addressed by box schemes that bring together produce from different sources. I spoke with Lorraine Upham, who by 2008 had been running The Organic Connection box scheme from her Paraparaumu Beach home for several years. After a good talk with Lorraine and three trial box deliveries to see if this is really what they want, her clients set up an automatic payment account for a certain size of box at a set price. They let her know what they *don't* want (up to a maximum of three opt-outs) and arrange a place for the box to be delivered. All the boxes are packed and customised in the Chantal Wholefoods warehouse in Napier, which has a big fresh produce section, and loaded into one courier truck for delivery from southern Hawke's Bay down to the Miramar peninsula at the southern end of Wellington. Some of them go to workplaces and others to homes.

Most customers like the element of surprise that comes with opening the box. People with small children often make a present-opening game of it, which helps the kids take ownership of new and unfamiliar foods. For those who have just met a choko, persimmon, Jerusalem artichoke or other unfamiliar food for the first time and are thinking 'What on earth do I do with this?' Lorraine provides tips and recipes in a regular email newsletter and also encourages her clients to contribute recipes. (Providing and contributing recipes via newsletters and fliers seems to be common to most box schemes.) Although Lorraine doesn't grow the food herself, she regularly visits the people who do, and is a strong advocate for more business and government support for organics.

The other way to get fresh organic produce delivered to your door is to make a small investment in a farm. Known as Community Supported Agriculture (CSA) the deal here is that each participating household pays a one-off flat fee to join a particular CSA scheme, and thereafter buys produce regularly through the scheme. New Zealand's first CSA scheme, Simply Good Food, is in the Wairarapa.[20] It started in 2007 and has trialled different business models to see what suited producers and customers best, and in 2011 reorganised itself as a co-operative. There are many different ways a CSA scheme can be organised.[21] Common to them all is ensuring that the producers have a reasonable return on their labour, and do not have to go into unsustainable debt to make farm improvements. Most schemes also support environmentally friendly farming and a good deal for customers.

Members of a CSA are generally welcome – often encouraged, or even required – to help out on the farm, so that they can see how their food is produced, and also contribute to keeping down the cost of its production. Simply Good Food CSA organises this by holding a Farm Day every six weeks throughout the year. It's a day out with a difference, involving hands-on encounters with food in paddocks, orchards and kitchens. In between Farm Days members of the CSA can obtain updates on the website, which advises what fruits and vegetables are coming into season, and how the weather is affecting the crops.

A further variation on box schemes and CSA, one that has been going longer but on a smaller scale, is good old mail order. These days it may be email order, but the principle is the same. The customer goes on the mailing list for a specialist food product, or a particular farm, writes or phones in what they want, and has it delivered to them. This system has been working successfully for some time with high-value products like cheese and wine. It is not best suited to fresh produce or bulk supplies, although some orchards courier seasonal fruit, while Terrace Farm, a biodynamic cropping farm beside the Rakaia River in Canterbury, provides a great service in freshly milled flours. They have different kinds of mills (stoneground and Zentrofan) that retain all the vitality of the whole grain, including its unstable oils. This means they are much more nutritious than industrially refined flours, but don't keep as well. That's not a problem if you can call the farm and order the flour to be milled for you. I have seen the big sacks of grain stacked in the barn at Terrace Farm, waiting for the customers to call and order up some really fresh flour. It was a comforting sight to see this most basic of foods being held for processing the way it was done for millennia before the oil age aberration in food production. Some farmers still know what to do, how to do it, and best of all *why* they are doing it – to keep a healthy and sustainable food culture alive.

Farms and market gardens are not the only places where things that are good to eat can be found, however, and nor do home kitchens have a monopoly on good cooking. In the next chapter we look at how to find free food in the wild, and where to find other cooks you can trust.

Ingredients for spicy eggplant and tomatoes (recipe opposite).

Nigel Slater's spicy eggplant and tomatoes

Ingredients

3 tbsp oil

500g small eggplants, cut into thick chunks

3 medium onions, peeled and sliced in thick segments

1 thumb-sized knob of ginger, finely sliced

600g tomatoes, quartered

500ml vegetable stock or water

small bunch of coriander, chopped

For the spice paste

3 cloves garlic

a little sea salt

seeds from 8 cardamom pods

1 tsp mustard seeds

2 tsp turmeric

2 tsp cumin seeds

2 small, hot fresh chillies, diced

Method

Heat the oil in a large frying pan or other shallow pan. Fry the eggplant chunks until they colour and soften slightly. Remove them and drain them on kitchen paper.

Add the onion slices to the pan and fry them *slowly* on a low heat until golden and translucent.

To make the spice paste:

Crush the garlic and salt together in a mortar with a pestle. Add the cardamom seeds and pound well, then add the mustard seeds, turmeric, cumin seeds and diced chillies, crushing it all into a thick paste.

Add the spice paste to the frying onions and cook for a few minutes. Add the ginger, then the quartered tomatoes, then the eggplant.

Pour in the stock or water, stir and leave to come to the boil. As soon as it starts to boil, turn it down to a simmer and cook until the eggplant is tender, the tomatoes are squishy, and there is still plenty of juice.

Stir in the chopped coriander leaves and serve with cardamom rice – basmati rice flavoured with the seeds of 6 cardamom pods, 8 black peppercorns and a broken cinnamon stick.

I got this recipe from a Nigel Slater column reprinted in the Christchurch *Press*. It is not in either of his most recent books, *Tender* and *The Kitchen Diaries*, but they do have lots of other mouth-watering eggplant recipes.

The Thursday morning market in Byron Bay, northern New South Wales, is a great place to buy Asian veges.

A selection of salad ingredients on sale at the Byron Bay market.

Salad greens come to the CBD – the City Farmers' Market in Auckland.

A great selection of carrots and a cheerful seller at the Hamilton Farmers' Market.

Almost too pretty to eat – a stall at the Matakana Farmers' Market.

Some of the stalls at the Matakana Farmers' Market have photos of the farmer/stall-holder down on the farm.

CHAPTER SEVEN

Food@Large

Food explorations

If you want to find good food in New Zealand it's best to get off the beaten track – sometimes off any track at all. Staying on the culinary highway today means shuttling between the supermarket, fast-food outlets and the microwave at home. It's a road to a dull and deadly diet. Yet just off that highway there are all sorts of better options. Some of them are even on actual main routes, like Auckland's Great South Road.

On my exploration of New Zealand's evolving food system I took this road out of town, heading for Otahuhu. I'm guessing that this suburb wouldn't be most people's first pick as the gourmet hub of the City of Sails, but I was drawn by the memory of a cheap yet excellent Vietnamese meal I had there in the 1980s, in a café that was obviously a home-away-from-home for new migrants. Extended families ate together at large tables, and it was touching to watch the fierce competition among the young, childless uncles to be able to hold and rock their infant nephews and nieces.

Otahuhu's little high street runs parallel to the main road, and it is well supplied with Pacific Island and Asian food and clothing stores. On the busy Great South Road there are all the multinational fast-food chains and one unique food store, the Soung Yueen Food Market. It virtually shouted at me: here you will find vegetables you have never seen before! There were also Chinese-style cuts of meat and novel types of charcuterie, not to mention hundreds of unfamiliar grocery items.

I recognised most of the dozens of fruit and vegetable varieties for sale, but there were three that had me mystified. I took them to the counter seeking enlightenment and was told that the skinny cucumber-like thing with ridges on it was a see qua, and that the pale green stems with a honeycomb pattern inside were taro stalks. I knew that the bunch of heart-shaped dark-green leaves I was holding was not what is usually sold under the name of Vietnamese mint, so I asked for the Chinese name. I was told that it translated as 'fish-smell plant', and that it can be used as a medicine for liver complaints.

I was eager to know who grew these plants and where, but there was a bit of a language barrier, my Chinese being limited to 'hello' and 'thank you', so that is a mystery to be solved another day. What they tasted like was easier to determine. After a light stir-frying, the fish-smell plant did not lose its rather stinky rotten-fish smell; the see qua was a bit woody; but the taro stalks were much tastier than I expected. I hit the web to find out exactly what these vegetables are, and how they are usually cooked, and found a wonderful colour chart of Asian vegetables.[1] It told me that I had just eaten a bath sponge – the see qua or sze gwa is a member of the loofah family. It is best cooked in soups and stews where it softens and soaks up other flavours; the fish-smell plant is a unique species from China that may be becoming an invasive weed in Australia; and the taro is a plant with an ancient global history and some startling new culinary applications – taro gelato, anyone?[2]

Somewhere in south Auckland right now there is probably a little girl who is refusing to eat up the delicious fish-smell plant that her mother just cooked for her, just as I used to turn up my nose at Brussels sprouts. Neither of us will ever cook this vegetable regularly, but I am glad that I made this exploration into a new world of fresh ingredients. I was equally glad to come to the market in Pukekohe, a bit further down the road, and see tables heaped high with puha and watercress, which were being sold by Maori stallholders and snapped up by Maori customers. I have never seen them for sale in the South Island, where people must forage for them. And forage they do, getting so far off the beaten food track that there is no track at all.

Foraging freely

The natural environment is full of food – you just have to know what you're looking for. This is true even in cities, which is just as well, since there are not many places left like the Urewera Ranges, where the Tuhoe people still gather traditional foods from their traditional land. Foods like 'bush bananas', the fruit of the puwharawhara (*Astelia* spp.). The elders who gave me a guided tour of the traditional uses of the Urewera forest plants in 1986 told me that this fruit was so prized in the old days that Maori wove a protective covering from the leaves of the plant around the fruits, to protect them from rats. The long leaves of the astelia can also be turned into remarkably strong rope, just by passing them through a flame.

Wild plants and their uses have always been an interest of mine, and I have been foraging for so long that I don't remember when I started. I do recall the al fresco meal that confirmed me in the habit. I was 11 years old and holidaying with family friends in Dunedin. With two other children I followed the Water of Leith upstream until we passed the last house on its banks and came to the first open paddock. There we saw a boy who was cooking something in a tin can over a small fire. We hopped over the fence to see what it was, and found it was a little native freshwater crayfish (koura), which he had just caught in the stream. He had enough to share, so for the first and thus far only time I enjoyed this delicacy. We returned the favour by providing the dessert – wild apples that we gathered, cut up and stewed in the same can.

Since then I have regularly eaten food gathered in the wild. I am not alone: during the writing of this book many people told me about their foraging experiences, and some of them were passing the skills on to their children. There is a lot of free fresh food around, even in the centre of cities, if you know what you are looking for and where to look for it. Some foragers guard the source of their delicacies carefully, like whitebaiters with a good pozzy. Carlo and Cherry de Negri know where the prized porcini mushrooms can be found in the wild in Hawke's Bay, and they're not telling. Similarly, I now know where you can find a native freshwater crayfish in a very surprising spot in Wellington, but I wouldn't tell just anyone. For more ordinary free foods, almost anywhere is a good place to start looking. Roadsides, vacant lots, riverbanks, public parks and shorelines may have something you can make into a meal, a beverage or a preserve. Around where I live I can gather plenty of wild New Zealand spinach and also silverbeet from the beach and sea cliffs in the cooler months. I can also pick great handfuls of flatleaf parsley, which is a weed in these parts, and make pesto with it. On the roadsides I find elderflowers, for cordial and 'champagne', in late spring, and blackberries in autumn, for jellies, desserts and breakfast fruit. Totting up the number of free wild foods I have munched on regularly over the years I found it came to around 25 items. This is quite a lot, but certainly less than half of what is actually available.

That's my estimate after reading the source books on the subject, Sheila Natusch's *Wildfare for Wilderness Foragers*, Gwen Skinner's *Simply Living: A gatherer's guide to New Zealand's fields, forest and shores* and Andrew Crowe's *A*

Field Guide to the Native Edible Plants of New Zealand.[3] These books are now out of print, but since they were written the web has become the first stop for foragers, in the form of Wellingtonian Johanna Knox's blog.[4] She has also set up an email list where foragers can swap tips and recipes. A great feature of Johanna's blog is the variety of photos of foraged food, both in the wild and as she prepares it. If you live in Christchurch you could join a network of foragers, Otautahi Urban Foraging.[5] This group has published a map of where all sorts of free goodies can be found around Christchurch. One member is a wild-food gatherer who specialises in coastal foraging and blogs about it.[6]

Foraging adds zest to walks around the town or in the country and sharpens the mind, since it involves working out where to find wild food, how to identify it and how to prepare it well. Richard Mabey, the English author of *Food for Free*,[7] calls this 'inconvenience food' and asks why 21st-century people with 'easy access to most of the taste sensations on the planet' would opt for 'bramble-scrambling, mud-larking, tree climbing' instead.[8] Ask anyone who has gathered a good feed for free how it feels compared with paying money for stuff from the supermarket and you have your answer. Humans evolved as hunter-gatherers – and heavens, it feels good to go back to the old ways every now and then.[9]

It is, however, now a much more complex act than it once was, especially in cities, with their multiple intersections of cultural and property boundaries. I was reminded of this when staying with an Australian Aboriginal friend in central Sydney in the late 1990s. She is descended from a long line of hunter-gatherers, most of whom gave up this lifestyle only very recently, and some of whom are still living it. The spirit of hunting and gathering is still strong in her and she is skilful at obtaining and preparing good food from the land in traditional ways. I have happy memories of sitting beside a Northern Territory billabong at sunset, eating morsels of tender barramundi with my fingers from a plate made of bark. My friend had caught the fish only 30 minutes before. It was cooked by wrapping it in well-soaked papery tree bark, then laying it on the embers of an open fire. I knew it was really wild food because I was told not to go too close to the banks of the billabong in case a crocodile jumped out and got me for dinner instead. We could hear them growling in the distance as we dined, which gave an interesting edge to our meal.

Taking things for free in the bush is straightforward, but the urban setting of property-mad whitefellas poses some social problems for a hunter-gatherer. A big mulberry tree laden with fruit was leaning over a fence on the Sydney lane where my friend lived, but she was afraid that gathering the surplus fruit might lead to a racist reaction. She therefore proposed doing it after dark. I offered to do it with her in daylight, and take any flak as a thieving Kiwi if anyone objected. She was happy with that, so we held a big sheet under the tree, gave it a shake, and gathered lots of fruit. Most of it went to Tranby Aboriginal College, a couple of blocks away, where the cook was very pleased to receive it. As we left the college my friend surreptitiously nipped a few ripe berries off the lillypilly tree out the front and shared them with me. I wished I had known they were edible when I was living in a flat in Grey Lynn with half a dozen lillypilly trees across the back boundary.

Nearly 10 years later and a lot further north in Australia I found more twists on free food gathering. At the Saturday morning market at Yeppoon in central Queensland the Murri Magic stall was serving 'Hot Dingoes' with a sauce made from wild-gathered indigenous ingredients along with farmed ones. Other wild sauces and pickles, plus herbal medicines made with wild-gathered ingredients, were also for sale. On the other side of the market a stall selling only plump organic avocados was getting rid of them fast, as they were going for half the usual price. I was introduced to the seller later, as we sat in a friendly group around the chai stall run by the local peace group, Pineapples for Peace. All my stereotypes about who goes in for foraging went for a tumble when I learned he was a retired (in his late thirties) stockbroker who was gathering surplus fruit from the trees in private gardens. This had improved his own diet, and was making good food available cheaply to others. He always asked if he could harvest the trees, and was seldom refused.

But imagine if one didn't even have to ask. That is the dream of artist A. D. Schierning, who has organised the planting of a 'freedom fruit garden' in an under-used reserve in Otara, next to Rongomai Primary School. She came up with the idea of freedom fruit gardens after learning from first-hand experience how difficult it is to feed a child well on a tight budget.[10]

Project Lyttelton is also exploring the possibility of planting pockets of reserve land around Lyttelton with fruit and nut trees that will supplement local diets for free. We can expect to see more such initiatives around the country in future, as they make so much sense, both environmentally and socially.

Sustainable swapping

More public fruit trees would surely make cities more nutritious as well as more beautiful. Sharing the surplus harvest from private gardens is another way of making sure that everyone has enough good food to eat. Again, this is something that hasn't happened in New Zealand on a large scale since World

War Two, when the citrus harvest from private gardens in the North Island was collected by service clubs and shipped to the South Island to make up for the lack of imported citrus fruits, which were a low priority during wartime.

Wild-gathered rosehips from Central Otago were another Vitamin C source during the war and for a decade afterwards. I still vaguely remember the scent and taste of rosehip syrup from my childhood, and when I lived in Otago I revived the memory by gathering rosehips for jelly and for tea.

Private gardens still produce far more fruit than the householders can consume at the height of the season, but not necessarily enough to go to a market. This inspired some enterprising and generous gardening geeks to create a virtual neighbourhood of food swappers and sharers. There are now several such websites, including Home Grown Market, OOOOBY (Out Of Our Own Backyards) and Locavore365.[11]

These sites are great ways to make connections with friendly food sharers in your neighbourhood and beyond, but there are of course excellent no-tech alternatives. Selling or swapping with workmates is one, or with the members of a community group that you belong to. I recently started doing the latter with the small community choir I sing with every Wednesday, selling an average of $18 worth of produce and preserves to members each week. I keep half the money and give the rest to the choir – an easy way to fundraise where everyone wins. Putting a sign at your gate that you have produce to sell or give away, or a notice to that effect on the nearest community noticeboard, is also low-tech and neighbourly. It ensures that your surplus will be consumed really, truly locally, with the added bonus of building positive relationships with the neighbours. Such activity was common up until the 1970s, when the supermarket and car combination took over from close-to-home provisioning. In the street of around 50 houses where I grew up during the 1950s and 1960s there were at least three households selling fresh produce grown on their quarter-acre sections. It was better, fresher and cheaper than anything else on offer – and could be again.

Friendly freeganism

Food garnered by foraging and swapping represents a resource that would not otherwise be utilised by humans, but would go back to replenish nature. At the other end of the spectrum are those who retrieve food from the waste stream of the industrial food system. This represents a resource that has been rejected by humans, and is en route to a tip where it will produce damaging pollution, whether from methane emissions (a powerful greenhouse gas) or leachate. Such food waste is not only a huge environmental problem, it is also a dreadful social disgrace. Hundreds of billions of tonnes of food are wasted in the world every year while hundreds of millions of people go hungry.[12]

The warriors against wasting food this way are mostly young inner-city dwellers, and they go by the name of freegans. Freegans are motivated to get food from the waste stream for two reasons – it's free and it makes environmental sense. Freeganism is a philosophy as well as a practice and freegans define themselves as embracing 'community, generosity, social concern, freedom, co-operation and sharing in opposition to a society based on materialism, moral apathy, competition, conformity, and greed'.[13]

How do freegans get their free food? There are three main ways: asking, foraging and dumpster-diving. This is the term coined in the US for taking discarded food out of the skips or bins behind supermarkets and other food retail outlets. Such food is often still fine to eat. The packaged food is generally less than a month past its 'best by' or 'use by' date, while the fresh produce is usually not rotten or bad, just a bit wilted. Collecting this food is legally marginal, so dumpster-diving tends to be a nocturnal activity. Some retailers make it easy to access their bins, while others make it difficult. Especially annoying to freegans is when good food is mixed with bad – baked goods with coffee grounds, or raw food with packaged food – meaning that everything is wasted (and may not even be good for composting).

Collecting food that would otherwise go to the dump is as much a political statement about waste in the industrial food system as a way of eating, although freegans often collect so much food that they have a surplus to share around. Some of this might go to the organisation Food Not Bombs (FNB),

My wild and free pantry

Vegetables
chickweed
dandelion greens
New Zealand spinach
potatoes
puha
pumpkins
silverbeet
watercress

Herbs and flowers
borage
calendula
elderflower
manuka leaves (for tea)
mint
parsley
thyme

Fruit and nuts
apples
blackberries
cape gooseberries
cherry plums
crabapples
konini berries
passionfruit
rosehips
walnuts

which was set up in the US in 1980 and now has hundreds of independent chapters all around the world, including two in New Zealand, in Christchurch and Wellington.[14] Food Not Bombs is dedicated to providing free food to those in need, whether their need is chronic, (such as the permanently homeless) or acute (victims of disasters). Most of their food comes by prior arrangement with retailers who give away their tired produce, day-old bread, short-dated packaged goods and so on.

In Christchurch some student supporters of FNB do a weekly early-morning run on their bikes to collect and distribute food this way. Some of the food goes to shelters for the homeless and other places in need of it, and some is cooked by FNB members to give away on the street, or to serve at social events. I attended one such event in Christchurch while writing this book, and found the food to be well prepared and tasty, albeit with a predominance of soups, stews and curries containing a multiplicity of vegetables. After the 2010 and 2011 earthquakes the Christchurch Food Not Bombs group found an additional role as an ad hoc community food provider. In July 2011 I received an email advertising a gathering in the centre of the shaky city, offering:

> Free Kai, Fun activities
> Plenty of seating
> @ The empty site
> Corner of Barbadoes & Kilmore Streets
> Midday onwards
> Bring music and join in with the community spirit.

Food not Bombs food is vegan, which is another characteristic of freeganism. FNB members, like many other freegans, take an ethical and environmental approach to eating. This usually includes opposing the cruelty and environmental burden of industrial animal farming. FNB makes the food it prepares for others vegan, which also avoids health issues from eating scavenged animal foods, although animal food from safe sources is also eaten.[15]

Convivial kitchens

Some of the food collected by freegans, and a lot of food donated by home and community gardeners, ends up in kitchens that provide for those who for one reason or another do not eat at home. I have no idea how many meals are cooked this way across the country, but the Christchurch City Mission alone served 15,660 dinners in its Night Shelter dining room in 2009.[16] The meals are prepared by volunteers, some of whom are professional chefs.

The Night Shelter dinners represent one end of the community dining spectrum, where the cooks and the diners are not likely to have family ties, or even belong to the same geographical communities or communities of interest. Most of the Night Shelter diners need more help than dinner, but everyone feels better after a good meal. The dinner table is a dignified and friendly place where they can let it be known what other sort of help they might need.

Most present-day urban community kitchens and dining rooms are not for people with such special needs, but rather are dedicated to meeting the need of every community to get together in an informal way. In this regard they are similar to New Zealand's oldest tradition of community cooking and eating, which is on the marae. An integral part of marae life is offering good hospitality, and the whare kai is an important part of the marae complex. Some community kitchens model themselves on the marae tradition of hospitality to all comers. The Gold Coin Café at Te Whare Roimata in inner-city Christchurch, for example, started providing a weekly two-course sit-down dinner for a gold coin donation in the mid-1990s. Local residents, many of them dependent on pensions and other benefits, make a booking for meals just as with any regular restaurant. For some elderly men living alone, who have limited cooking skills, it may be the only proper meal they have all week, and the most friendly one. Food comes partly from the community garden run by the Te Whare Roimata Trust, and partly from donations in kind or in money.

(After the Christchurch quakes Te Whare Roimata had to relocate to temporary premises and the Wednesday dinner has had to be changed to a Thursday lunch. But all are still welcome and produce still comes from the community garden.)

Inner-city neighbourhoods often have a mix of class and ethnicity, with students, pensioners, refugee migrants, solo parents and other low-income folk living in the cheaper rental accommodation. This mixture was very evident when I was living in Mount Victoria in Wellington in the early 1980s, and was a regular diner at the Friday-nights-only café at the Crossways Community House, which was the only place where different strands of the community could come together. Every Friday night a different community group would raise funds by putting on simple cheap meals, consisting of two or three choices of a main dish with salads, and home-baked cakes for dessert. Great memories of my Friday night meals there include an impromptu song and dance concert by some elderly Greek men, and spotting one of the stars of the BBC television drama *When the Boat Comes In* dining with one of the locals, who happened to be an old friend.

Community cafés really do help build community, and this is appreciated even by those who can afford to eat at flash restaurants. There was huge community opposition to Crossways being sold by its owner, the Presbyterian Church. As feared, the building was sold privately and the café closed in 2008.[17] Before that happened there was a debate over whether the Wellington City Council should fund a facility whose purposes included a community café. The majority view was that this part of Wellington was richly supplied with commercial eateries of all kinds, from takeaway places to upmarket restaurants, so there was no need for ratepayers' money to go toward a community kitchen. This view shows little understanding of the huge difference between community and commercial cooking and dining, with the former being socially as well as personally nourishing. The positive social-multiplier effects may be harder to measure than the economic-multiplier effects of a commercial food business, but that does not mean they are not valuable. As well as their contribution to social cohesion and conviviality in the neighbourhood, community kitchens and cafés are also potential training grounds in the everyday cooking, serving and dining skills that all New Zealanders need for healthy survival.

SOLE food on the menu

Discerning diners who want their restaurant meals to *be* good as well as taste good need to do a bit of research, since cafés and restaurants that base their menus on really fresh, local organic produce and sustainably produced and traded foods are still very rare. The *Organic Explorer* guide is the place to start locating such eateries.[18]

In my home town the kitchen-garden connection is reinforced beautifully by the Curator's House restaurant in the Christchurch Botanic Gardens, which has an organic herb and vegetable garden on site that is used by the cooks for produce and as an educational resource for home gardeners.[19] The food at the Curator's House is excellent, and a great showcase for the environmental sustainability philosophy and practice of the restaurateur, Javier Garcia. It is also lovely to be able to take a stroll under the espaliered fruit trees and admire the vegetable beds between courses on a summer evening. Unfortunately this restaurant fell victim to the earthquake of 22 February 2011, but they hope to reopen as soon as possible.

Similarly, Restaurant Schwass is generally agreed to be one of the top places for SOLE food gourmets, and any other kind of gourmet, in Christchurch, owing to owner-chef Jonny Schwass's passion for using local, seasonal and organic ingredients.[20] Schwass has a zero-waste policy: every part of an animal, fruit or vegetable is used, indicating the chef's deep respect for the food and those who provide it. Trainees in Schwass's kitchen soon learn that vegetable peelings and animal bones are a resource, not rubbish. Restaurant Schwass also cuts waste by offering only a *prix fixé* menu, with five choices in each of the entrée, main course and dessert sections, plus five different properly matured cheeses to choose from for a cheese board. The winter 2010 *prix fixé* menu was $68 for a three-course meal, which is incredibly good value for money.

Schwass says of restaurant cooking, 'It is easier to add more to a dish and to make it clever and more complicated. This is often to cover poor produce or bad technique and shows a real immaturity for the craft of cooking … It is my firm belief that the focus should be on the quality of the raw component of any dish … In the kitchen we have a duty to uphold the veracity of the ingredient handed to us by our growers and farmers.' Schwass's philosophy of dining as a civilised and civilising act is clearly expressed at the bottom of his menu: 'Use of mobile phones in our dining room will cause our ovens to stop.'

Restaurant Schwass's building in Ferry Road was destroyed in the February 2011 earthquake, but while waiting for new premises his chefs kept cooking according to the Schwass philosophy, catering functions in people's homes. One of them hosted an eight-course fundraising dinner in his own home, with the guests donating the fresh produce for the meal from their gardens.

Fresh ingredients transformed into top-quality yet reasonably priced food was a feature of Christchurch's first organic Japanese restaurant, the Aiki, which opened in 2001 and closed in 2007. Sadly, it seems it was ahead of its time. There were just not enough locals who appreciated what a culinary treasure it represented, although many local Asian restaurateurs ate at the Aiki, knowing the food was superior. They served their own customers cheap food and put some of the profit toward eating organically themselves. 'They don't even feel guilty about it!' the Aiki's owner, Ui Chida, said to me. 'I can't do that kind of business. I'd feel guilty if I did that.' Such restaurateurs clearly don't have Ui's passion for food and health. 'I think about food all the time,' she told me.

> I really love food and cooking – but that doesn't mean that I just want anything. What you eat is so important because it goes directly into your body. I have never respected those people who are just into gourmet food, because they don't care about health. They just want the most tasty, delicious, expensive food. They go everywhere to get that sort of food – and that's completely wrong for me. You can't think about food without thinking about your health, and about the health

of the earth. It's all connected – it's so simple. Whatever you do, you have to think about how it is related to other things. That's why I don't make a lot of money! [But] I don't think in that profit-first way.

Certainly, it is currently hard to make a good living from serving really good food when so many diners put cheapness before their own health, the health of the environment and even true gastronomy. As with other food businesses aiming to befriend rather than trash the natural environment, cafés and restaurants can struggle to find the investment they need to grow their business and put it on a financially stable footing. However, increasing numbers are now starting to make a go of it. New Zealand's first organic café, Hislops Café, on State Highway 1 on the north side of Kaikoura, is a well-established and successful business that has been going for over 10 years.[21] Initially started as a way to use the organic produce of Paul and Elizabeth Hislop's family farm locally, rather than sending it out of the region, the café is now a popular destination for tourists and locals.

When it first opened there were some sticky moments with a few potential patrons who did not understand or appreciate the Hislops' philosophy of food, which is that food should be served as God created it, in its whole form, or as close to it as possible. Also that there is a connection between looking after one's own health and caring for the planet. So a few people went away grumpy because they couldn't have artificial sweeteners in their coffee, or buy cigarettes. These days there are far fewer people who don't get what the Hislops are trying to achieve, and probably quite a few more people who might not know much about the philosophy, but know good food when they taste it.

A feature of Hislops Café is the bread they bake from grain they grow and mill themselves. Bread doesn't get fresher or better than this, and the quality of this humble but important staple part of our diet serves as a good guide to how much a café's owners care about nutrition and taste generally. Any cafés worth patronising regularly will either bake its own bread, or buy in bread from an artisan baker. The flavour in the bread will come from the high-quality wholegrain flours used to make it, and the long slow fermentation process it goes through before baking. This is not, by the way, what you get from fast-food chains and supermarkets that claim to bake their own bread. This may be legally correct in that they do put dough into a hot oven on the premises and take it out when it's brown. However, that dough is rarely (if ever) mixed and kneaded and slow-raised and shaped there. It usually comes pre-shaped and frozen or partially baked from a factory far away, where it was made at speed using cheap, low-nutrition flours, a raft of flavouring and preserving additives and high levels of salt and/or sugars. These are *not* part of good bread.

SOLE drink in the glass

There are now several organic wineries and breweries in New Zealand, their products on a par with other top-class wines and beers. I would pick a Seresin's wine or a Green Man beer before any same-priced, same-style non-organic wine or beer any day. There are also plenty of non-fermented fruit juices available, of course, and a very ancient fermented beverage not made from fruit at all, but from honey: mead. You could make it at home, but as with other fermented drinks the best results tend to come from experienced craft brewers and vintners. At the Haewai Organic Meadery I found out how good this very environmentally friendly and utterly local drink can be.[22] Coral Hyam and Jacob de Ruiter brew their nectar in an historic cottage at the front of their wonderfully wild garden on Wellington's equally wild south coast. They specialise in mead made from native flower honeys – pohutukawa, tawari, kamahi, rewarewa and the honeydew honey from native beech forests – but they have also made it from exotic plant honeys, including thyme and even the feral fennel that grows on the open hillsides of Wellington.

Over a most satisfactory sampling session, Coral pointed out to me the ways in which mead is more environmentally friendly than industrially produced wine. Instead of displacing native plants with an exotic monoculture, as large-scale grape-growing does, mead made from native honeys positively encourages protecting and extending naturally growing forests. Nor does it require any of the destructive additions made to industrial wine-growing, such as tanalised posts, sprays and fertilisers, and it requires much less by way of fossil fuels since tractors and other machines are not used. The only fuel required is that used to truck the hives to and from the nectar sources. Bees are also multi-purpose creatures, essential for pollinating a good deal of our food and fodder crops – an environmental service of incalculable value.

Mead has the same subtly different range of flavours as wine, but the honey it is based on comes from a more genuinely diverse range of sources. Coral therefore considers that producing and consuming mead is a practical way of valuing and promoting biodiversity. Also cultural diversity, for she finds that her best customers are not New Zealand-born. Having learned to produce and drink wine from European immigrants, it seems we have yet to learn to understand and value mead, or to notice that over 90 per cent of New Zealand's vineyards are now owned by foreign conglomerates that are not averse to

increasing profits by industrialising the production of grapes and the processing of the wine.

'Living well is the best revenge' is an excellent form of advice commonly
given to jilted lovers. Don't sit around moaning about how badly you have been
treated. Pick up, pack up and move on to something better. Organic native
honey mead for me symbolises just how good it can get living off the industrial
food grid, and for other species as well. Bee-keeping is a traditional adjunct to
growing food for yourself and others, and represents another important facet
of moving away from dead food to lively food.

It also represents a choice that many people may not be aware they have,
since the industrial food system is a monolith that dominates mainstream com-
munication channels as well as retail outlets. The last chapter of *Food@Home*
looks at what changes need to be made, both personally and politically, in order
to choose good food, and ensure good food options are widely available.

Elderflower cordial

(makes 350–400ml of cordial)

Ingredients

20 elderflower heads, washed in
cold running water

1½ cups *cold* water (hot water
makes the flowers go brown)

1½ cups sugar

1½ tsp citric acid

Method

Lay the flowerheads on a chopping board and strip off the flowers with a fork. Put the flowers in a jug with the cold water, and leave to stand 8–16 hours (covered).

Strain the elderflower-scented water into a clean jug; squeeze the liquid out of the flowers. Add the sugar and citric acid, and stir well until dissolved.

Strain the cordial into screw- or swing-top glass bottles that have been sterilised by filling them with boiling water. It will keep in the fridge for 5–6 weeks; in the freezer for 5–6 months. To serve, dilute to taste with water or soda water. Add ice and/or a slice of lemon or lime.

Apple harvest - first picking from the Gravenstein Red tree.

Moorpark apricots ripening.

Homegrown strawberries and blueberries in a well-used berry trug.

A backyard apple harvester at work.

Blackberries gathered in a handy hanky.

Claire & Michael Dann pick raspberries.

$3·00

A bored watercress seller at the Pukekohe market.

CHAPTER EIGHT

Alimentary Action

Creating more eating options

Eating off the industrial grid is easy enough for individuals or households with all or some of the necessary resources – access to a bit of land, gardening skills, cooking skills, the money to buy good-quality foods that one can't grow oneself and food literacy – the knowledge of what is good to eat, where to find it and how to prepare it for eating. Fifty years ago almost every New Zealand household had enough land to grow food and enough money to buy food, and almost every household had a food-literate person or persons with gardening and cooking skills.

This system wasn't perfect. Too many toxic chemicals were already being used in home and market food production, and the national diet was too high in animal foods and sweet stuff, and too low in whole plant foods. But very few were excluded from good eating for lack of the key resources on which healthy household diets are based.

Today food has become highly politicised as food corporations and food industry groups have become more wealthy and powerful than any other industry except the oil industry. Governments have set up expensive food 'safety' and 'standards' bureaucracies that purport to be working for the public good, but in fact have a dual purpose, and their role of facilitating trade means they do what the food industry wants much more often than they do what consumers want.[1] If everyone is to eat well again, there must be changes in public policy and practice regarding food. This will take time – and meanwhile we all have to eat.

So far in *Food@Home* we have looked at a range of starting places for improving access to good food and home food production skills, including options for those on a low budget. These are all necessary if a better food system is going to replace the current system, but unless they can be applied on a much wider scale they will not be sufficient. Eating well should not be a privilege reserved for the well educated and the well off. Good food should be seen as a basic human right, second only to the right to life itself.

How can this happen? Who cares enough about good food to advocate for it publicly, and what changes are they advocating?

Alimentary activism

In 1941 New Zealand was experiencing another kind of food crisis. The country had been at war for two years, young men who would otherwise have been producing food on farms and in market gardens had joined the armed forces, and those forces had to be fed. There were shortages of basic foodstuffs such as potatoes, food supplies were disrupted, and so were supplies of the imported seeds, petrol, fertilisers and chemicals that New Zealand agriculture had begun to depend on.

The government response to this crisis was to create an alternative agricultural labour force, the Women's Land Army, to divert commercially grown produce to feeding the forces, and to provide some resources and encouragement to civilians to 'Dig for Victory' by increasing their home vegetable production.[2] Some citizens were already ahead of the government when it came to encouraging the healthy home production of plant foods, and in 1941 they created the world's first organic growing organisation, the New Zealand Humic Compost Club.[3] That organisation still exists today, under the name of the Soil and Health Association, and publishes a bi-monthly magazine, *Organic NZ*.[4] Its membership has grown from hundreds to thousands, and as well as providing organic gardening and farming information and education the association also campaigns and lobbies for healthy and sustainable food and farming policies and practices. Its current flagship campaign is 'Organic 2020 – a vision for New Zealand', which is a work-in-progress of defining issues, setting goals and finding ways to move New Zealand's primary production in a more healthy and sustainable direction.[5] It also campaigns to reduce pesticide use and to ban the worst pesticides, to stop the genetic engineering of animals and plants in New Zealand and the sale of genetically engineered foods, and to improve food safety generally.

Its influence on national food and agriculture policies has waxed and waned, depending on which parties and especially which ministers are in power. Sympathetic ministers have provided some funding for organic research, development and marketing; unsympathetic ones have taken it away, and put in place policies that are pro genetic engineering and against basic organic-related research.

The Green Party is the only parliamentary party with strong policies on sustainable farming and healthy food. However, until 2011 it had never had more than nine MPs in parliament, and has never been in government, so it has been unable to break parliamentary support for chemical/oil-based agriculture and genetic engineering.

It is not for want of trying. Green MP Sue Kedgley entered parliament with a background in safe-food campaigning[6] and Jeanette Fitzsimons, Green co-leader until 2009, was both an organic farmer and a leader of the campaign against genetically engineered food. The first major Green policy launch for the 1999 election campaign was the Safe Food policy and Fitzsimons said at the December 1998 launch:

> Safe food will be the issue of the decades which kick off the next millennium …
> The next generation and the generation to follow will have to deal with the health
> and environmental effects of this government's handing over of food regulation to
> big industry. The results so far are growth hormones in meat, spray residue in our
> vegetables and genetically engineered packaged supermarket products …[7]

In July 2010 the Green Party's website had 63 pages devoted to its campaigning on food issues over the previous 12 years.[8]

Like the Soil and Health Association, the Green Party's ability to influence food policy, and the direction of government spending on food and agriculture has been largely dependent on its relationships with other parties, and particularly with the relevant ministers. Agriculture and Food Safety ministers in the Labour-led governments of 1999–2008 were not at all sympathetic to Green aspirations for a 100 per cent pure-food New Zealand, and nor was the Labour leadership. They went so far as to make differences on genetic engineering a deal-breaker during talks around possible coalition formation in 2002. The Green request for an extension of the moratorium on the field release of genetically engineered plants and animals was completely ruled out.

The Greens were more successful in influencing the quality of food available to children in schools, first by running the well-supported Children's Food Awards, and second by campaigning for better food in schools. Strongly supported by health professionals, this saw the Labour-led government introduce a National Administration Guideline in June 2008 which required all schools to 'promote healthy food and nutrition for all students; and where food and beverages are sold on school premises, make only healthy options available'. This guideline was rescinded by the National Minister of Education Anne Tolley in April 2009, apparently for ideological reasons, since she was advised in January 2009 that the guidelines were being well implemented. She was also told that numerous studies have shown poor nutrition and health adversely affects educational achievement, and Pacific and Maori students are especially vulnerable in this respect. For example in a recent study of seven South Auckland secondary schools 58 per cent of students were found to be overweight or obese. The same study reported that school tuckshops were the primary source of lunch for around half of these students.[9]

While the Ministry of Health has been generally supportive of the Green work on healthier food for children, when healthier is defined as less fatty and sugary, successive health ministers and the ministry have shown little or no interest in campaigns to improve the inherent quality of the non-fatty and non-sugary foods that New Zealanders are eating, or campaigns against food that is grown in ways that decrease its nutritional value and expose it to chemical contamination. Nor is the ministry interested in the effects of food additives, or genetically engineered food. This research has been delegated to the New Zealand Food Safety Authority (NZFSA), which was first established as a semi-autonomous body within the Ministry of Agriculture and Forestry (MAF) in 2002, became a stand-alone agency in July 2007, and was sent back to MAF in July 2010.[10] Wherever located, the NZFSA has shown a consistent preference for backing the big players in the food industry, rather than listening to concerns expressed by consumers and independent experts.

This is well documented by another alimentary activist group, the Safe Food Campaign, which has had little success in getting the NZFSA to take on board genuine scientific and consumer concerns about pesticide residues, aspartame, GE foods, food dyes and other additives.[11] Nor have independent academics had any success. On the contrary, Lincoln University Professor of Farm Management and Agribusiness Keith Woodford found that the NZFSA behaved completely inappropriately with regard to properly assessing the safety of New Zealand milk. In documents obtained under the Official Information Act Professor Woodward found an internal memo sent by the acting head of the NZFSA that said that the authority's strategy with regard to handling the concerns raised in his book *The Devil in the Milk* included 'maintaining drinking milk' (i.e. don't crash the market for milk), and the desired outcome of the NZFSA's strategy was 'at the end [we] can say we have checked'.[12]

Thus far, it has to be said, trying to change the food system from the top down seems like a futile endeavour. There are just too many powerful vested interests involved. They are influencing government both directly through their contacts with politicians, and indirectly through their easy access to governmental and quasi-governmental bodies that set and monitor food guidelines and regulations. Before we get a better food system this way we will need to build a better democracy. Meanwhile, if the NZFSA says it is safe to eat, don't take this as gospel.

Working from the grassroots up is not so frustrating, although without some support and investment from central and local government most of the good-food alternatives canvassed in this book will not become readily available to the majority. Nevertheless, there is much satisfaction to be had in working with others to create a farmers' market, a school garden or a community cooking class. Nor is it a case of either/or – in fact the most effective activists are those who practise what they preach. Someone who has volunteered her time to work with children to create a school garden, and then taught them how to cook what they have grown, is better placed than most people to advocate strongly for the importance of keeping junk food out of schools, and for properly funded school gardening and cooking programmes.

Healthy policy prescriptions

If we were going to put the same amount of money into creating a good food system that we have put into creating a bad one, where would it be best invested? Is there a yardstick we can use to measure whether a change will have a big impact? I think there is, and the measure I would use is: to what extent does this change set up *learning and nurturing food relationships*? I say this because I have come to the conclusion that the most broken part of the industrial food system, the worst and most defining feature of it, is that it takes food out of its traditional context of family and community relationships. During the millions of years that *Homo sapiens* evolved as a hunter-gatherer species, and for all but the last 100 years since the invention of agriculture some 10,000 years ago, the vast majority of human beings have had personal relationships with most of the people who hunted, found, grew or cooked their food.

Food production and preparation for all those thousands of years was a co-operative endeavour, based on the family unit and the household. Households co-operated internally, with food production and preparation tasks shared among family members; and externally, sharing labour for major tasks, such as grain sowing and harvesting, and animal herding. The survival of families and communities depended on skill and co-operation in food matters. In the so-called Cradle of Civilisation – the Middle Eastern region where cities and irrigated agriculture first developed, stretching from present-day Turkey through to southern Iraq – food production and consumption was, and often still is, the primary basis for human relationships.

Not surprisingly then, it is also the basis for celebrations of the sacred. The most important Jewish religious celebration, the Passover Seder, is a home-based ritual meal where the foods eaten and the wine drunk, and the ways in which they are consumed, all have historical and spiritual significance.[13] The Seder was the famous Last Supper eaten by Jesus and became the basis of the ritual of the Roman Catholic Mass and Protestant Holy Communion. In Islam the feasting of Eid al-Fitr that marks the end of the month of Ramadan fasting is preceded by Sadaqa Al-Fitr, the charity of fast-breaking, in which every household is obligated to donate food to those in need.[14] Every world religion connects food and spirituality, with feasts and/or special foods to mark significant days on the religious calendar, and offerings of food made on altars and distributed to the needy. Monks in the Theravadan Buddhist tradition depend entirely on food that is cooked and given to them by others. This tradition promotes and cultivates the virtues of generosity and gratitude, which are sadly lacking in industrialised life.

In English the words 'holy' and 'health' are both derived from the old Germanic root word for 'whole'. For as long as humans have had written records, we know that the health of the family was demonstrated daily by sitting down together to a wholesome meal, after saying prayers of thanks that signified the holiness of this event. Thanks were also said to those who produced and cooked the food. The relationships between paddock and plate, producer and consumer, parent and child were whole because they were not separated by long industrial chains of production and supply. Nor were they blighted by food retailing and marketing industries that encourage the separation of all these relationships. 'Happy Meals', 'It's the real thing', 'Finger-lickin' good', 'You deserve a break' and other constantly repeated slogans of the food industry have replaced prayers of thanks as the words we most often hear before meals.

Industrial food is the most radical experiment in human health conducted in the whole history of humankind, and the results are serious. We need to prioritise having healthy, holy food systems again, and that means returning to *authentic relationships* of food production and consumption: home-based and community-based relationships. This cannot be done by order from above, but requires voluntary action from every household and community. There are, however, some public policies and investments that would help households and communities make these changes. They all involve restoring what we have lost in the *content* of food relationships. These are the values of honesty, nurturing and sharing, and the wisdom that comes with experiential knowledge of good food.

The *form* of the new food relationships, however, will be very different from the largely self-provisioning households that were the norm almost everywhere two centuries ago, and perhaps even from the network of small fresh-food retailers that was standard 50 years ago. The food evolution taking place in New Zealand is throwing up new forms for rebuilding producer/ consumer relationships that show a lot of promise for building a better food system, and they deserve public support.

1. Restoring relationships between food producers and consumers

Farmers' markets reconnect producers and consumers in a way that no other form of food retailing can match. They are the best way to restore the broken producer/consumer relationship, and in the process provide better access to good food, and they need to be everywhere. A weekly market within walking distance (or easy public transport access) for every urban dweller would be the optimum. In 2010 there were only 55 farmers' markets in New Zealand that were operational every week. That's only one weekly market for every 80,000 New Zealanders, which is far too few. Not only are there not enough farmers' markets, but also they are unevenly distributed, and tend not to be in the places where the need for affordable fresh food is greatest.

In the Auckland region, for example, the weekly farmers' markets are at Matakana, Orewa, Waiheke, Oratia, Clevedon, Pukekohe, Grey Lynn, Parnell and the CBD. Most of these places are not areas of high need. Although some Auckland suburbs have mixed weekly markets where some fresh food is sold, it is not sold by those who produced it. So for most Aucklanders the supermarket is still their main place to buy raw food, and they have almost no chance of meeting someone who produced what they are eating. Furthermore, the people who can afford to pay more for fresh fruit and vegetables have easier access to getting them cheaply in farmers' markets than those who can afford to pay least.

This looks like a market failure in farmers' markets. At this rate it seems unlikely that Mangere or Meadowbank will have a weekly farmers' market any time soon. Is there anything that can be done that would address this mismatch in supply and demand, without requiring huge amounts of money and bureaucracy? The Canadian cities of Toronto and Vancouver are ahead of New Zealand in this regard. They have identified the main barriers to farmers being able to supply weekly suburban markets – lack of a suitable permanent market site, lack of management structures and experience, and the start-up costs such as transporting produce to the market and stall overheads – and found a variety of ways to lower them by convincing local and central government authorities of the need to do so. Local government can be involved in providing sites, and also management structures and training; central government, especially the ministries of Health and Agriculture, can be involved in helping cover start-up costs via grants and loans. Many New Zealand farmers' markets are organised as trusts, providing a suitable vehicle both for managing the market and for liaising with local and central government in the interests of maximising the social, environmental and economic value of the market. As soon as there is a genuine will to restore New Zealanders' healthy relationships with fresh food and those who produce it, ways will be found.

2. Restoring gardening knowledge and relationships

If every suburb eventually has a weekly farmers' market, why bother growing food at home? It is cheaper than buying it, of course, and gardening is an excellent form of outdoor exercise and recreation, suitable for all ages and body types, that requires no fancy gear and not much equipment, uses almost no fossil fuels, and is not dangerous (if one avoids toxic chemicals). But the clincher is that home-grown food is the freshest, tastiest and most nutritious food that one can ever eat.

Anyone who has ever eaten sweetcorn taken straight from the plant to the pot knows this is true. The longer a corn cob is off the plant, the less delicious it becomes, as its tingly sugars turn into dull starches. This happens with other vegetables as well, just not quite so quickly or dramatically. So taste is my main reason for growing at home, although enjoyable exercise and saving money are close seconds.

I was lucky in getting my motivation to grow food at home at the same time and in the same place as I got my first instruction in gardening – as a child in my home garden. In addition to growing easy things like radishes I used to stake out the Gravenstein apple tree, the first to fruit in the season, and sit underneath waiting for the first ripe apples to fall of their own accord. Most children of my generation had this sort of opportunity; most of the current generation do not. They are missing out on so much that is truly worth having. How can it be restored to them?

A patchwork of gardening knowledge restoration projects is developing around the country already, as we saw in Chapter 3. But it is very patchy indeed. Some schools now have food gardens but most do not. Some communities have community gardens; the vast majority do not. Professional training in organic horticulture and garden management has been severely pruned, and funding for adult education classes has also been reduced. On the plus side, gardening advice is now more readily and cheaply available than ever before, on websites and in magazines. But virtual gardening is no substitute for the real thing, and multiplying opportunities for people to engage in hands-on gardening, so that it once again becomes every child's birthright, seems to be the way to go.

For this to happen there needs to be more consistent and coherent support for school gardens, and gardening education generally. There also needs to be a change in the way in which community gardens, and other forms of urban agriculture, are viewed by civic authorities, involving a shift from passive toleration to active support and encouragement. There is no one-size-fits-all way to achieve these goals, but there are some good models to follow that are already established in New Zealand and elsewhere.

Boosting the role that community gardens can play in gardener education, fresh-food provision, environmental protection and community cohesion just means boosting the numbers of gardens, and this is done easily enough by any city that makes a commitment to doing so. Seattle in the US has made such a commitment, and for nearly 40 years the P-Patch Program run by the Department of Neighborhoods (in association with the P-Patch Trust) has been actively promoting and supporting organic community gardens. Seattle sees its community gardeners playing the following positive roles in the life of the city:

- Growing community;
- Nurturing civic engagement;
- Practising organic gardening techniques;
- Fostering an environmental ethic and connecting nature to people's lives;
- Improving access to local, organic and culturally appropriate food;
- Transforming the appearance and revitalising the spirit of their neighbourhoods;
- Developing self-reliance and improving nutrition through education and hands-on experience;

- Feeding the hungry;
- Preserving heirloom flowers, herbs and vegetables;
- Budding understanding between generations and cultures through gardening and cooking.[15]

The P-Patch Program actively encourages citizens to identify suitable sites for community gardens in their neighbourhood, and provides dedicated staff to help the community make the necessary steps to create a community garden, from technical issues such as site choice and soil quality to social issues like garden co-ordination and management. Seattle has identified the valuable role that its community gardens play in improving connections between different ethnic and cultural groups in the city. In New Zealand the Ranui Community Garden shows how this could also happen here. It doesn't happen automatically just because it is a good idea. It requires champions in both the community and the council.

School gardens also need champions within the teacher and parent community, as Lily White has found. But for every school to have a food garden, especially schools in poorer communities, those champions need solid support from outside the school. They need seed money to buy garden tools and materials to establish the garden, and they need ongoing funding to meet the wages and overheads of a professional garden facilitator/educator. Where should this money come from?

Until now, as we have seen, it has come from just about everywhere except Vote Education. Mostly it has come from government authorities and private charitable organisations with an interest in promoting health and/or protecting the environment. On the West Coast of the South Island, for example, the District Health Board initiated the Tucking In programme in 2007. It was taken up jointly by the charitable trust Sport West Coast, which still exists and is very active, and the Ministry of Health's Healthy Eating Healthy Action programme, which is no longer active as its funding was stopped in 2009. With help from a lot of other sources, including businesses that donated garden materials, other community groups, the West Coast Regional Council (which gave advice on composting), and the Tai Poutini Polytechnic (which provided a horticulturist to grow seedlings), food gardens were set up in every school and pre-school on the West Coast, from Karamea to Haast.[16]

The West Coast is an area with a lot of land, not many people (just over 31,000), a high level of need for better food – 61 per cent of Coasters over 15 years old are classified as overweight or obese – and significant constraints on being able to purchase it: 49 per cent of those over 15 have an annual income of

$20,000 or less. There are other groupings of around 30,000 New Zealanders who have similar health and income challenges. They are mostly to be found in densely settled suburbs in Auckland, Wellington and Christchurch. These are areas that do not have the same sense of collective identity as the West Coast, and they certainly don't have their own health boards, sports trusts or other organisations that might take up a Tucking In-style programme.

While it is highly appropriate and desirable that school gardens are created via partnerships between community trusts and government departments, there is still a need for a coherent national policy of establishing a food garden in every school and pre-school in the land. School gardens fulfil so many functions – health, environment, education, recreation – that at present they are slipping through the cracks of the silo departments of state that deal with each of these important facets of life.

Is there a way in which all the governmental and non-governmental organisations with an interest in promoting school gardening can get together and work out the most cost-effective way to fund a garden and a garden educator in every school? Who will champion that? For many years schools that cannot afford or do not need to employ a full-time music teacher have been serviced by itinerant music teachers who give group and private instruction on a part-time basis. Could garden educators be employed on the same basis, with costs shared across several schools in the same district? Again, as soon as there is a will, ways will be found, if we can just start the necessary dialogue between all those concerned.

That dialogue should include the question, who will teach the teachers? When organic food gardening is re-established as an important skill for life, rather than a niche industry, then re-establishing the organic teaching gardens and educators at polytechnics and universities will also make sense, and will be an urgent priority. Their graduates will be equally qualified to grow organic food commercially, and to show home and school gardeners how to do it. But what use is this coming bounty of good food if we don't know how to cook it?

3. Restoring cooking and dining knowledge and relationships

Australian farmers' market advocate Jane Adams has a wish for schools in her country, as she told the Farmers' Market Conference in Blenheim in June 2008: 'The new Australian Prime Minister wishes a computer for every child in every school in Australia. My wish is different. I wish that every child in every school in Australia knew what really good, healthy food tastes like.'

Her wish is shared by top Australian cook Stephanie Alexander, who set about making it come true in 2001 when she was given the opportunity to create a kitchen garden and a cooking-from-the-garden programme at Collingwood College in Melbourne. After four years she wrote up the experiment, which has been a raging success and is now being copied by other schools, in a book called *Kitchen Garden Cooking with Kids*.[17] This also contains child-oriented instructions for mouth-watering recipes for seasonal dishes prepared by the pupils at Collingwood College. The Stephanie Alexander Kitchen Garden Foundation, set up in 2004, provides support and encouragement to other schools wishing to set up kitchen garden programmes using the same philosophy and methods.[18] The philosophy is expressed in the Kitchen Garden Foundation's value statement:

> We believe that:
> - The best way to encourage children to choose food that is healthy is to engage them in fun, hands-on experiences in growing, harvesting, preparing and sharing fresh, delicious food from the earliest possible age.
> - No one embraces change in their behaviour if they think it will be unpleasant, uncomfortable or too difficult. Cautionary messages that food is 'good for you' or 'bad for you' do not resonate with young people.
> - Children are more likely to experiment with foods they have grown or prepared themselves.
> - Lifelong eating habits are developed early.
> - Children need positive models in their lives to reinforce that eating with others is a joyful activity, and one that they can enjoy as long as they live.
> - Many young children do not receive such positive experiences at home, and therefore schools should consider including rich and interdisciplinary programs that will fill this gap, as well as giving practical skills that will enable young people to take more responsibility for their own physical well-being.
> - The causes of obesity are complex and there is not one single solution, but children who are encouraged to take a broad and active interest in food and the table from a very young age are more likely to maintain a positive attitude to food throughout their lifetimes.[19]

Within five years the Kitchen Garden Foundation had over 100 schools around Australia participating in its programme. An academic evaluation in 2009 found that children in these schools were more likely than children in comparison schools (all of which had school gardens and a few of which had school kitchens) to try new foods, say they liked cooking a lot, and to know more about cooking and gardening and have more confidence and skills in cooking and gardening. Other benefits of the programme that were identified were the links it created between school and community, and school and home, with children in the programme more likely to take good food knowledge home and put it into practice.[20]

In 2008 the Garden to Table Trust was formed in Auckland to bring a modified form of the Stephanie Alexander programme to New Zealand, and currently three pilot schools in Auckland are involved.[21] In both Australia and New Zealand the champions of educating children in good food production and preparation have found that a major barrier to overcome is the lack of kitchens and dining rooms in schools. Following the 1980s decision in New Zealand not to teach cookery to students as part of the core curriculum for what was then known as Forms 1 to 4 (11- to 14-year-olds), a lot of existing school kitchens went into disuse and disrepair, or were removed altogether. In New Zealand it has been mainly gardeners who have championed a return to cooking in schools, but it would be great if some well-known cooks joined them. British chef Jamie Oliver's efforts to improve school food in Britain are well known in New Zealand thanks to television, but New Zealand schools need action programmes that make the link between garden and table. For this to happen we need champions from the community, and within the education establishment.

It is hard to believe that everyone in the Ministry of Education is ignorant or unconcerned about the growing deficit in food knowledge and skills among New Zealanders, or has bought the current party line that education should be only for work, not for life. Perhaps there are some closeted good-food champions in there, just waiting for shouts of encouragement from the community to begin making space in the core curriculum for garden-to-table programmes. This has already started to happen in Victoria, thanks to Stephanie Alexander's efforts, and it can happen here if we demand that it does.

The home front

If we don't make changes where we have the most power to make them, in our own homes, then no amount of good public policy will make up for private failure to become food literate and learn how to eat well. There is not much point in getting junk food out of school tuckshops and teaching cooking at school if children are fed on takeaways at home, and there is no point in learning to cook if the meals produced are replicas of industrial fast food minus a few additives. As Australian food historian and philosopher Michael Symons has pointed out, it is not necessary to reject everything that comes with industrialisation, but rather to learn to use our new powers in a more satisfying way. 'By taking time to grow our own vegies and chooks, by seeking out genuine supplies of farmhouse cheese and crusty bread, we re-engage with our natural supports. By returning to the goal of generosity, we re-engage with our social supports.'[22]

These are admirable goals – but how to achieve them? Here are the key actions that I have identified. They can be taken in any order, one or several at a time, and over any timeframe, so anyone can make up a sequence that suits their needs most conveniently.

Eating

- Eat at least one home-cooked meal per day, every day, at a dinner table with all the members of the household. Turn off any distractions (television, radio) and tune into the food and each other.
- Talk to each other about what is in the meal, where and how it was produced, how it was cooked and how it tastes.

Cooking

- If there are children (or adults) in the household who do not know how to cook, involve them in preparing a meal or learning other cooking skills (such as baking and preserving).
- Invest in a good basic cookbook that emphasises garden produce and memorise the ingredients and methods for the dishes that you and your household enjoy most; *or* take a vegetarian cooking class to learn such dishes; *or* surf the web for some new fresh-produce recipes – or do all three.

Growing

- If you have limited space and/or have never grown vegetables before, start with leafy greens – lettuce, silverbeet, spinach, kale, Chinese cabbage, mesclun – and herbs before moving on to crops that require more space and/or growing skills.
- Invest in a comprehensive organic gardening book and follow its advice for the next crops you want to grow; *or* join a gardening group where you can get such advice from more experienced gardeners; *or* subscribe to a gardening magazine or e-news service – or do all three and you will never be at a loss for what to do.

Finding

• Explore the most convenient and most economical ways of obtaining fresh produce and whole foods close to your home, and set up an efficient system for getting them.

• Buy fresh produce at supermarkets only if they have the same or higher-quality goods at lower prices.

Storing

• Learn how to store fresh and dry foods correctly.

• If necessary, designate or create proper storage spaces: a pantry for dry-goods, coolstore sheds for long-keeping garden produce, cool cupboards for fresh produce.

Splurging

• Redefine 'food treat' to mean 'fruit or vegetable fresh from the garden', rather than processed or fast food. Anticipate and enjoy the seasonal change in treats, from cherries and strawberries in summer through to persimmons and mandarins in winter.

• If the garden is looking a bit bare, remember that there are SOLE-food treats to suit every budget, from fair-trade organic chocolate bars to meals at SOLE-food restaurants. Make sure you have some on hand, or know where to get them.

I have taken all these steps myself – some of them several times, as, for example, when I have moved to a new city and had to sort out my sources all over again. With each of them I apply the good old MEME (Minimum Effort Maximum Effect) principle. Here's how I put it into practice.

You do have to cook at home if you want to eat well, but you don't have to spend all day doing it to produce delicious food. You do need to eat a variety of fresh produce to stay healthy, but you don't have to master a huge number of recipes to eat that variety of foods while staying interested in your meals. What you need are 20–30 family-favourite main-dish recipes, covering all the seasons, which can be prepared in 30–40 minutes. This recipe bank can be built up over the course of a year or more. The recipes should focus on the vegetables you like most and grow most of, or on a carbohydrate that can have vegetable flavours added to it. Examples of the first kind of recipe are ratatouille (eggplant, tomato, capsicum and zucchini), niçoise salad (new potatoes, green beans, lettuce, tomatoes, radishes), mixed vegetable stir-fries and vegetable soups. In the second category are vegetables combined with pasta, rice, potatoes, polenta (coarse cornmeal), couscous, burghul wheat or another grain. In spring, for example, such a dish could be a risotto made with asparagus, in summer a risotto with zucchini and red peppers fried with a little garlic, and in winter it could be made with leeks cooked in a little butter and water.

As with cooking, so with shopping. You need to give the supermarket a swerve if you want truly good food, but you don't need to run all around town picking up a cabbage here and some yoghurt there. Make a master list of the food you buy most often, find out where you can get the most SOLE-food versions of what is on your list at a reasonable price, and shop there. Apply the same efficiencies of effort to gardening. Don't make a rod for your back trying to get your vege beds to resemble the pretty potagers in the designer garden books (unless you enjoy that sort of thing). Dead, rotting weeds don't look very pretty as mulch, but they do a better job of keeping the soil moist and nourished than dry straw, they cost nothing and no hauling is required to get them in place. A good food garden is one that reliably produces good food, not one that could win a garden beauty contest.

Remember that the Food@Home evolution is all about living better with less from the supermarket and fast-food outlets, and more from the garden and kitchen. It is about taking time to slow down and smell the sweetpeas as well as the green peas. It is about home-made cake as well as home-grown carrots; it is about taking tea in the garden on a summer's afternoon.

Time for (a Victorian afternoon) tea

Although there is much to criticise in New Zealand's legacy of industrial British food, there is one food and drink tradition established by the Victorian middle classes that fully deserves to be honoured and continued. Taking afternoon tea in the garden, or on a verandah, is a ritual of physical and spiritual refreshment that is rightly celebrated by the English, and appreciated by many other nations as well. At its best, it is the epitome of Slow Food. It can be as simple or as elaborate as you please.

In an historic cottage in Diamond Harbour, once the childhood home of the landscape and flower painter Margaret Stoddart, for two glorious pre-earthquake years Annie Baxter served 'Victorian cream teas' on Sunday afternoons. There was a choice of dainty sandwiches, buttermilk scones served with little pots of jam and whipped cream alongside, and regal cakes that were light and rich with eggs from Annie's own hens (which free ranged in an olive grove, no less). Annie dressed the tables, and herself and her staff, in appropriately Victorian garb: flowery chintz and white damask for the tables, black floor-length gowns and starched lacy white aprons and caps for the women. The tables were set with tiny vases of flowers and flowery china. The tea came in silver-plate pots. It all felt as special as it looked. Annie created an atmosphere of warm hospitality that made one want to linger over yet another cup of tea, and maybe just another *little* slice of cake.[23]

It is one of the truths of life that leaving home, and going on a long and sometimes painful journey, is one of the best ways to learn how to really appreciate what is good about home. The collective journey away from producing and consuming food at home has certainly been long and often times painful, and lots of young travellers are still in danger of living the fast-food life and dying young. Yet the seeds that will make a difference are being sown in pots and gardens around the nation right now, and in summer there will be cucumber for the sandwiches and strawberries for the scones at the afternoon tea table. Be sure to appreciate your share – and share some with others.

Bread and butter pickles

Ingredients

1 litre water

1 dessertspoon dsp salt

2 medium cucumbers, finely sliced

1–2 small onions

¼–½ cup sugar

1 cup cider vinegar

1 tsp mustard seed

1 tsp celery seed

6 black peppercorns

a good pinch of turmeric

Method

Make a brine in a large bowl with the water and salt.

Soak the cucumber slices in the brine overnight.

Drain and add the sliced onion.

Heat the other ingredients together in a large pot, stirring well.

Add the vegetables and heat thoroughly but don't boil.

Pour into sterilised jars while hot and seal.

Brigitte whisks up an omelette for visitors to a Waiheke Island Garden.

A December harvest gift box.

Jersey Bennes potatoes – first harvest, November 2010.

Cavallo Nero kale.

An olive orchard in Katikati.

A Painted Lady runner bean shows the reason for its name.

Meyer lemons are a cross between true lemons and a mandarin or orange. The fruit are smaller and sweeter than true lemons, with thinner skins.

Rock melons growing in my new glasshouse.

The beautiful tangelo is a hybrid citrus fruit that is delicious as juice and in all sorts of recipes.

Zucchini seedlings emerging.

The root of the yacon, a vegetable from South America, is sweet and juicy and good in salads, and the leaves have medicinal uses.

A New Zealand Kitchen Garden Planning Guide

How to use this guide

This guide is designed as a quick reference to:

- when (what time of year) the usual range of annual vegetable crops should be sown or planted;
- how often they need to be sown or planted to ensure a regular supply;
- where (inside or outside) to sow or plant them; and
- how many seeds or plants are needed to feed a household of four people.

When to sow/plant

How warm is your garden? The main factors that affect a garden's temperature are:

- its latitude, e.g. kumara struggles to grow below 43 degrees south (just south of Christchurch), but does well above 40 degrees south (north of Whanganui and Hastings);
- its altitude – gardens at sea level are on average warmer than gardens in the hills;
- its aspect – gardens facing north and getting full sun all day are warmer than south-facing gardens. Especially if there is no shelter from prevailing cold winds.

With these three factors in mind, the general rule about when to start planting your garden in spring, and how late to keep planting in autumn, is that the further north you live, the earlier you can start and the later you can finish.

Be aware, however, that an unsheltered garden on top of a hill facing south in Northland may very well be colder, and more prone to frosts in September and May, than a sheltered beachside garden in Southland that faces north.

So the sowing and planting times given in the guide are not one-size-fits-all. They give the range from earliest to latest sowings possible. Where the garden is located and how warm/frost-free it is has to be your final guide. Experienced gardeners in your locality will know, so make friends with some and you will always get your timing right. Also note that while no plants like it very cold, some don't like it too hot. Lettuce, spinach and other leafy greens in particular will start flowering and setting seed instead of making leaves if they are planted in the heat of high summer. So stagger sowings of such plants to miss the worst heat, and/or grow them in cool parts of the garden, and/or pick 'slow bolt' varieties to avoid this problem.

How often to sow/plant

Slow-growing crops that take more than 12 weeks to get to harvestable size, such as tomatoes, pumpkins, main-crop potatoes and eggplants, are usually sown/planted only once in the growing season. The self-reliant vege gardener will stagger the plantings, however, putting in some tomato plants as early as possible, and some as late as possible, in order to extend the fresh tomato season.

Fast-growing crops like lettuce, silverbeet and other leafy greens, which can be ready to eat in 6–7 weeks from sowing, must be sown 4–5 times during the growing season in order to keep up supplies.

In-between crops that take 8 to 12 weeks to be ready to eat, such as cabbages, cauliflowers, beetroot, carrots, beans, peas, onions, leeks, should be sown 2–4 times. The lower number is for the 'keepers' like carrots and onions, which can be sown in greater quantities than crops best eaten fresh and green, like beans and cabbages.

The planning guide on page 168 gives a conservative indicator of the average number of weeks from first sowing the seed (indoors or outdoors) to first harvest of the crop outdoors. This number is your guide to how often you need to sow/plant that crop – once or twice if it is a big number, five or even six times if it is a small number and your garden has a long growing season. It is also your guide to when to sow or plant more. If a crop takes eight weeks to mature, the time to make a new sowing is three to four weeks after the first one. Keep records of how quickly things grow in your unique garden conditions, and change the numbers in the guide if necessary to personalise the guide for your own garden.

Where to sow/plant

A few hardy crops like broad beans and garlic can be planted outdoors in early winter, and others like peas and mesclun will tough it out in cold soil in late winter. Most vegetable seeds and plants sown or planted outdoors before the soil has warmed up in spring and the frosts have departed will not thrive. For frost-tender and slow-maturing crops, such as tomatoes and pumpkins, this poses a problem that the gardener solves by planting the seeds indoors, and growing the plants in pots until it is safe to put them out in the garden. 'Indoors' can be as fancy as a heated greenhouse, or as basic as a warm kitchen windowsill. 'Pots' can be as expensive as new plastic or terracotta, or as cheap and environmentally friendly as reused food containers like yoghurt pots with drainage holes punched in the bottom, or even the cardboard tubes from toilet rolls, which make fantastic biodegradable plant containers for pumpkins, tomatoes and other vegetables that go out late.

The planning guide gives the time range for sowing both indoors and outdoors, and for planting outdoors.

How many to sow/plant

The aim of the self-reliant vege gardener is to have the full range of seasonal crops ready to harvest in any given week. This requires knowing both how much the household is likely to want to eat of any given crop, and how much seed/how many plants should have been sown or planted from six to 20 weeks previously to give that result. The answer to the first question is very household-specific, but reasonably reliable estimates can be made for the answer to the second question.

In the planning guide the total quantity of seeds or plants required to feed four people over one growing season is given, including crops that are stored, like onions and potatoes. It assumes that the gardener will follow the wise practice of overplanting, i.e. sowing more than is strictly necessary to compensate for any losses due to failures of germination, attacks by pests, rogue frosts, hailstorms and all the other natural and unnatural vissicitudes that plague the gardener.

Since seeds come in widely differing sizes and weights, from big broad beans to light lettuce, and since one cannot usually see into the packets in which they are sold, the guideline to buy 'one packet' may seem a bit vague. But it is not quite as vague as it seems, since it is based on my knowledge of how many sowings/plants can be got from a typical packet of those particular seeds.

Self-reliant gardeners will usually have more seed than is needed immediately on hand in any case, simply because they are growing a number of different varieties of each crop. So the guide gives only the minimum needed. Adjust the numbers upwards to suit your own unique needs – and remember to store surplus seeds in a cool, dry place, protected from light and critter attack in a tin, box or other suitable container.

Planning Guide
(S stands for Sow, and P for Plant.)

Vegetable	Time in weeks from sowing to first harvest	Total quantity seed/plants for 4 people	Time(s) to sow/plant indoors	Time(s) to sow/plant outdoors
Artichoke (Jerusalem)	20	6 tubers	x	Aug–Sept/S
Beans (broad)	14–20	1 large packet	x	May–Jun/S
Beans (dwarf & climbing)	8–10	2 packets dwarf 1 packet climbing	x	After last frost, until January/S
Beetroot	8–10	1 packet	x	Aug–Mar/S
Broccoli	8–9	1 packet	July–Feb/S	Sept–Mar/ S & P
Brussels sprouts	11–13	1 packet	Aug–Dec/S	Sept–Jan/ S & P
Cabbage	9–16	1 packet	July–Feb/S	Sept–Mar/ S & P
cabbage (Chinese)	7–11	1 packet	June–Feb/S	Aug–April/ S & P
Carrots	9–11	1–2 packets	x	Aug–Dec/S
Cauliflower	8–12	1 packet	July–Feb/S	Sept–Feb/ S & P
Celeriac	15–19	1 packet	Aug–Oct/S	Sept–Nov/ S & P

Vegetable	Time in weeks from sowing to first harvest	Total quantity seed/plants for 4 people	Time(s) to sow/plant indoors	Time(s) to sow/plant outdoors
Celery	16–20	1 packet	Sept–Nov/S	Oct–Dec/ S & P
Cucumber	10–12	1 packet	Aug–Oct/S	Oct–Dec/ S & P
Eggplant (aubergine)	18–20	8–10 plants	July–Sept/S	Oct–Nov/P
Garlic	18–24	100 cloves	x	May–July
Kale (collards)	8–10	1 packet	x	Sept–Mar/S
Kumara	20–24	40–50 tubers	July–Aug sprout tubers	Sept–Dec/ P
Leeks	8–10	1 packet	Aug–Dec/S	Oct–Feb/ S & P
Lettuce	6–8	1–2 packets	July–Mar/S	Aug–Mar/ S & P
Marrow	16–18	1 packet	Aug–Sept/S	Oct–Dec/ S & P
Mesclun (salad mix)	6–8	1–2 packets	x	All year/S
Onions	16–18	1 packet	Aug–Mar/S	Sept–Jan/ S & P
Parsnips	15–16	1 packet	x	Sept–Mar/S
Peas	10–11	1–2 packets	x	Aug–Mar/S
Peppers (capsicum)	12–16	1 packet	Aug–Sept/S	Oct–Nov/P
Potatoes	12–16	5–6kg tubers	x	Aug–Dec
Pumpkin & squash	14–18	1–2 packets	Aug–Sept/S	Oct–Nov/P

Vegetable	Time in weeks from sowing to first harvest	Total quantity seed/plants for 4 people	Time(s) to sow/plant indoors	Time(s) to sow/plant outdoors
Radish	4–6	1 packet	x	Sept–Feb/S
Rocket (arugula)	6–8	1 packet	x	Aug–Mar/S
Shallots	16–20	100 bulbs	x	June–Sept
Silverbeet	7–8	1 packet	July–Feb/S	Aug–Mar/S & P
Spinach	7–9	1 packet	Aug–Feb/S	Sept–April/S & P
Spring onions	8–9	1 packet	July–Feb/S	Sept–Mar/S & P
Swedes	8–16	1 packet	x	Nov–Feb/S
Sweetcorn	14–16	1 packet	Aug–Sept/S	Sept–Nov/S & P
Tomatoes	14–16	1 packet	Aug–Sept/S	Oct–Dec/S & P
Turnips	8–10	1 packet	x	Sept–Mar/S
Yam (oka)	20–24	30 tubers	x	Oct–Nov
Zucchini (courgettes)	12–14	1 packet	Aug–Sept/S	Oct–Dec/S & P

Space for adding more vegetables to this list...

A Guide to Harvesting and Keeping Home-grown Fruit and Vegetables

This guide starts with a general introduction to vegetable and fruit harvesting and keeping, before moving on to alphabetical charts that briefly cover best practice in harvesting and storing all the common home-garden vegetables and fruits in New Zealand. The introduction covers the basic principles and techniques of good harvesting and storage, and explains why certain things are done the way they are.

Vegetables and fruits belong in 'families', such as root veges, leafy greens, berryfruits, pipfruits, which have similar requirements when it comes to harvesting and storage. When a year goes by between one harvest and the next, as it does with asparagus, garlic, persimmons and several other short-season and/or once-a-year crops, it is easy to forget both principles and techniques.

Vegetables

Harvesting home-grown vegetables is usually simple. When the vegetable is fully grown, pick it, cut it or pull it up. In this guide to harvesting home-grown produce that is usually what is suggested. However, for some veges there are a few extra things that it is good to know when harvesting, in order to prolong its flavour and/or storage life.

Raw garden produce that can be stored for more than two months generally needs a space that is:

- cool but not frosty;
- dry, but with medium to high humidity;
- dark, but able to be lit;
- insect and rodent proof; and

- well-ventilated.

There are a few big exceptions to the first two rules – see below.

Ideally, there should be enough space in the storage place to store potatoes in small sacks or large boxes, to keep carrots and other root crops in boxes, to line up pumpkins in rows on shelves and to hang onions in strings or net bags from the ceiling. Fruit for storage needs even more airy space – see page 180.

The classic storage space that meets all these requirements is a cellar, but very few New Zealand homes have one. Alternatives might be a laundry or other room that is not ordinarily heated, a very large closet, an enclosed porch, or a purpose-built super-pantry. Outside there may be a shed or garage that could be fully or partially converted. However, it must not be a place where paint, petrol or other toxic and/or volatile chemicals are used or stored, as they could taint the produce.

When storing whole vegetables for the long term the aim is to give each kind of produce the conditions it needs for staying healthy and edible for as long as possible. To keep stored produce healthy – free from diseases, fungus, and rot – the most important step to take is to store only perfect specimens, with no cuts, bruises, insect holes or other damage that will limit their storage life and could infect their box mates. If produce can be prevented from touching its fellows in storage this also lessens the risk of rot and disease spreading.

There are various ways to do this. Root crops such as beetroot, carrots, celeriac and turnips are best stored in a wooden or cardboard box with a slightly damp, but not wet, packing material separating each layer. Sharp sand (i.e. coarse washed sand) is the traditional packing material, but sawdust or wood shavings (from untreated timber, of course), peat, straw, shredded paper and compost are all options. Wherever the following storage guide says 'box of sand' you can substitute one of these alternatives.

Pumpkins should be stored in rows with a gap between each one, and it is good to plait onions and garlic into strings, not just because it looks pretty and is handy for the cook, but also because it minimises touching and maximises air circulation. Potatoes are best stored in hessian sacks, which allow them to 'breathe', or layered between sheets of newspaper in cardboard boxes.

Produce to be stored should be clean and dry, so try to harvest crops on dry days, when the soil is not wet. Do not wash anything to be stored. Brush excess soil off root crops with a soft brush or a gloved hand, but do not scrub them. If the vegetables come in different sizes, choose the largest ones for longer storage and store them separately from the smallest ones, which should be eaten first, as they do not keep as well.

All produce keeps better in the cool and dark, as warmth and light are the usual signals for sprouting. Cool means 0–5ºC. Some crops like it a bit warmer – potatoes, pumpkins and squashes would rather be stored at 5–10ºC. Most stored fresh produce likes reasonably high humidity (around 85 per cent, with a 75 per cent minimum) but onions, shallots and garlic prefer below 75 per cent. No vegetables improve with accidental freezing, so storage places should not go below zero at any time. In the storage guide below, the humidity and temperature storage preferences of each crop are given where relevant.

Given the opposite temperature and humidity preferences of the two most important stored vegetable crops, potatoes and onions, it is probably best to store them in different places if possible. For the other crops, make a call on how much to pander to their preferences depending on how important that crop is to your household.

Wherever and however raw produce is stored, it is a good idea to give it a thorough check-over every week or so for signs of trouble like rot, disease, insect or rodent incursion, and to deal with any such problems immediately before the rest of the stored food is spoiled. As the old saying goes, one bad apple spoils the barrel.

A lot of shelf space in the house, preferably in a dedicated pantry or storage closet, is needed for home-grown produce that is processed into preserves. It is best if the shelves are not more than two large jars deep, to make it easier to see what is in the jars, and to get them off the shelf. Furthermore, in this earthquake-prone country it is a very good idea to either have securely fastened cupboard doors in front of shelves full of preserves, or to have some other way, like an edge to the shelf and/or a strong length of fishing line secured along the front, to ensure the jars stay on the shelf if they get a shake-up.

Storage places for preserves and dried foods should be cool, dry, dark and insect and rodent free, and again, it is sensible to check regularly to see that no mishaps have occurred. The most common mishaps are improper sealing of jars of bottled fruit, leading to leakage, and mould growing on improperly sealed jams and pickles or inadequately dried and stored beans and peas. In all cases the affected food should be put in the compost bin, as some moulds are toxic.

Storage in the fridge

When using a refrigerator to store fresh fruit and vegetables, be aware that:
- the desirable average temperature range for a fridge is 1–5ºC, anything above 5ºC is not safe for animal foods and not efficient for vegetable foods;

- most fridges will be warmer at the top than at the bottom;
- the air in a properly functioning fridge is very dry.

All these factors affect where to put fresh produce in a fridge and how to store it. Vegetables that prefer high humidity are best refrigerated in ways that keep them moist, such as by putting them in plastic bags with air holes, or left open so that they can breathe and won't go slimy. Extra moisture can be added depending on the needs of the vegetable – none for hard vegetables like carrots, parsnips and turnips; the water left after washing and shaking for leafy greens like lettuce and spinach. More environmentally friendly alternatives to plastic bags are loosely woven cotton bags, muslin or cheesecloth, or damp teatowels. For asparagus, silverbeet and lettuces with roots attached, the vegetable can be stood upright in a container with some water in it, instead of being bagged.

For short term, no-energy-cost storage a great alternative to the fridge is the food safe – for those lucky enough to live in an older house that still has one. When it is part of the house it is usually on a south- or east-facing wall, and consists of a spacious cupboard with slatted shelves, with a recessed or sheltered opening covered with fine flyscreen mesh. No sun or rain gets in; lots of cool air does. In winter the temperature in New Zealand goes down to low fridge temperatures, and in summer the safe can be kept cool by placing an open pan of cold water to evaporate on the lowest shelf. As well as being a good place to store vegetables it is also better than a fridge for storing butter, cheese, and opened jars of jam and honey. Since energy costs are sure to rise, and since a safe is a better storage method for some foods anyway, it is worth considering adding one to the 21st-century kitchen, along with decent-sized low cupboards or drawers for compost buckets and recycled materials.

Storage in the garden

One final food storage tip – *the garden* is usually the best place to store fresh food. Most root crops can be left in the ground over winter, and even in coastal Otago and Southland it is possible to leave green vegetables like silverbeet, cabbages, kale, celery and leeks in the garden over the winter months. They won't grow much, if at all, but they will stay green and edible. In both summer and winter, make it a general rule to harvest only what is needed for each day's meal requirements to enjoy the freshest, tastiest, most nutritious food possible.

VEGETABLE	Harvesting	Keeping/Storing

HT = Higher storage Temperature preferred (5–10ºC)
LT = Lower storage Temperature preferred (0–5ºC)
HH – Higher storage Humidity preferred (75–95 per cent)
LH = Lower storage Humidity preferred (65–75 per cent)

VEGETABLE	Harvesting	Keeping/Storing
Artichoke (globe)	Cut the mature but unopened flower bud with a short length of stalk.	Best eaten at once, but can be stored in the fridge for 1 week, with the stalks standing in water that is changed daily. LT; HH.
Artichoke (Jerusalem)	Can be left in the ground and lifted as needed, except in areas with hard frosts, where they should be covered with a thick layer of straw.	Will keep fresh in a plastic bag in the fridge for 3–4 weeks. LT; HH.
Asparagus	Cut spears at the base when they are 15–20cm in length.	Best eaten at once, but will keep 3–4 days if stood upright in a jug of water with 3cm of water in it, ideally in the fridge. LT; HH.
Beans (broad)	Baby pods can be harvested and eaten whole; 'adolescent' pods are opened and the immature beans eaten. Don't let broad beans get to 'adult' size unless wanted for drying.	Freeze young beans; dry mature beans. Dried beans: LT; LH.
Beans (dwarf, runner)	For fresh eating, harvest when pods are small, young and tender. For drying, leave the pods to mature on the plant until they are brown and the beans inside are almost dry enough to store.	Freeze young beans; dry some varieties of mature beans. To dry beans: harvest when almost dry, leave the pods in a warm, dry, airy place until all moisture is gone. Shell and store in glass jars in a cool, dark, dry place. Dried beans: LT; LH.
Beetroot	Harvest as soon as mature (size varies with variety). Don't let them get too large and woody.	Gently remove any soil from perfect beets, and store them in boxes of sand in a cool place. LT; HH.
Broccoli	Cut the full head or sprouts (depending on variety) when they are still tight and firm. (In some varieties the stem is also harvested.)	Freeze.

VEGETABLE	Harvesting	Keeping/Storing
Brussels sprouts	Sprouts mature gradually on the plant over several months, so harvest only as needed, when the sprouts are small and tightly closed.	Freeze. In heavy-frost areas the whole plants can be pulled up, hung in a cool place, and sprouts picked from them for the next few weeks.
Cabbage (heading)	Cut the head when it is tight and firm.	Keep in the fridge for up to a week. Winter cabbages (i.e. late-maturing, big-head varieties) can be stored in crates of straw or shredded paper in a cool place – remove outer leaves and ensure the cabbage is dry first. Or make sauerkraut or kimchi – the healthiest way to keep and eat cabbage. LT; HH.
Cabbage (Chinese, looseleaf)	Pull up the whole plant of small Asian cabbages (e.g. pak choy), pick leaves as required from kale, collards and other looseleaf brassicas.	Wash and keep in an unsealed plastic bag in the fridge for up to a week.
Carrots	Harvest when fully grown. (Size will depend on variety.) Late crops that have stopped growing can be left in the ground until needed.	If storing above ground, lift the crop in April or May, and store in boxes of sand in a cool place. LT; HH.
Cauliflower	Cut the heads with a bit of stalk on them when they are fully grown but still 'tight and white'.	Keep in the fridge for 1–2 weeks, or in winter hang in a cold place for 3–4 weeks. LT; HH.
Celeriac	Start harvesting when they are tennis-ball size. Leave in the ground until needed, covered with a thick layer of straw if hard frosts are likely.	If storing above ground, lift the crop in May or June. Remove the leaves, brush off soil, and store in boxes of sand. LT; HH.
Celery	Cut full-grown stalks as required, or pull up the whole plant.	Stand stalks upright in a jug of water in the fridge or other cool place to keep them fresh for 3–4 days. LT; HH.
Cucumber	Harvest when just mature. (Size depends on variety.)	Wrapped in cling film and stored in the fridge they will stay succulent for up to 2 weeks.

VEGETABLE	Harvesting	Keeping/Storing
Eggplant (aubergine)	Harvest when the skin is fully coloured and shiny. Dull-skinned eggplants are past their prime; green ones are bitter and unsafe.	Will keep around 2 weeks at the top of the fridge. HT; HH
Garlic	Harvest the whole crop in midsummer when the tops start to die down and the bulbs are big and full. Pull up on a sunny day and leave in a warm place to dry for 1–2 days.	Plait the tops together to make strings, or tie into loose bunches, or remove the tops and store the bulbs in mesh bags. Use the smallest bulbs first as the larger ones keep longer. LT; LH.
Herbs	Herbs for long-keeping are best harvested just before they start flowering, on the morning of a dry day.	Herbs that retain their flavour and aroma well when dry (e.g. thyme, sage, oregano, marjoram) can be dried by hanging in bunches or spreading on trays in a warm, airy, shaded place. Herbs that do not keep their flavour when dried (basil, mint, parsley, coriander) are better frozen. (Freeze in ice-cube trays with water to make cubes for flavouring soups and stews.)
Kumara/* (sweet potato)	Harvest the whole crop as soon as it is mature (the leaves will be starting to go yellow and brown). Harvest on a warm day when the soil is dry. Handle very carefully as kumara tubers are easily damaged.	Kumara require warmer storage temperatures than other crops (not less than 12ºC, but no more than 20ºC) and high humidity. Commercial kumara crops are cured for long-term storage in a hot (30–35ºC) and humid (85–90% humidity) place for 5–7 days. The home gardener has to improvise something as close as possible – a glasshouse might be suitable. The traditional method of storage* was a purpose-built storehouse half buried in earth to keep the temperature warm and stable. It is a good idea to store kumara in open, shallow crates or trays so that rot and disease can be quickly seen and dealt with. HT; HH.
Leeks	Harvest when the desired size. Can be left in the ground over winter.	Will keep in the fridge for up to 10 days.

VEGETABLE	Harvesting	Keeping/Storing
Lettuce	Loose-leaf lettuces: harvest leaves as required. Heading lettuces: cut when the head is fat and firm.	Wash, leave water on the leaves, and store in an open or perforated plastic bag or wrapped in a damp teatowel in the fridge. LT; HH.
Onions	Pull up the whole crop on a dry sunny day, and leave in a warm place to dry for 1–2 weeks.	Plait the tops into strings, or remove the tops and put the onions in mesh bags. LT; LH.
Mushrooms (button or open)	Pick as required, at the desired stage of maturity. Twist the stems to pick; don't cut.	Store in paper bags in the fridge for up to 10 days. LT; HH. Mushrooms can be dried in a dehydrator, in the oven, or by stringing small ones loosely and hanging them in a dry, airy place.
Parsnips	Can be left in the ground when mature to pull up as required. Any still in the ground at the end of winter should be lifted and stored or they will go to seed.	Store in the fridge for 2–3 weeks, or in boxes of sand in a cool place for 3–4 months. LT; HH.
Peas	Pick as close to cooking (or freezing) as possible, for the sweetest eating.	Freeze. Some varieties of pea are suitable for drying (as for beans).
Peppers (capsicum/chilli)	Harvest when full size and fully coloured.	Keep in the fridge for 1–2 weeks. LT; HH. Can be frozen, or preserved in oil. Chilli peppers can be dried by stringing them loosely and hanging in an airy dry place.
Potatoes	Harvest new season's potatoes just as required. Main-crop potatoes can be left in the ground when mature for a month or two, and harvested as required. For potatoes that are to be stored, lift the whole crop on a dry, sunny day, and leave the potatoes in a dry sunny place for a few hours, or a warm, dry shaded place for a few days, to cure them ready for storage.	Potatoes must be kept in a dark place and/or inside lightproof containers, as light causes toxic greening. Thick hessian sacks are good; cardboard boxes with newspaper sheets between each layer of potatoes are also good. Grade the potatoes into small, medium and large and store each grade in separate containers.

VEGETABLE	Harvesting	Keeping/Storing
		Eat the small ones first and the large ones last. HT; HH.
Pumpkin & squash	Harvest when fully mature. Those to be stored should be left on the vine until the first frost. Cut the pumpkin from the vine, leaving a 5–6cm length of stalk attached.	Ensure the pumpkins' skins are dry and clean, but do not wash or scrub them. Store in rows on shelves, leaving gaps between them, or hang in nets. HT; LH.
Radishes	*Salad radishes*: harvest often for the tastiest radishes – left too long in the ground they get woody, hot and tasteless. *Asian radishes* (e.g. daikon) can be left in the ground until required.	Salad radishes will keep for up to 10 days in the fridge. LT; HH. Asian radishes can be lifted and stored in boxes of sand in a cool place for 3–4 months. LT; HH.
Silverbeet	Pick leaves as required.	Stand the stalks in a jug of water in the fridge or other cool place, or wash the leaves, leave the water on, store in the fridge in an open or perforated plastic bag for up to 3 days. LT; HH.
Spinach	Pick leaves as required.	Wash the leaves, leave the water on, store in the fridge in an open or perforated plastic bag for up to 3 days. LT; HH.
Swedes	Leave in the ground and harvest as required.	Can be stored in boxes of sand in a cool place. LT; HH.
Sweetcorn	Harvest the cobs as soon as they are ripe, and just before required. The sugar in corn starts turning into tasteless starch from the moment it is picked.	Will keep (but not well) in the fridge for 3–4 days. LT; HH. Corn kernels can be frozen.
Tomatoes	Pick when fully ripe, as required. At the end of the tomato season, green tomatoes can be ripened off the vine by keeping them in a warm place. The process can be speeded up by putting them in a plastic bag with a couple of ripe tomatoes, or a ripe banana.	Store at room temperature. Fully ripe tomatoes can be kept in the fridge, but will lose flavour. HT; LH.

VEGETABLE	Harvesting	Keeping/Storing
Turnips	Pull up as soon as mature, which is before the tops get to tennis-ball size.	Keep in the fridge for 3–4 weeks, or in boxes of sand in a cool place for 3–4 months. LT; HH.
Yams (oka)	Yams begin to mature as days begin to shorten, in autumn. Harvest them carefully, and leave in the sun to dry before storing them.	Perfect yams (no cuts or bruises) will keep for 3–4 months in a cool, dark place. LT; HH.
Zucchini (courgettes)	Harvest at the desired size – check the plants regularly, as the desired (small) size is quickly outgrown, and the marrows that result are not such good eating.	Zucchini are best eaten immediately, but will keep in the fridge for 3–4 days. LT; HH.

* More on kumara harvesting and storage, and a photograph of a traditional storage house, can be found at www.panui.org.nz/Currentkumaracuring.htm

Fruit

There are very few fruits that will keep ripening, and improve in sweetness and flavour, if stored for more than a few days. Luckily they include two of the fruits most commonly grown at home in New Zealand, apples and pears, and also that other great source of winter vitamins, kiwifruit.

However, not all apples and pears are created equal when it comes to keeping their flavour as good in month three as it was in month one. Thus to prevent serious disappointment it is important to know which varieties are the best keepers. The New Zealand-grown apples you see on sale at the end of winter and beginning of spring are the good keepers – they include Braeburn, Fuji, Granny Smith and Pink Lady. There are also older, traditional varieties, such as Sturmer and Bramley's Seedling, which keep well but are seldom seen on sale these days. When buying apple trees be clear about whether you want apples for eating straight away or for storing.

Other tree crops that keep well off the tree are bananas and avocados. Casimaroa/white sapote, cherimoya, mango and papaya are also in this group – for those lucky people in Northland who can grow these. Avocados are unusual in that they will only ripen after picking. While bananas are best left on the tree until they are almost ready to eat, so long as they are full size when picked they will continue to ripen until edible (and beyond). Once they are ripe, both avocados and bananas can be stored in the fridge for a few days more to keep them in peak condition, although it turns the skins of the bananas black.

No other fruits ripen off the tree, if ripening is defined as improving in flavour and sweetness. Some other fruits will improve in texture (going from hard to soft), juiciness, and/or colour after picking, but they will not improve in sweetness or flavour, and if kept too long may still look good but not taste good. These fruits include:

- apricots
- blueberries
- feijoas
- figs
- melons
- nectarines
- passionfruit
- peaches
- persimmons
- plums
- tamarillos

With these fruits it is important to wait until they are fully grown and ripe before picking them.

Most of the stonefruits indicate that they are fully ripe when they are fully coloured, i.e. they have no green patches at all, although some, such as nectarines, may still be quite hard. Ripe apricots should be eaten straight away, as they lose flavour and go mealy very soon after harvest, but nectarines, peaches and plums will get softer and juicier if left in a paper bag at room temperature. Passionfruit that are kept until their skins go wrinkly are juicier. Persimmons come in astringent and non-astringent varieties (the astringent ones are more cold-tolerant and easier to grow down south). Astringent persimmons should be picked when fully coloured but still hard, and then left to soften before they are ready to eat. Non-astringent persimmons are best eaten when they are still firm and crisp. Feijoas picked a day or two before ultimate ripeness should be left for a week to 10 days to finish ripening.

Finally, there are fruits that will not ripen or improve in any way at all after picking. These must be picked when they are as sweet, soft and juicy as they will ever get. These fruits include:

- blackberries and boysenberries
- cherries
- citrus fruits – grapefruit, lemons, limes, mandarins, oranges
- currants (black, red, white)
- gooseberries
- raspberries
- strawberries

With a few exceptions, which are covered in the list below, the fridge is a very bad place to store fruit. It will stop any further ripening that might have been possible, and in some cases change the flavour and aroma of the fruit. However, the edible life of some fully ripe fruits (bananas, berries, kiwifruit) can be prolonged by keeping them in the fridge for a short time. Fruit kept in this way that is to be eaten raw should always be taken out of the fridge and brought back to room temperature before eating, or it will lack aroma and flavour.

Fruit to be eaten within a few days of harvest should in most cases be kept at a pleasant room temperature (around 16–18°C). It should be kept out of direct sunlight and away from other strong heat sources. It is best kept in shallow baskets or bowls that allow for air circulation around the fruit, and prevent squeezing and squashing of soft fruits (which is a sure way to hasten decay). It is a good practice to check the fruit every day and remove any pieces that are showing signs of rot or decay that might spread.

Fruits that can be ripened off the tree, which includes vegetable fruits such as tomatoes, can be ripened more quickly by putting them close to riper fruit, especially inside a paper bag. Ripe apples and bananas are often recommended as good companions for all other kinds of less ripe fruit. This is because ripe fruit gives off a gaseous hormone called ethylene. Fruits that can ripen slowly off the tree, like apples and bananas, are good producers of this gas. If they are kept close to other fruit in a confined space, like a paper bag, the ethylene they give off stimulates ripening in the other fruit.* The downside to the amazing power of ethylene is that it can accelerate ripening when you don't want it to, for example when storing apples for long keeping. Hence the recommendation in the list below to store the different varieties of apple that ripen at different rates separate from each other.

Gases can be friend or foe when it comes to keeping fruit, but water is always an enemy. Moisture promotes and spreads rot, fungus and other problems. For this reason it is best to harvest the fruit when it is completely dry. If you need to wash fruit after harvest (to remove dirt, for example) then make sure it is well dried before adding it to the fruit bowl. For the same reason, it is not good to store fruit in fastened plastic bags without breathing holes, as this keeps moisture close to the fruit, and does not allow it to evaporate. If organic home-grown fruit needs to be washed at all, this should be done just before eating it or cooking with it.

For long-term storage in a box or a tray where the produce is touching other fruits it is best to wrap each piece in paper to minimise the spread of decay. Old newspaper is fine for this, but stronger papers like waxed or wrapping paper (it's a good way to recycle) are even better.

Fruit to be stored long term needs to be kept in the same cool (0–5°C), dry, dark conditions as vegetables being stored long term. Humidity should be at the higher end of the scale. Check stored fruit regularly, and remove any that show signs of decay before they infect the rest. Citrus fruits are especially prone to attracting moulds that spread quickly.

Fruit should be handled gently and carefully at all times. Not even hard fruits such as quinces and thick-skinned fruits like oranges are impervious to the consequences of being banged about and squeezed hard, while thin-skinned soft-fleshed fruits like feijoas, peaches and the like need special care to avoid bruising, scratching and other damage that will shorten the life of the fruit.

* For more information on ethylene and fruit ripening see www.scientificamerican.com/article.cfm?id=origin-of-fruit-ripening

FRUIT	Harvesting	Keeping/Storing
Apples	Pick as soon as full size and fully coloured.	Store late-maturing varieties only. Use only perfect fruit. Either wrap each one in paper and store in one-layer boxes, or set out on trays and shelves with a little space between each apple. Keep each variety of apple in a separate boxe or on a separate shelf, to stop fast-ripening ones from spoiling late-ripening fruit.
Apricots	Pick when perfectly ripe – there should be no green on the apricot at all, including where it meets the tree.	Eat immediately, or preserve by freezing or bottling.
Avocados	Harvest when full size, 1–2 weeks before required for eating.	Store on the tree. To ripen, keep at room temperature, close to ripe fruit. To keep ripe avocados at the point of ripeness, store them in the fridge for up to 10 days.

FRUIT	Harvesting	Keeping/Storing
Bananas	Ideally, leave on the tree until on the point of ripeness, but can be picked at any stage after reaching full size/maturity, and ripened indoors.	Once fully ripe, to delay decay, bananas can be stored in the fridge (although the skins will go black).
Blackberries, boysenberries, raspberries	All the 'seedy' berry fruits must be picked when fully ripe, and also dry. Do not harvest during or just after rain, or before the dew has dried in the morning. Wet fruit does not keep as well as dry fruit.	Eat immediately; or store in the fridge for 3–4 days in shallow containers. Layer the berries in the container, sprinkling a little white sugar between each layer.
Blueberries	Harvest when fully ripe, on a dry day.	Best eaten at once, but can be kept in the fridge in a shallow container that is covered in cling film (or placed inside an unfastened plastic bag). Keep for 3–4 days maximum.
Cherries	Harvest when fully ripe but still firm. Leave the stalks on.	Best eaten at once, but can be kept in a cool (5–10°) place for 3–4 days maximum.
Currants (black, red, white)	Harvest when fully ripe, on a dry day.	For fresh eating, currants can be stored in the fridge for 8–9 days, in a shallow container covered with cling film (or inside an unfastened plastic bag). Or preserve them immediately by freezing or bottling whole, or turning into jam, jelly or cordial.
Feijoas	Feijoas fall from the bush at the point of ripeness, so collect them from the ground below every day, or pick them just before the fruit is ready to fall. (It should come away easily. If it does not, it will not finish ripening off the tree.)	Feijoas can be stored in a cool, dark, dry place for 4–5 weeks. Store in one or at most two layers in rigid, shallow trays or boxes, and ensure good air circulation around the fruit to stop the ethylene it gives off from ripening it all too quickly.

FRUIT	Harvesting	Keeping/Storing
Figs	Harvest when fully ripe. Damaging figs – as birds do when they peck holes in them – will hasten their ripening, but this is best tried in small batches.	Best eaten at once, but can be kept in a cool (5–10°) place for 3–4 days maximum.
Gooseberries	Gooseberries for cooking and preserving can be harvested as soon as they are full size and just starting to soften; dessert gooseberries for eating fresh should be left to colour and become softer and juicier. Harvest when dry.	Eat or preserve at once, if possible. If not, store in the fridge in a shallow container that is covered with cling film or placed inside an unfastened plastic bag. Keep dessert gooseberries no longer than 3 days; cooking gooseberries for 6–7 days.
Grapes	Pick when fully ripe and sweet, with the stalk still attached to the bunch. Harvest on a dry day.	If the stalk is placed in a bottle or jar of water, and the grapes in their bottles are stored in a cool, dark place, they will stay fresh for up to 2 months.
Grapefruit	Harvest when fully ripe, on a dry day.	For short-term keeping (1 week) place grapefruit in small baskets that allow air circulation and keep at room temperature. Grapefruit will also keep in the fridge for 3–4 weeks. Warm them back to room temperature well before eating, or they will be less juicy.
Kiwifruit	Pick when full size, but still hard.	For eating immediately, leave at room temperature with ripe fruit (in a paper bag for faster ripening). For long storage up to 8 weeks keep in a cold (0°) place with high humidity (90–95 per cent), stored in shallow trays or boxes. Kiwifruit are very sensitive to ethylene, and good producers of it, so keep away from other ripe/ripening fruit, keep well ventilated, and remove any fruit that starts to ripen in cold storage to the kitchen. Fully ripe kiwifruit can be kept in the fridge for a week or so.

FRUIT	Harvesting	Keeping/Storing
Lemons, limes	Pick when fully coloured, as required.	Best stored on the tree and picked as needed, but for longer-term keeping off the tree lemons will keep in the fridge in an unsealed or holey plastic bag for up to a month.
Mandarins	Pick when fully coloured and juicy.	Keep in a basket in a cool place and eat within 1 week.
Melons	All types of melon must be picked when fully ripe. Muskmelon varieties (rockmelons or cantaloupes, honeydew, Charentais and other scented melons) will usually indicate this by their fragrance, and some will start to 'slip' from their vines. Watermelons are harder to judge – see the footnote for a good online guide.* Cut any melon neatly from the vine, don't pull it.	Melons will soften if kept at room temperature, but will not get sweeter or tastier. Eat muskmelons as soon as possible, as they do not improve with keeping, although they can be put in a holding pattern in the fridge for a few days. Watermelons can be kept in a cool, dark place for up to a week. All cut melons should be kept in the fridge, in a plastic bag.
Nashi	Pick when fully ripe – still crisp but juicy.	Nashi can be kept in the fridge for up to 3 months.
Nectarines	Pick when full size and fully coloured. Firm fully coloured fruit will soften off the tree, but those with any green on them will not.	If soft, eat at once. If firm, ripen further in in a paper bag with a another ripe fruit in it.
Oranges	Pick when fully ripe and juicy.	For immediate eating keep in a basket in a cool place. For long-term storage (6–8 weeks) oranges can be wrapped in paper and stored in boxes in a cool (0–5°), dry, dark place.
Passionfruit	Passionfruit fall off the vine when fully ripe – encourage them to do so by gently shaking the vine when it has full-size and fully coloured fruits on it. Pick every day at the start of the season, to prevent fallen fruit from being scorched by the sun.	Leave ripe passionfruit in a cool, dark place to go wrinkly and sweeter and juicier – better for eating raw. At this point passionfruit can be kept in the fridge for up to 2 weeks.

FRUIT	Harvesting	Keeping/Storing
Peaches	Pick when full size and fully coloured. Firm, fully coloured fruit will soften off the tree, but those with any green on them will not.	If soft, eat at once. If firm, ripen further in in a paper bag with another ripe fruit in it.
Pears	All pears are best picked when full size but still firm. The fruit is ready if the stalk comes away easily from the branch when the pear is lifted and given a slight twist. You can also test a sample pear or two by cutting to see if the pear has some juice – non-juicy pears will not ripen off the tree. Handle carefully, as pears have thin skins and bruise easily.	Early-season pears should be left in a moderately warm place (18–20°C) to finish ripening, and eaten or preserved as soon as ripe. Late-season pears (such as Winter Nelis) can be stored as for apples, but will not keep as long – check regularly.
Persimmons	Harvest persimmons as soon as they are fully coloured, but still hard. Cut the fruit from the branch using secateurs, leaving the calyx intact. Fruit can be left on the tree until they soften, but this is a waste of time and fruit unless the tree is protected against birds and possums.	Non-astringent persimmons should be eaten from 2 days to 2 weeks after picking. Astringent persimmons should be stored on shelves (stem side down) in a cool place until they soften. Speed up softening by putting persimmons in a paper bag with a ripe apple. If too many soften at the same time the pulp can be scooped out and frozen for later use.
Plums	Pick when full size and fully coloured. Firm, fully coloured fruit will soften off the tree, but those with any green on them will not.	If soft, eat at once. If firm, ripen further in in a paper bag with other ripe fruit in it.
Quinces	Pick as soon as the fruit is pale yellow all over. Use secateurs to cut the fruit from the branch.	For immediate use, keep the quinces in a warm room and when they start to scent they are ready to use. They can then be kept in the fridge for 2–3 weeks if necessary. For later use, store quinces (perfect ones only) in a cool, dry place for 3–4 weeks.

Strawberries	Pick strawberries when they are plump and red all over. Do not harvest during or just after rain, or before the dew has dried in the morning. Wet fruit does not keep well.	Best eaten at once, but can be kept in the fridge for 3–4 days in shallow containers. Layer the berries in the container, sprinkling a little white sugar between each layer.
Tamarillos	Pick when the fruit is a good size and fully coloured. If there is any green on the top of the fruit where it joins the stalk it is not fully ripe, and it will not ripen after harvest.	Keep in the fruit bowl for up to 1 week, or in the fridge for up to 2 weeks.
Tangelos	Pick when fully ripe.	Store as for oranges.

* How can you tell when a watermelon is ripe? See http://faq.gardenweb.com/faq/lists/cornucop/2002071935010165.html

Heritage fruit tree sources

Mail-order sources of heritage fruit trees include (from north to south):

Kaiwaka Organics: www.kaiwakaorganics.co.nz
Forgotten Fruits: www.forgottenfruits.co.nz
The Edible Garden: www.ediblegarden.co.nz
Mapua Country Trading: www.mapuacountrytrading.co.nz
Sutherland Nursery: http://sutherlandnursery.co.nz

The best garden centres will also stock some heritage trees. Check out the catalogues of the mail-order nurseries so that you know what to look for and ask for. Some Seed Savers groups also have an interest in fruit trees, so check out your nearest group and see if they have anything to share or swap.

ENDNOTES

Chapter One: Culinary Confusion

1   This and other information on the ingredients and nutritional value of McDonald's products in New Zealand can be found at http://mcdonalds.co.nz/our-food/nutrition.

2   The food industry lobby and its political power are described in Marion Nestle, *Food Politics: How the food industry influences nutrition and health*, University of California Press, Berkeley, 2002.

3   This and other experiments in the longevity of fast food are recorded in Morgan Spurlock, *Don't Eat This Book*, Penguin Books, London, 2005, pp. 115–17.

4   Martin Tobias, *Looking Upstream: Causes of death cross-classified by risk and condition, New Zealand, 1997*, Public Health Intelligence Occasional Bulletin no. 20, Ministry of Health, Wellington, 2004: www.moh.govt.nz/moh.nsf/wpgIndex/Publications-Looking+Upstream.

5   WHO Information sheet on fruit and vegetables: www.who.int/dietphysicalactivity/fruit/en/index2.html.

6   Ministry of Health data, 'Major causes of death, numbers and WHO age-standardised rates by sex, 2007': www.moh.govt.nz/moh.nsf/indexmh/mortality-demographic-data-2007.

7   Carolyn Gibson, *Fries With That? How to lose weight and keep it off in an upsized world*, New Holland, Auckland, 2009; New Zealand Ministry of Health, *A Focus on Nutrition: Key Findings of the 2008/09 New Zealand Adult Nutrition Survey*, Wellington, 2011: www.moh.govt.nz/moh.nsf/indexmh/dataandstatistics-survey-nutrition.

8   *A Focus on Nutrition*, ibid.

9   Rachel Carson, *Silent Spring*, Houghton Mifflin, Boston, 1962: www.ourstolenfuture.org; www.rspb.org.uk/ourwork/farming.

10   For more on the environmental and human health impacts of factory farming see Colin Tudge, *So Shall We Reap*, Allen Lane, London, 2003.

11   Christine Dann, *A Cottage Garden Cookbook*, Bridget Williams Books, Wellington, 1992.

12   Mary Browne, Helen Leach and Nancy Tichborne, *The Cook's Garden: For cooks who garden and gardeners who cook*, Reed, Auckland, 1980; *More from the Cook's Garden: For cooks who garden and gardeners who cook*, Reed Methuen, Auckland, 1987.

13   Jill Brewis and Dennis Greville, *The Grower's Cookbook: From the garden to the table*, Penguin Books, Auckland, 2008.

Chapter Two: Growing@Home

1   Lynda Hallinan's blog is at www.lyndahallinan.wordpress.com.

2   See *Counting for Nothing* (Allen & Unwin/Port Nicholson Press, Wellington, 1988) by
     Marilyn Waring for a book-length explanation of what we are doing wrong when it comes
     to national and international accounting for genuine welfare, and see the research on
     Genuine Progress Indicators at www.gpiatlantic.org, and the Happy Planet Index at www.
     neweconomics.org for how we could do better at measuring – and hence protecting –
     human and environmental health and wealth in sustainable and fair ways.

3   More facts and figures on the greater productivity of home gardening and on its contribu-
     tion to the household and national economy can be found in Edward Hyams, *English
     Cottage Gardens*, Whittet Books, London, 1970, pp. 158–77.

4   'Dig for Victory' gardens are making a comeback in Britain, both as
     replicas of the actual wartime gardens (www.fortiesexperience.co.uk/Dig_for_Victory_
     garden/1940sdigforvictorygarden.html) and as part of the growing move to create more
     allotment and community gardens for healthy diet, recreation and environmental sustain-
     ability reasons. (See 'Echoes of Britain's wartime Dig for Victory as community gardens
     gain ground' at www.guardian.co.uk/money/2008/aug/10/property gardens.) There is a
     lovely personal memoir of a Victory Garden that fed six families at www.transitiontowns.
     org.nz/node/1355. In the US in 1943 the Kitchen Gardeners International newsletter
     reports that there were some 20 million private gardens that produced 8 million tons of
     food. Kitchen Gardeners International (www.kitchengardeners.org) is encouraging people
     to turn redundant lawns into edible gardens and in 2008–09 it ran a successful campaign
     aimed at getting President Obama to turn part of the White House lawn into a Victory
     Garden. (Michelle Obama is in charge of it.)

5   Just how much difference it made in Cuba has been studied and summarised in 'Impact
     of energy intake, physical activity, and population-wide weight loss on cardiovascular
     disease and diabetes mortality in Cuba, 1980–2005' by M. Franco et al, *American Journal
     of Epidemiology*, 12 December 2007, 166 (12), pp. 1374–80: http://aje.oxfordjournals.org/
     cgi/content/full/166/12/1374. More information on the benefits of going off the industrial
     diet can be found in Garry Egger and Boyd Swinburne, *Planet Obesity: How we're eating
     ourselves and the planet to death*, Allen & Unwin, Sydney, 2010, Chapter 5.

6   Hohepa Kereopa's experience and views on food and gardening can be found in Paul
     Moon, *A Tohunga's Natural World: Plants, gardening and food*, David Ling, Auckland, 2005,
     pp. 16–17.

7   Green Guide World Environment Day 2008, Fairfax Media, p. 10.

8   Patch from Scratch: www.patchfromscratch.co.nz.

9   Urban agriculture is now a worldwide movement, and urban farms and market gardens
     can be found in big cities on every continent. The Resource Centres on Urban Agriculture
     and Food Security (www.ruaf.org) is an international clearing-house of information on
     urban agriculture, while the Vancouver-based City Farmer organisation (www.cityfarmer.
     org) has been supporting, documenting and promoting urban agriculture in Canada and
     elsewhere since 1994. Three urban agriculture projects in Auckland are documented
     in *Organic NZ* (www.organicnz.org/112/urban-agriculture-in-auckland). 'Container
     Farming Organic food production in the slums of Mexico City' by Rodrigo A. Medellín
     Erdmann (http://journeytoforever.org/garden_con-mexico.html) shows just how much
     food can be produced in very little space and with few resources. More information
     about Romita Urban Garden including a photo is available at www.cityfarmer.info/

promoting-urban-agriculture-in-mexico-city-sembradores-urbanos.

10   The 26,000ha of greenhouses in the Almeria region of Spain is the largest grouping of greenhouses in the world. Ironically, for a production method that is so resource- and water-intensive and polluting that it is destroying the health of the region, such a huge amount of white polythene has a bizarre climate change upside. It is so large that it creates an albedo effect, reflecting the sun's rays to such a degree that Almeria, unlike the rest of Spain, is not experiencing the warming due to global greenhouse gas emissions that is affecting the rest of the country.

11   Edward Hyams, *English Cottage Gardens*, Whittet Books, London, 1970, pp. 158, 160.

12   Rachel Knight also shares her knowledge and sells her produce via her website: www. thekitchengarden.co.nz.

13   Earth Talk: www.earthtalk.co.nz.

14   See the trust's website for more on the garden and the trust's other educational activities: www.permaham.boo.co.nz.

15   Find out more about this tree and how to grow it in New Zealand at www.edible.co.nz/ fruits.php?fruitid=35.

16   Enviroschools: www.enviroschools.org.nz.

Chapter Three: Community@Garden

1   For the definitive work on the first gardens and gardeners in New Zealand, see Helen Leach, *1000 Years of Gardening in New Zealand*, A. H. & A. W. Reed, Wellington, 1984.

2   www.whiteglovestv.co.nz/Anatonio.html.

3   Hohepa Kereopa provides a good account of how things used to be done up until the 1960s in 'The approach to gardening', in Paul Moon, *A Tohunga's Natural World: Plants, gardening and food*, David Ling, Auckland, 2005.

4   Kiwi Maara is produced by White Gloves TV. Read more about the show and its present-ers at www.whiteglovestv.co.nz.

5   Read about Te Waka Kai Ora and its activities on its website: http://tewakakaiora. wordpress.com.

6   Find out more about the Spud in a Bucket programme and the rest of Taahuri Whenua's work at www.tahuriwhenua.org.nz.

7   ARGOS has a page on the establishment and early work of He Whenua Whakatipu at www.argos.org.nz/ngaitahu_home.shtm.

8   Read about the rest of the trip at www.kaitiakitanga.net/projects/1-1-1 raglan trip.htm and look at the main site www.kaitiakitanga.net too, for it is a wonderful resource on the indigenous approach to sustainability.

9   This research is cited in Brian Halweil, *Eat Here: Reclaiming homegrown pleasures in a global supermarket*, W. W. Norton, New York, 2004. A lot more information on the positive social benefits of community gardening in other parts of the US is given in Janet A. Flammang, *The Taste for Civilization: Food, politics, and civil society*, University of Illinois Press, Urbana and Chicago, 2009, Chapter 12.

10   Stephen Trinder with Christine Blance and Ross Paterson, *Community Gardening*, Christchurch Community Gardens Association, Christchurch, 2006, p. 2.

11   More on the Framework Trust and its work at www.framework.org.nz.

12   A brief biography of Mother Aubert, including reference to her medicinal use of native plants, can be found at www.compassion.org.nz/publication/aubert.htm.

13   See www.guerrillagardening.org.

14   See www.guerrillagardening.org/community/index.php?board=90.0.

15   The policy is at www.aucklandcity.govt.nz/council/documents/gardenpolicy/default.asp. It goes nowhere near the vision of urban permaculturist Betsy Kettle in her article 'Urban agriculture in Auckland': www.organicnz.org/page/2020-9.

16   See some pictures of the garden and gardeners and read more about it at www.ranui.org. nz/page.php?view=ranui_community_garden.

17   For information on Vertical Composting Unit technology see www.zerowaste.co.nz/default,149.sm.

Chapter Four: Dining@Home

1   James Ng, *Windows on a Chinese Past*, Volume II, Otago Heritage Books, Dunedin, 1993, p. 179.

2   Ibid.

3   For more information on the poor diet of low-income households in 19th- and 20th-century Britain and the millions who were clinically malnourished as a result, see David Goodman and Michael Redclift, *Refashioning Nature: Food, ecology and culture*, Routledge, London, 1991, pp. 31–33.

4   For why and how many of our immigrant ancestors ate so badly, and were driven to emigrate, see Tony Simpson, *A Distant Feast: The origins of New Zealand's cuisine*, Godwit, Auckland, 1999.

5   For how the rich ate in Victorian Britain, see Simpson, *A Distant Feast*.

6   For more information on these first productive gardens see Christine Dann, *Cottage Gardening in New Zealand*, Bridget Williams Books, Wellington, 1990, pp. 17–25.

7   Michael Murphy, *Handbook of Gardening for New Zealand*, Whitcombe and Tombs, Christchurch, 1885.

8   David Veart, *First Catch Your Weka: A story of New Zealand cooking*, Auckland University Press, Auckland, 2008, p. 31.

9   E. B. Miller, *Economic Technical Cookery Book*, Mills, Dick and Co, Dunedin, p. 173. Although brutal to vegetables, Miller's book does not advocate brutality to women, unlike the Education Board's *Home Science Recipe Book*, which included an (illustrated!) version of the adage 'The woman, the donkey and the walnut tree, the more you beat them, the better they be.' Apparently this was considered to be a suitable illustration to head the page on 'Batters' (p. 44). No wonder I later came to think of manual training classes as 'sex role indoctrination' classes, since girls and boys were taught quite different skills and values. Such a pity, when both genders could have been taught good cooking.

10   For a Kiwi version see the French Salad Dressing recipe in Barbara Milburn, *Fifty French Dishes for New Zealand*, Price Milburn, Wellington, 1970, p. 10, which suggests that 'topmilk added makes a delicious change' to the tablespoon of cream in the recipe. I have never seen or even heard of a home-made vinaigrette with cream in it before, so I checked the bible of French cooking, *Larousse Gastronomique*, to see if this was in the original recipe. There I found that although basic vinaigrette is indeed only vinegar, oil, salt and pepper, a range of other things may be added, and one of those is cream. However, fresh herbs are much more common (and healthy).

11   Graham Kerr, *Entertaining with Kerr*, A. H. & A. W. Reed, Wellington, 1963. Kerr's career in New Zealand and his influence on New Zealand cookery are described by David Veart, *First Catch Your Weka*, 2008, on pp. 235–43, and there is more on his subsequent media-chef career at http://en.wikipedia.org/wiki/Graham_Kerr.

12 Tui Flower, *Tui Flower's Modern Hostess Cookbook*, A. H. & A. W. Reed, Wellington, 1972.

13 In *The Taste for Civilization: Food, politics, and civil society* (University of Illinois Press, Urbana and Chicago, 2009) Janet Flammang puts 'the time crunch' first in her book on food, politics and civil society, documenting the ways in which shopping time has squeezed cooking time in contemporary America and how the home cook's lot has become harder, not easier, as a result of the proliferation of supermarkets at the expense of small local food stores, markets and street stalls.

14 Using *Wise's Business Directories* I tallied the numbers and types of food stores in Christchurch for over three decades (in 1968, 1978, 1988 and 1998), to track the steep decline of local fresh food stores and their replacement by a much smaller number of supermarkets and the rise in takeaway food outlets. *Wise's Business Directory* is no longer published (is this because of a steep decline in small independent businesses generally?) so it is not possible to track changes in food retailing this way any more.

15 The latest New Zealand mortality figures are at www.moh.govt.nz. The most recent and comprehensive global study on the dietary causes of cancer and how to prevent it (*Food, Nutrition, Physical Activity, and the Prevention of Cancer: A global perspective* – available at www.dietandcancerreport.org) sets out the evidence for the connection between high animal food and low fresh vegetable food consumption and cancer. According to the World Health Organisation, 'Low fruit and vegetable intake is among the top 10 risk factors contributing to attributable mortality … Up to 2.7 million lives could potentially be saved each year with sufficient global fruit and vegetable consumption … Worldwide, low intake of fruits and vegetables is estimated to cause about 19 per cent of gastrointestinal cancer, about 31 per cent of ischaemic heart disease and 11 per cent of stroke. Of the global burden attributable to low fruit and vegetable consumption, about 85 per cent was from cardiovascular disease (CVD) and 15 per cent from cancers. (See www.who.int/dietphysicalactivity/fruit/en/index2.html.)

16 'Unhealthy food advertising outstrips healthy ads' at www.scoop.co.nz/stories/GE0807/S00021.htm.

17 See Kamala Hayman, 'Global brand urged for diet', *Press*, 10 August 2004.

18 One of the key findings of the Food and Nutrition Monitoring Report 2006 was that the average household spent $6.50 each week on confectionery, but only $5.90 on fresh fruit. See www.scoop.co.nz/stories/PA0610/S00434.htm for more from the Minister of Health's media release on this report.

19 Read about the Slow Food Movement and its members at www.slowfood.com.

20 R. J. Brodie and M. J. Mellon, *Cheese: A consumer survey of Christchurch households*, Research Report no. 102, Lincoln University, Agricultural Economics Research Unit, 1979.

21 The song, animated cartoon and parodies can be heard and seen at http://folksong.org.nz/chesdale/index.html.

22 Tony Simpson, *An Innocent Delight: The art of dining in New Zealand*, Hodder and Stoughton, Auckland, 1985, pp. 266–70.

23 Read more about Evansdale cheese and how it came to be made at http://localfoodenthusiasts.com/2010/03/21/evansdale-cheese-otago-new-zealand and www.evansdalecheese.co.nz.

24 Laura Shapiro, *Something from the Oven: Reinventing dinner in 1950s America*, Viking Books, New York, 2004, p. 253.

25 See www.familyfresh.blogspot.com. They have now kept their mission up for over a year. There are heaps of other websites on getting kids to eat more fresh food, why they really

need to do so, and what works in motivating them to start munching on carrots, not cookies. www.keepkidshealthy.com/nutrition/kids_vegetables.html is a good place to start looking.

26   Barbara Kingsolver, *Animal, Vegetable, Miracle: Our year of seasonal eating*, Faber, London, 2007; Linda Cockburn, *Living the Good Life: How one family changed the world from their backyard*, Hardie Grant Books, Prahran, Victoria, 2006.

27   How widespread this practice was, and how bad the food was, are discussed by Lisa Chaney in her biography of the great English cook and food writer Elizabeth David. David recalled the nursery food in her grand country home (where her wealthy parents could certainly have afforded to feed their children better) as consisting of boiled meat and over-boiled vegetables. ('Vegetable marrows were yellow, boiled and watery. There were green turnip tops, spinach, Jerusalem artichokes. I hated them all.') Puddings were either slippery (junket) or stodgy (jam roly-poly). Lisa Chaney, *Elizabeth David: A Biography*, Pan Books, London, 1999, pp. 20–22.

28   See the delightful essay 'Food and drink in the Potter universe' by 'Susanna/pigwidgeon37' (www.hp-lexicon.org/essays/essay-food.html) for details on the diabetic disaster and cho-lesterol catastrophe that is standard young wizard fare. For the real world, where people do get fat and sick when they eat this sort of food regularly, see Joanna Blythman's *Bad Food Britain*, where she excoriates the British fondness for bad food and describes its multiple negative effects. Joanna Blythman, *Bad Food Britain: How a nation ruined its appetite*, Fourth Estate, London, 2006.

Chapter Five: Cooking@Home

1   Ann Vileisis, *Kitchen Literacy: How we lost knowledge of where food comes from and why we need to get it back*, Island Press/Shearwater Books, Washington, 2008.

2   G. A. Kennelly, *The Home Vegetable Garden*, NZ Department of Agriculture Bulletin no. 342.

3   Catherine Harris, 'Cuts end popular night classes', *Dominion Post*, 13 February 2010.

4   www.supergran.org.nz has some cheap and cheerful – if often a bit stodgy or sweet for my taste – recipes to share.

5   A good selection of the cooking schools and their classes is listed at www.nzs.com/recre-ation/cooking-classes. Interesting that cooking classes are now classified as 'recreation', isn't it?

6   They are the Healthy Kitchen Cooking School, formerly of Greendale in Canterbury and now in Christchurch and Cambridge, Waikato (www.healthykitchen.co.nz); another Christchurch-based teacher (www.nourish.org.nz); and a Northland couple who offer a range of classes (www.vibrantearthcreations.com).

7   Email getgrowing@nzgardener.co.nz to subscribe.

8   *Digby Law's Vegetable Cookbook*, Hodder and Stoughton, Auckland, 1978.

9   Christine Dann, *A Cottage Garden Cookbook*, Bridget Williams Books, Wellington, 1992.

10   Mary Browne, Helen Leach and Nancy Tichborne, *The Cook's Garden: For cooks who garden and gardeners who cook*, Reed, Auckland, 1980; Mary Browne, Helen Leach and Nancy Tichborne, *More from the Cook's Garden: For cooks who garden and gardeners who cook*, Reed Methuen, Auckland, 1987.

11   Jill Brewis and Dennis Greville, *The Grower's Cookbook: From the garden to the table*, Penguin Books, Auckland, 2008.

12   Sally Cameron, *Grow It Cook It*, Penguin Books, Auckland, 2009.

13   Rosalind Creasy, *Cooking from the Garden*, Sierra Club Books, San Francisco, 1988.

14   Read about Fearnley-Whittingstall and his activities at www.rivercottage.net.

15   Nigel Slater, *Tender: A cook and his vegetable patch* (vol. 1), Fourth Estate, London, 2009; Nigel Slater, *Tender: A cook's guide to the fruit garden* (vol. 2), Fourth Estate, London, 2010.

16   Margaret Brooker, *At its Best: Cooking with fresh seasonal produce*, Tandem Press, Auckland, 2003.

17   Julie Biuso, *Fresh*, New Holland, Auckland, 2000.

18   Lois Daish, *A Good Year*, Random House, Auckland, 2005.

19   Digby Law, *A Pickle and Chutney Cookbook*, Hodder and Stoughton, Auckland, 1986.

20   Gilian Painter, *A New Zealand Country Harvest Cookbook: Delicious traditional and new recipes for jams, preserves, chutneys, pickles and baking*, Viking, Auckland, 1997.

21   Chris Fortune, *Pick, Preserve, Serve: Enjoy local and home-grown produce year-round*, David Bateman, Auckland, 2008.

22   For more on the unpleasant fate of genetically engineered animals in New Zealand see the May/June and July/August 2010 issues of *Organic New Zealand*.

23   Jean Hewitt, *The New York Times Natural Foods Cookbook*, Hutchinson Group, Auckland, 1979.

24   This way of avoiding bad food is advocated in Michael Pollan's *In Defence of Food*, Allen Lane, London, 2008.

25   Anna Thomas, *The Vegetarian Epicure*, Vintage Books, New York, 1972; Anna Thomas, *The Vegetarian Epicure Book Two* Alfred A. Knopf, New York, 1979.

26   See http://en.wikipedia.org/wiki/Caesar_salad for the origins and history of Caesar salad, and for my recipe with back-story see http://ecogardenernz.blogspot.com/2010/10/have-lettuce-lemons-garlic-make-caesar.html.

27   Nigel Slater, *Real Fast Food: 350 recipes ready to eat in 30 minutes*, Michael Joseph, London, 1992.

28   www.cs.otago.ac.nz/research/foss/Bridge/eipomoea.htm.

29   www.otago.ac.nz/titi/hui/Main/Talks2/Oliver.htm.

30   www.scoop.co.nz/stories/PA0807/S00488.htm.

31   For details on Harris's work look him up on www.slowfoodfoundation.org.

32   www.kaiwakaorganics.co.nz.

33   http://localfoodenthusiasts.com/2010/02/15/honestly-grown-heritage-potatoes.

34   See the list of apples and their harvest times at www.treedimensions.co.nz/freshorganic-fruit.php.

35   For more on this apple, and other research into high-nutrient fruit and vegetables in New Zealand, see http://treecropsresearch.org/montys-surprise.

36   A landrace is a breed that is well adapted to local conditions, giving good yields without requiring high inputs. The science underlying landrace breeding, epigenetics, which involves understanding the ways environmental influences affect the genome, is relatively new. A lay summary of what epigenetics is about can be found at http://en.wikipedia.org/wiki/Epigenetics and a full scientific account in Jörg Tost (ed.), *Epigenetics*, Caister Academic Press, Norwich, 2008.

Chapter Six: Almost@Home

1   The Farmers' Market Association website with the latest on new farmers' markets around the country is at www.farmersmarket.org.nz.

2   Felicity Lawrence tells almost identical stories from growers in Britain in *Not on the Label*,

Penguin Books, London, 2004, pp. 87–97. She also covers just what damage this unnecessary trucking of food around the country is doing to the environment and society.

3   www.matakanavillage.co.nz/farmmkt01.htm.

4   I thought I had made a mistake in my notes here, scribbling the 1 of 15 per cent so that it looked like a 7. But no – checking on the web I found Mainland Poultry chief executive Michael Guthrie quoted as saying that 'international issues' had driven feed prices up 80 per cent in the past 18 months. The issues he identified included drought in Australia, which decimated world grain production; floods and biofuel production in the United States; growing demand for grain from China and India; low world grain stocks; and dairying taking over cropping land in New Zealand. See http://homepaddock.wordpress.com/2008/07/12/grain-price-rises-pushes-food-prices-up.

5   www.cityfarmersmarket.co.nz.

6   www.clevedonfarmersmarket.co.nz.

7   www.hamiltonfarmersmarket.co.nz.

8   www.napier.govt.nz/index.php?cid=events/eve_markets.

9   www.lytteltonfarmersmarket.co.nz.

10   www.lyttelton.net.nz.

11   Read all about the activities of Fresh Farm Markets at www.freshfarmmarkets.org.

12   Judith Cullen, *Dinner in a Basket: Judith Cullen cooks from the market*, Longacre Press, Dunedin, 2007; Vicki Winn, *Market Day: A taste of life at New Zealand farmers' markets*, New Holland, Auckland, 2007.

13   Daish's article 'The Price of Soup' was published in the *Listener*, 28 October 2000, pp. 40–41.

14   www.foodhawkesbay.co.nz/index.cfm/our_activities/food_trail.

15   www.northlandnz.com/food_and_wine/northland_food_wine_trail_map.htm.

16   www.thecoromandel.com/HomegrownFoodTrail.pdf; www.thecoromandel.com/home-grownfestival/index.html.

17   www.nzine.co.nz/features/northcanterburytrail.html.

18   www.hawkesburyharvest.com.au.

19   http://hawkesbury.yourguide.com.au/news/local/news/general/barn-offers-food-for-all/344425.aspx.

20   www.simplygoodfood.co.nz.

21   The source book on Community Supported Agriculture is *Sharing the Harvest: A citizen's guide to community supported agriculture* by Elizabeth Henderson and Robyn van En (2nd edn., Chelsea Green, 2007). The Robyn van En Center at Wilson College, Pennsylvania, is an online and on-the-ground source of information and support for CSA practitioners in the US and elsewhere.

Chapter Seven: Food@Large

1   www.marketfresh.com.au/images/downloads/AsianVegGuide.pdf.

2   All you need to know about how to source, grow and cook taro in New Zealand can be found at www.taro.co.nz/ and the recipes for taro gelato are at www.taro.co.nz/recipe.html.

3   Andrew Crowe, *A Field Guide to the Native Edible Plants of New Zealand*, 3rd edn, Godwit, Auckland, 1997; Sheila Natusch, *Wildfare for Wilderness Foragers*, Collins, Auckland, 1979; Gwen Skinner, *Simply Living: A gatherer's guide to New Zealand's fields, forest and shores*, A. H. & A. W. Reed, Wellington, 1981.

4   http://starcooked.blogspot.com/search/label/Foraging.

5   www.facebook.com/pages/Otautahi-Urban-Foraging/136897606208?ref=sgm.

6   http://wild-foods-nz.blogspot.com.

7   Richard Mabey, *Food for Free*, revised edn, Collins, London, 2001.

8   See his 2006 review essay on gathering wild food and writing about it at www.guardian. co.uk/books/2006/sep/02/featuresreviews.guardianreview4.

9   The book and BBC television series *Wild Food* look at what the last hunter-gatherers in Britain ate some 30,000 years ago, at the lives and foods of contemporary hunter-gatherers in Australia and Africa, and at the wild plant foods that are still abundant in Britain today. It is a fascinating look at why including some wild food, and effort to get it, in the modern lifestyle still makes a lot of sense. Ray Mears and Gordon Hillman, *Wild Food*, Hodder and Stoughton, London, 2007.

10   www.radionz.co.nz/news/stories/2010/04/19/1247fe58d9b7.

11   www.homegrownmarket.co.nz; http://ooooby.ning.com; www.locavore365.org.

12   Tristram Stuart's book *Waste: Uncovering the global food scandal* (Penguin Books, 2009) covers this subject in detail.

13   http://en.wikipedia.org/wiki/Freeganism.

14   www.foodnotbombs.net/story.htm.

15   'All our food is vegetarian, that is, no meat, dairy or eggs. This is for many reasons, but for now, two will do. First, the potential for problems with food spoilage are greatly reduced when dealing strictly with vegetables. With the process we use, we rarely hold the food we collect for more than a couple of hours. Second, teaching people about the economic and health benefits of a vegetarian diet is directly connected to a healthy attitude about ourselves, each other and the planet as a whole. It is also a direct challenge to the injustice of the military/industrial economic system. This is not to suggest that it is our policy that everyone should be vegetarian or that eating meat is wrong. We encourage awareness of vegetarianism for political, spiritual and economic reasons. We only prepare food that is strictly from vegetable sources so people will always know and trust that Food Not Bombs food has this standard whenever they come to our table. At times, we take already prepared dairy and meat products that might have been donated to us and take it to soup kitchen that aren't vegetarian because we believe eating is more important than being politically correct; however, we never cook with animal products.' From www.foodnotbombs.net/seven.html.

16   www.stuff.co.nz/the-press/news/3490887/Small-oasis-of-calm-for-lifes-basics.

17   Although those on the right wing of the political spectrum often espouse the view that 'there is no such thing as society, only individuals', one of the most persuasive pleas made for keeping Crossways in community hands was on the blog of former ACT MP Stephen Franks: www.stephenfranks.co.nz/?p=468.

18   www.organicexplorer.co.nz.

19   www.curatorshouse.com/dining/About.

20   www.jonnyschwass.com/index.php/Restaurant_Schwass.

21   www.hislops-wholefoods.co.nz.

22   www.haewai.co.nz.

Chapter Eight: Alimentary Action

1   The chief executive of the New Zealand Food Safety Authority, Andrew McKenzie, was the biggest of the big public-service CEO spenders on food and drink entertainment between July 2008 and June 2010, racking up $66,105 on wining and dining himself and

others at the taxpayer's expense during that time. His most expensive meals (including a \$464 lunch for himself and two others) were in foreign capitals, where he travelled for market access meetings, and he also entertained lavishly at Wellington's better restaurants. McKenzie was 'unavailable for comment' to the media on this subject, but the authority's acting deputy director-general, Carol Barnao, said that 'much of his discretionary credit-card spending was cost-recovered from the industry, which supported the authority's work'. (Quoted in Martin Kay, John Hartevelt and Andrea Vance, 'Eat, drink and be merry on the Kiwi taxpayer', *Press*, 6 August 2010). This quasi-apology raises more questions than it answers. What 'support' does industry give the Food Safety Authority, and what does it get in exchange? Market access for products of dubious quality?

2   Matt Morris, 'A History of Christchurch Home Gardening from Colonisation to the Queen's Visit: Gardening culture in a particular society and environment', PhD thesis, University of Canterbury, 2006; Chapter 5: 'Sustenance', Christine Dann, 'Digging for Victory: Wartime kitchen gardening in New Zealand', a Heritage Week talk (unpublished), 2009.

3   Ibid.

4   www.organicnz.org.

5   www.organicnz.org/96/organic2020.

6   Sue Kedgley, *Eating Safely in a Toxic World*, Penguin Books, Auckland, 1998.

7   www.greens.org.nz/press-releases/safe-food-greens-first-major-policy-launch.

8   www.greens.org.nz/food.

9   www.greens.org.nz/press-releases/govt-wrong-dump-school-food-guidelines-says-public.

10   www.nzfsa.govt.nz/about-us.

11   www.safefood.org.nz.

12   Keith Woodford, 'The role of the NZFSA in investigating health issues concerning A1 and A2 milk', p. 7: www.lincoln.ac.nz/staff-profile? staffId=Keith.Woodford.

13   A good description of the Seder and the foods eaten at it is available at http://en.wikipedia.org/wiki/Passover_Seder.

14   See http://islam.about.com/od/ramadan/a/sadaqafitr.htm.

15   www.cityofseattle.net/neighborhoods/ppatch.

16   HEHA newsletter, Issue 6, November 2007: www.moh.govt.nz/moh.nsf/indexmh/heha-newsletter-issue6#news.

17   Stephanie Alexander, *Kitchen Garden Cooking with Kids*, Penguin, Camberwell, Victoria, 2006.

18   www.kitchengardenfoundation.org.au.

19   www.kitchengardenfoundation.org.au/goals.shtml.

20   The evaluation is available at www.kitchengardenfoundation.org.au/evaluation.shtml.

21   Find out more about the Garden to Table Trust and its activities at http://gardentotable.org.nz.

22   Michael Symons, *The Shared Table Ideas for Australian Cuisine*, AGPS Press, Canberra, 1993, p. 19.

23   Diamond Harbour's loss is Oamaru's gain. After being quaked-up in Canterbury Annie Baxter put her considerable energy into creating a teashop and tea store in a 19th-century building in Oamaru. Called Annie's Victorian Teas and Store, it is on the corner of Tees and Itchen Streets, the gateway to the historic whitestone precinct.

RECOMMENDED READING

Alexander, Stephanie, *Kitchen Garden Cooking with Kids*, Penguin Books, Camberwell, 2006

Allhoff, Fritz and Dave Monroe (eds), *Food and Philosophy*, Blackwell, Malden, Oxford, 2007

Biuso, Julie, *Fresh*, New Holland, Auckland, 2000

Blythman, Joanna, *Shopped: The shocking power of British supermarkets*, Harper Perennial, London, 2005

Blythman, Joanna, *Bad Food Britain*, Fourth Estate, London, 2006

Brooker, Margaret, *At its Best: Cooking with fresh seasonal produce*, Tandem Press, Auckland, 2003

Browne, Mary, Helen Leach and Nancy Tichborne, *The Cook's Garden: For cooks who garden and gardeners who cook*, Reed, Auckland, 1980

Browne, Mary, Helen Leach and Nancy Tichborne, *More from the cook's garden: For cooks who garden and gardeners who cook*, Reed Methuen, Auckland, 1987

Cameron, Sally, *Grow It Cook It*, Penguin Books, Auckland, 2009

Carson, Rachel, *Silent Spring*, Houghton Mifflin, Boston, 1962

Cockburn, Linda, *Living the Good Life: How one family changed the world from their backyard*, Hardie Grant Books, Prahran, Victoria, 2006

Colborn, Theo, Dianne Dumanowski and John Peterson Myers, *Our Stolen Future*, Abacus, London, 1997

Cox, Stan, *Sick Planet Corporate Food and Medicine*, Pluto Press, London, 2008

Creasy, Rosalind, *Cooking from the Garden*, Sierra Club Books, San Francisco, 1988

Crowe, Andrew, *A Field Guide to the Native Edible Plants of New Zealand*, 3rd edn, Godwit, Auckland, 1997

Daish, Lois, *A Good Year*, Random House, Auckland, 2005

Dann, Christine, *A Cottage Garden Cookbook*, Bridget Williams Books, Wellington, 1992

Egger, Garry and Boyd Swinburn, *Planet Obesity: How we're eating ourselves and the planet to death*, Allen & Unwin, Sydney, 2010

Ettlinger, Steve, *Twinkie, Deconstructed*, Hudson St Press, New York, 2007

Flammang, Janet A., *The Taste for Civilization: Food, politics, and civil society*, University of Illinois Press, Urbana and Chicago, 2009

Flower, Tui, *Tui Flower's Modern Hostess Cookbook*, A. H. & A. W. Reed, Wellington, 1972

Fortune, Chris, *Pick, Preserve, Serve: Enjoy local and home-grown produce year-round*, David

Bateman, Auckland, 2008

Gibson, Carolyn, *Fries with That? How to lose weight and keep it off in an upsized world*, New Holland, Auckland, 2009

Greville, Dennis and Jill Brewis, *The Grower's Cookbook: From the garden to the table*, Penguin Books, Auckland, 2008

Halweil, Brian, *Eat Here: Reclaiming homegrown pleasures in a global supermarket*, W. W. Norton, New York, 2004

Harvey, Graham, *We Want Real Food*, Constable, London, 2006

Hyams, Edward, *English Cottage Gardens*, Whittet Books, London, 1970

Kedgley, Sue, *Eating Safely in a Toxic World*, Penguin Books, Auckland, 1998

Kerr, Graham, *Entertaining with Kerr*, A. H. & A. W. Reed, Wellington, 1963

Kingsolver, Barbara, *Animal, Vegetable, Miracle: Our year of seasonal eating*, Faber, London, 2007

Kneen, Brewster, *Farmageddon: Food and the culture of biotechnology*, New Society Publishers, Gabriola Island, 1999

Lang, Tim and Michael Heasman, *Food Wars: The battle for mouths, minds and markets*, Earthscan, London, 2004

Lappe, Anne and Terry Bryant, *Grub: Ideas for an urban organic kitchen*, Jeremy P. Tarcher/Penguin, New York, 2005

Law, Digby, *A Vegetable Cookbook*, Hodder and Stoughton, Auckland, 1978

Law, Digby, *A Pickle and Chutney Cookbook*, Hodder and Stoughton, Auckland, 1986

Lawrence, Felicity, *Not on the Label*, Penguin Books, London, 2004

Lawrence, Felicity, *Eat Your Heart Out*, Penguin Books, London, 2008

Leach, Helen, *1000 Years of Gardening in New Zealand*, A. H. & A. W. Reed, Wellington, 1984

Madeley, John, *Food for All: The need for a new agriculture*, Zed Books, London, 2002

Madeley, John, *Hungry for Trade: How the poor pay for free trade*, Zed Books, London, 2000

Magdoff, Fred, John Bellamy Foster and Frederick H. Buttel (eds), *Hungry for Profit: The agribusiness threat to farmers, food and the environment*, Monthly Review Press, New York, 2000

McMichael, A. J., *Planetary Overload: Global environmental change and the health of the human species*, Cambridge University Press, Cambridge, 1993

McQueen, Humphrey, *The Essence of Capitalism: The origins of our future*, Sceptre, Sydney, 2001

Mears, Ray and Gordon Hillman, *Wild Food*, Hodder and Stoughton, London, 2007

Montgomery, David R., *Dirt: The erosion of civilizations*, University of California Press, Berkeley, 2007

Moon, Paul, *A Tohunga's Natural World: Plants, gardening and food*, David Ling, Auckland, 2005

Natusch, Sheila, *Wildfare for Wilderness Foragers*, Collins, Auckland, 1979

Nestle, Marion, *Food Politics: How the food industry influences nutrition and health*, University of California Press, Berkeley, 2002

Painter, Gilian, *A New Zealand Country Harvest Cookbook: Delicious traditional and new recipes for jams, preserves, chutneys, pickles and baking*, Viking, Auckland, 1997

Patel, Raj, *Stuffed and Starved: Markets, power and the hidden battle for the world food system*, Black Inc, Melbourne, 2007

Pearce, Fred, *When the Rivers Run Dry: Water – the defining crisis of the twenty-first century*, Beacon Press, Boston, 2006

Pfeiffer, Dale Allen, *Eating Fossil Fuels: Oil, food and the coming crisis in agriculture*, New Society Publishers, Gabriola Island, 2006

Pollan, Michael, *The Omnivore's Dilemma*, Bloomsbury, London, 2006

Pollan, Michael, *In Defence of Food*, Allen Lane, London, 2008

Popkin, Barry, *The World is Fat: The fads, trends, policies, and products that are fattening the human race*, Avery, New York, 2009

Salatin, Joel, *Holy Cows and Hog Heaven: The food buyer's guide to farm friendly food*, Polyface Inc, Swoope, Virginia, 2004

Schlosser, Eric, *Fast Food Nation: The dark side of the all-American meal*, Perennial, New York, 2002

Simon, Michele, *Appetite for Profit: How the food industry undermines our health and how to fight back*, Nation Books, New York, 2006

Simpson, Tony, *An Innocent Delight: The art of dining in New Zealand*, Hodder and Stoughton, Auckland, 1985

Skinner, Gwen, *Simply Living: A gatherer's guide to New Zealand's fields, forest and shores*, A. H. & A. W. Reed, Wellington, 1981

Slater, Nigel, *Real Fast Food: 350 recipes ready to eat in 30 minutes*, Michael Joseph, London, 1992

Slater, Nigel, *Tender: Volume I, A cook and his vegetable patch*, Fourth Estate, London, 2009

Slater, Nigel, *Tender: Volume II, A cook's guide to the fruit garden*, Fourth Estate, London, 2010

Smith, Alisa and J. B. MacKinnon, *Plenty: Eating locally on the 100 mile diet*, Three Rivers Press, New York, 2007

Spurlock, Morgan, *Don't Eat this Book*, Penguin Books, London, 2005

Steel, Carolyn, *Hungry City: How food shapes our lives*, Chatto & Windus, London, 2008

Stuart, Tristram, *Waste: Uncovering the global food scandal*, Penguin Books, London, 2009

Symons, Michael, *One Continuous Picnic: A gastronomic history of Australia*, 2nd edn, Melbourne University Press, Victoria, 2007

Symons, Michael, *The Shared Table: Ideas for Australian cuisine*, AGPS Press, Canberra, 1993

Thomas, Anna, *The Vegetarian Epicure*, Vintage Books, New York, 1972

Thomas, Anna, *The Vegetarian Epicure Book Two*, Alfred A. Knopf, New York, 1979

Thomas, Mark, *Belching out the Devil: Global adventures with Coca-Cola*, Ebury Press, London, 2008

Trinder, Stephen, with Christine Blance and Ross Paterson, *Community Gardening*, Christchurch Community Gardens Association, Christchurch, 2006

Tudge, Colin, *So Shall We Reap*, Allen Lane, London, 2003

Veart, David, *First Catch Your Weka: A story of New Zealand cooking*, Auckland University Press, Auckland, 2008

Vileisis, Ann, *Kitchen Literacy: How we lost knowledge of where food comes from and why we need to get it back*, Island Press/Shearwater Books, Washington, 2008

Waring, Marilyn, *Counting for Nothing*, Allen & Unwin/Port Nicholson Press, Wellington, 1988

Warren, Piers, *How to Store your Garden Produce: The key to self-sufficiency*, Green Books, Totnes, 2008

INDEX

5+ a Day campaign 73

Aboriginal food
    gathering 128–29
Adams, Jane 111, 152
additives 12–13, 146
Agriculture Research Group on
    Sustainability *see* ARGOS
Aiki restaurant 135
Akaroa 78
Alexander, Stephanie 154, 155
animals, welfare of 16–17, 92, 132
apples 97, 131, 141, 180,
    182, 183; Altländer
    Pfannkuchenapfel 97; Beauty
    of Bath 97; Braeburn 180;
    Bramley's Seedling 180;
    Cornish Aromatic 97;
    Cox's Orange 97; Fuero
    Rous 97; Fuji 97, 180;
    Gala 97; Granny Smith 97,
    180; Gravenstein 97, 140;
    Hetlina 97; Jonathan 97;
    Kidd's Orange; 97; Monty's
    Surprise 97; Peasgood
    Nonesuch 97; Pink
    Lady 180; Reinette Marbrée
    d'Auvergne 97; Rose 25;
    Sturmer 180
apricots 140, 181, 183
ARGOS (Agriculture Research
    Group on Sustainability) 49
artichokes: globe 175;
    Jerusalem 168, 175
arugula *see* rocket
Asian foods 92, 104, 122, 125

asparagus 171, 174, 175
aspartame 146
Astelia spp 126
aubergine *see* eggplant
Aubert, Suzanne 57
Auckland 25, 53, 56, 59, 75, 109,
    114, 149
Auckland Botanic Gardens 22,
    44
    Auckland City Council 59
    Auckland Regional
    Gardens 41
Australia 112, 116, 128–29,
    153–54
avocados 180, 183
Awhitu Peninsula 39
azolla 40

babaco 25
bananas 25, 26, 180, 182, 184
Banks Peninsula 78, 107, 154
Barry's Bay cheeses 77
Basque Gardens 53
Baxter, Annie 158, 198
beans 166; broad 167, 168, 175;
    climbing 168; dwarf 168,
    175; Painted Lady 162;
    runner 175
Beeton, Mrs 68
beer 137
bees 137
beetroot 166, 168, 172, 175
Bellamy, David 95
biodynamics 48, 64, 119
biointensive gardening 48
Biuso, Julie 91

blackberries 83, 127, 131, 141,
    181, 184
Blok, Roger 97
blueberries 107, 108, 140, 181,
    184
bodyweight 14–15
borage 131
box gardens *see* container
    gardening
box thorn 66
boysenberries 181
bread 13, 14, 22, 65, 67, 68, 71,
    82, 93, 105, 110, 132, 136–37,
    156, 160
Brewis, Jill 90
Britain 29
British culinary tradition 12, 48,
    67, 80
broccoli 95, 168, 175
Brooker, Margaret 91
Brown, Gail 109
Browne, Mary 90
Brussels sprouts 168, 175
buckwheat 104, 108
Bulls 83
Burger King 14
Byron Bay market (NSW) 122

cabbage trees 47
cabbages 86, 166, 168, 176
Caesar salad 82, 93
cafés 18, 69, 70, 72, 77, 114, 115,
    125, 133–34, 136
calendula 131
Cameron, Sally 90
cancer 14, 97

cape gooseberries 131
capsicums 157, 169, 178
carbohydrates 13
carob 25
carrots 23, 30, 100, 166, 168, 172, 176
Carson, Rachel 16
casana 25
Casci, Glenys 43
cauliflowers 166, 168, 176
celeriac 169, 172, 176
celery 169, 176
Central Otago 130
Central Tree Crops Research Trust of New Zealand 97
Chantal Wholefoods 118
cheese 76–78, 80, 83, 85
cherimoya 25
cherries 181, 184
cherry plums 131
chickens 14, 16–17, 54, 66, 86
chickweed 35
Chida, Ui 135
children 51, 73, 79, 112, 145, 150, 153–54; food for 80; gardens for 41; gardening with 33; obesity in 15–16, 146
Children's Food Awards 145
chilli peppers 178
Chiltern Seeds (UK) 98
China 66
Chinese in NZ 65–66, 70, 125
Chinese cabbage 168, 176
Christchurch 19, 36, 51, 52, 54, 55, 60, 64, 72, 128, 133, 135
Christchurch Botanic Gardens 134
Christchurch City Mission 132–33
Christchurch Polytechnic Institute of Technology (CPIT) 39
Christchurch South Community Garden 54, 55, 60
Christofferson, Stella 98, 99, 109
cider 27
citrus fruits 25, 130, 181, 183
City Farmers' Market (Auckland) 27, 109, 123
Clevedon Farmers' Market 98, 109, 149
climate change 92, 191
co-operatives 112, 117
Cockburn, Linda 79
coconut 101
cold frames 46
Collingwood College

(Melbourne) 154
comfrey 35, 59
Common Ground 57
community groups 56, 89, 111, 130
community gardens 18, 48, 52, 55, 58–60, 112, 151–52
community kitchens 111, 132
Community Supported Agriculture (CSA) 18, 112, 119
compost 11, 28, 30, 32, 53, 54, 57, 60, 108, 144, 152, 172–73
conservation 41
container gardening 31, 32, 33, 167
convenience foods 71–72
cookbooks 68, 70, 90–93, 112
cooking classes 88, 89, 111–12; see also education
cooking skills 78–79, 88, 155, 156
Coromandel Home Grown Food Festival 116
Coromandel Home Grown Food Trail 116
Cottage Garden Cookbook 90
courgettes see zucchini
crabapples 131
crayfish 127
Creasy, Rosalind 90
cress 65
Crop and Food Research, Lincoln 95
Crossways Community House 133–34
Crum, Bob 107–08
Cuba 29
cucumbers 160, 169, 176
Cumberland, Tanya 39
Curator's House Restaurant 134
Curl, Romi 98
currants 181, 184

dairy industry 76, 78
dairying, organic 112
Daish, Lois 113
dandelions 32, 35, 131
dates 25
Davies, Sarah 32, 38
de Negri, Carlo 110, 127
de Negri, Cherry 110, 112, 127
de Ruiter, Jacob 137
Dennison, Colin 77
Department of Scientific & Industrial Research (DSIR) 94–95
diabetes, Type II, 14, 16, 73

Diamond Harbour 158
'Dig for Victory' campaign 29, 144, 190
dill 43
diseases in plants 172, 173
diseases, diet-related 72–73, 74
dolichos 65
Don, Rev. Alexander 65, 66
dumpster-diving 131
Dunedin 107, 127

Earth Talk 39, 40
Eco Gardener (blog) 20
Eco-Seeds 98
education about gardening 38, 39, 41, 56, 73, 152; see also cooking skills
eggplants 121, 157, 166, 177
elderberry wine 27
elderflowers 127, 131, 139
Eltham dairy factory 76
Enviroschools Programme 42
ethylene 182, 183
Evansdale cheeses 77

falafel 93
farm-gate sales 18, 112, 115, 116, 117
Farmers' Market Association of New Zealand 19, 105, 110
Farmers' Market Conference (Blenheim, 2008) 153
farmers' markets 18, 19, 20, 27, 37, 70, 89, 91, 97, 98, 105–24, 147, 149, 150–53
fast food 16, 73, 80, 93
fats 13
Fearnley-Whittingstall, Hugh 91
feijoas 181, 183, 184
fennel 137
fertilisers 28, 137, 144
figs 25, 181, 184
Fitzsimons, Jeanette 145
flax 39
flour 119, 136–37
Flower, Tui 70
Fonterra 78
Food and Wine Trail (Northland) 115
food banks 111
Food Barn co-operative store 117
Food Hawke's Bay 115
Food Not Bombs 131–32
food trails 18, 112, 115
food waste 53, 117, 130, 134–35
FoodPrints education programme 111

foraging 18, 126–31
Fortune, Chris 91, 107
Framework Trust 56
freeganism 130–31
Fresh Farm Markets (Chesapeake
    Bay, USA) 111
Fresh Mouth (blog) 79
frost 25, 166, 167, 171, 175, 176,
    179
fungus 172, 182

Galvin, Sister Loyola 56–57, 63
Garcia, Javier 134
garlic 24, 167, 169, 171, 173, 177
gastronomy 74, 75, 81, 112
genetic engineering 16, 92, 95,
    144, 145
geraniums 85
gherkins 35, 102, 157
Gibson, Carolyn 15
Gold Coin Café 133
Golden Bay 25
gooseberries 181, 185
grapefruit 25, 181, 184
grapes 184
green manure 30, 31
Green Party of Aotearoa New
    Zealand 145
greenhouses 36–37, 191
Greville, Dennis 90
Grey Lynn 53, 55, 62, 149
Grey Lynn Community
    Gardens 53, 55, 62
Ground Café 111
Growing Today see Lifestyle Block
guava, red 25
guerrilla gardening 58

Haewae Organic Meadery 137
Hall, Nadine 36
Hallinan, Lynda 19, 26, 27, 30
Hamilton Farmers' Market
    109–10, 123
Hamilton Gardens 40, 44, 46
Hamilton Permaculture Trust 40
Harris, Graham 96
Hawke's Bay 115, 118, 127
Hawke's Bay Farmers'
    Market 107, 110
Hawkesbury Food for All
    Project 117
Hawkesbury Harvest
    (Sydney) 116
He Whenua Whakatipu 49, 50
Healthy Eating Healthy Action
    programme 152
Healthy Kitchen, The 89

heart disease 14, 193
hebes 57
heirloom varieties 97, 98; see also
    seeds
herbs 45, 83, 101, 177
Hewson, Kate 52
Higginson, Andrea 53
Hislop, Paul and Elizabeth 136
Hislops Café 136
Home of Compassion,
    Wellington 56–57
Home Science Recipe Book 69
Homegrown 90, 91
honey 109, 137
horseradish 110
Horse's Flat 65
Hua Parakore 48
humus 30
Hyam, Coral 137
Hyams, Edward 37

ice-cream bean 41
insect damage 171, 172, 173
intensive farming 16–17
International Federation
    of Organic Agriculture
    Movements 38
Ireland 67
Italy 76

jam 12, 158, 173, 174, 184, 194,
    195

Kahl, Holger 25
Kaikoura 136
kaitiakitanga 50
Katikati 161
Kaiwaka Gardens 96, 97, 98,
    102, 103
Kaiwaka Organics Heritage
    Garden Centre 98
Kaiwhenua Organics Trust 50
Kakariki see University of
    Canterbury
kale 161, 169
Karikaas 78
Katzen, Mollie 93
Kedgley, Sue 145
Kelmarna Organic City Farm 56,
    63
Kereopa, Hohepa 30, 50
Kerr, Graham 70
Kids' Edible Gardens 51
Kings Seeds 99
Kingsolver, Barbara 79
Kitchen Garden, The 40, 46
kitchen gardens 34, 35, 37, 40, 87,

134, 154
kiwifruit 83, 182, 184
Knight, Rachel 38
Knox, Johanna 128
Koanga Gardens see Kaiwaka
    Gardens
kohanga reo 41, 48
konini berries 131
koura 127
kumara 47, 61, 94–95, 96, 102,
    169, 177
Kumara Box, The 115
kura kaupapa 48
labelling of food 27, 106
Labour Party of New
    Zealand 145
landrace breeding 98, 195
Law, Digby 90, 91
Leach, Helen 90
leeks 158, 166, 169, 177
lemons 181, 184; Meyer 163
lettuces 82, 99, 158, 166,
    169, 174, 178; iceberg 99;
    buttercrunch 99
Lifestyle Block 36
lilly pilly tree (Acmena smithii)
    129
limes 101, 181, 184
Lincoln University 146
locavores 79, 130
Loyola, Sister see Galvin, Sister
    Loyola
Lyttelton Market 107, 111

Mabey, Richard 128
Maddison, Deborah 93
mahinga kai 49
Mahoe Farmhouse cheese 78
Mahurangi Pekin Ducks 108
mandarins 181, 186
manuka 25, 66, 131
Maori food gathering 126–27
Maori gardens 47–50, 94
Marlborough 91, 107–08
marrows 169
Martin, Bill 39
Matakana Farmers' Market 108,
    124, 149
Matariki 60
Maunga Kiekie 47
Maw, Ivan 34
Maw, Vanya 34–35
Maynard, John 31, 44
McDonald's 13, 75
mead 137
meat 11, 12, 17, 29, 54, 66, 67,
    68, 69, 86, 92, 93, 109, 110,

125, 145
melons 181, 186;
   rock melons 163;
   watermelons 188
mesclun 169
mezze 103
micro-nutrients 12–13
milk 13, 67, 79, 77, 78, 85, 86,
   110, 112, 146
Miller, Mrs, *Economic Technical*
   Cookery Book 69
Ministry of Agriculture and
   Forestry 146
Ministry of Education 41, 155
Ministry of Health 146, 152
mint 131
Moon, Paul 30
mould 14, 173, 183
mulberries 128–29
mulching 28, 41, 158
Murphy, Michael, *Handbook or*
   Gardening for New Zealand 68
mushrooms 127, 178

Napier 118
Napier Farmers' Market 105, 110
nashi 186
nectarines 181, 186
nettles 35
New South Wales 116
New York 55
New York Times Natural Foods
   Cookbook 92
New Zealand Adult Nutrition
   Survey 2008/09 15, 16
New Zealand Food Safety
   Authority 146, 147
New Zealand Gardener 19, 26,
   57, 90
New Zealand Humic Compost
   Club 144
New Zealand Qualifications
   Authority 56
Ng, Dr James 65
Ngai Tahu 49
Ngati Te Ata 39
Niche Seeds 99
Noble, Cheryl 40
nopales 35
North Canterbury Food and
   Wine Trail 116
nuts 65, 107, 131; walnuts 100,
   131

obesity 15–16, 29, 73, 78, 146,
   154
oka *see* yams

olive oil 69
Oliver, Jamie 155
olives 27, 162
onions 65, 166, 169, 173, 178,
OOOBY (Out Of Our Own
   Backyards) 130
oranges 181, 184, 186
Oratia 149
Orewa 149
organic certification standards 48
organic growers 106, 107, 118
organic shops 19, 99, 114
Organic Connection 118
Organic Garden City Trust 52
Organic New Zealand 144
organoponico garden 23, 64
Otago 65, 97, 107, 130, 174
Otahuhu 125
Otara 129
Otautahi Urban Foraging 128

P-Patch Program 151–52
Painter, Gilian 91
papaya 25
Parnell 149
parsley 127, 131
parsnips 169, 178
passionfruit 131, 181, 186
Patch from Scratch 32, 33
pea straw 32
peaches 181, 183, 187
pears 180, 187
peas 44, 65, 83, 166, 169, 178
Penrith City Council 116
permaculture 40, 48, 57, 108
Permaculture in New Zealand
   (website) 40
persimmons 41, 83, 171, 181, 187
pesticides 28, 144, 146
pesto 127
Piko Whole Foods 19
Pineapples for Peace 129
plums 108, 181, 187
Pollan, Michael 195
Pollan solution 92
pomegranates 25
Ponsonby People's Union 75, 117
potatoes 22, 31, 48, 49, 67, 96,
   131, 158, 166, 169, 172,
   178; Jersey Bennes 162;
   Karuparera 97; Maori
   varieties 96; MoeMoe 97;
   Pink Fir Apple 96, 97;
   Urenika 97
Pountney, Charmaine 39, 42
Prencipe, Gianni 49
preservatives 12–13

preserving fruit 11–12, 27, 83,
   91, 107, 110, 127, 130, 152,
   156, 173
Prince, Bernadine 111
produce box schemes 18, 39, 112,
   118–19
Project Lyttelton 111, 129
Pu Hao Rangi Trust 95
puha 32, 35, 126, 131
Pukekohe 126, 142, 149
pumpkins 21, 23, 28, 98, 131,
   166, 167, 169, 172, 179;
   Australian Butter 98; Red
   Kuri 98
Purau 25, 62
Purau Valley Produce 107
puwharawhara 12

quinces 103, 183, 187

radishes 158, 170, 179
Raglan 50
Rainbow Valley Farm 108
raised beds 23, 32–33, 45, 53,
   54, 57
Ranui Community Garden 59,
   152
raspberries 21, 101, 142, 181
ratatouille 157
Rehua Marae, Christchurch 94, 95
Reid, John 49
relish 104
Restaurant Schwass 134
Reynolds, Richard 58
rice 65–66, 98, 111, 121, 158
ripening of fruit 180–81
rocket 170
rosehips 130, 131
Round Hill, Southland 65
Rudolph Steiner School,
   Christchurch 64
Running Brook Seeds 21, 98,
   99, 109

Safe Food Campaign 146
Safe Food policy (1999)
salad dressings 69, 192
salads 69, 122, 123, 158
Schierning, A. D. 129
school gardens 19, 42, 51, 112,
   146, 152–53
schools 41, 49, 50, 51, 111,
   145–46, 154–55
Schwass, Jonny 134
Seattle 151
see qua *see* sze gwa
Seed Savers 99

SEED schools 42
seeds 18, 22, 28, 32, 33, 35, 51, 97, 98, 99, 109, 144, 159, 166–68
shadbush 85
shallots 170, 173
Shapiro, Laura 78
silverbeet 23, 86, 127, 131, 166, 170, 174, 179
Simply Good Food 119
Simpson, Tony 77
Slater, Nigel 91, 93, 121
Slow Food Movement 75–76, 158
smallholdings 36, 37
Smith, Adam 112
Soil and Health Association 144, 145
SOLE (Seasonal, Organic, Local, Ethical) 19, 20, 78, 134, 137, 157
South America 96
Southland 66, 174
Spencer, Colin 93
spinach 85, 170, 179; New Zealand 127, 131
spring onions 170
Spud in a Bucket 49
squash 21, 22, 169, 179
Stephanie Alexander Kitchen Garden Foundation 154
St Benedict's Urban Farm 53
St Columba's Anglican church, Auckland 53–54, 56
Stoddart, Margaret 158
storage 87–89, 157, 171–74, 182–83
strawberries 83, 140, 181, 188
Supergrans 89
Sustainable Backyard Garden 40–41, 45
Sutherland, Oliver 95
swapping of food 129–30
swedes 170, 179
sweetcorn 150, 170, 179
sze gwa 126

taewa see potatoes, Maori varieties
Tahuri Whenua 49
Tai Poutini Polytechnic 152
tamarillos 25, 181, 188
tangelos 164, 188
Taranaki 76
taro 45, 47, 126
Te Kura Toitu o Te Whaiti Nui-a-Toi 50
Te Maioha, Antonio 47
Te Waka Kai Ora: Maori Organics Authority of Aotearoa 48
Te Whare Roimata 133
Terrace Farm 119
Thomas, Anna 92, 93
thyme 131, 137
Tichbourne, Nancy 90
tikanga Maori 48
Tolley, Anne 146
tomatoes 28, 62, 83, 121, 157, 166, 167, 170, 179, 182; Brandywine Pink 24, 99; Yellow Pear 99; Black Krim 99; Tigerella 99
Treaty of Waitangi 49 see also Waitangi Tribunal
Tree Dimensions orchard 97
Tucking In programme 152
Tuhoe 125
turnips 170, 172, 180

Unitec 38, 60, 62
University of Canterbury 52–53, 64
Upham, Lorraine 118
Urewera Ranges 126

vanilla 25
veganism 132
Vegetarian Epicure, The 93
vegetarianism 197
vermicast 55, 108
Vertical Composting Unit 60

Victory Gardens see Dig for Victory

Waiheke Island 64, 149, 161
Waikato Farmers' Market 115
Wairarapa 119
Waitangi Tribunal 95
walnut liqueur 27
walnuts see nuts
wartime food 29, 130, 144
wasabi 25
water chestnuts 40
watercress 126, 131, 142
waterlilies 108
Wellington 39, 44, 46, 56, 127, 132, 133, 137
West Coast 152–53
West Coast District Health Board 152
West Coast Regional Council 152
Whaingaroa 50
Wham, Peter 53
Whangarei Growers' Market 105, 107
wheat 48, 67
White, Lily 51, 152
Wihongi, Dell 95
wild food 35, 66, 126–29
Wilkinson, Chris 105
Wine Country Food Trail 115
Women's Land Army 144
Woodford, Professor Keith, The Devil in the Milk 146
workplace gardens 32
World War II 29
World Wide Fund for Nature 41
worm farms 55, 56
Wyenova Farm 36

yacon 164
yams 170, 180
Yen, Doug 94
zucchini 104, 157, 164, 170